Z80 Users Manual

Z80 Users Manual

Joseph J. Carr

Reston Publishing Company, Inc.
Reston, Virginia
A Prentice-Hall Company

Library of Congress Cataloging in Publication Data

Carr, Joseph J.
  Z80 users manual.

  Includes index.
  1. Zilog Model Z-80 (Computer)   I. Title
QA76.8.Z54C37   001.64   80-13174
ISBN 0-8359-9517-8
ISBN 0-8359-9516-X (pbk.)

© 1980 by
Reston Publishing Company, Inc.
A Prentice-Hall Company
Reston, Virginia

10 9 8 7 6 5

Contents

Preface

For the past several years we have been seeing an explosive revolution in electronic semiconductor technology. Starting in the early part of the 70s decade, *microprocessor* integrated circuits have been available. These devices began simply, and were only part of the circuitry needed to implement a complete digital programmable computer. Today, however, the field has grown to the point where thousands of small computers, based on microprocessor chips, are in regular use all over the country. The chips have improved also. The early devices, such as the Intel 8008 and 8080 devices, have been eclipsed by later models. Zilog, Inc. introduced their Z80 device, and it improved on the old 8080 device. Zilog's Z80 is an eight-bit device. Originally operating at 2.5 mHz, the later Z80A operates at a faster 4-mHz rate. The newer Zilog devices, only recently released, include the Z8 and Z8000-series.

Although there are many eight-bit machines on the market, I am an unabashed Zilog, Inc. fan. I personally *like* the Z80; it seems so reasonable. This makes me even more eager to see the Z8 and Z8000 devices. My own personal microcomputer, with almost 30 K of memory, is based on the Z80 device. It is astounding to me that this desk-top machine has more computing power than the roomful of IBM 1620 computer that I was allowed to use as a freshman engineering student in the late 1960s.

JOSEPH J. CARR

1
Z80 Architecture

The Z80 is an integrated circuit microprocessor designed and manufactured by Zilog, Inc. (10460 Bubb Road, Cupertino, CA, 95014), and second-sourced by Mostek, Inc. (1215 West Crosby Rd., Carrollton, TX 75006). The Z80 is similar to, but advanced over, the Intel 8080 microprocessor. In fact, a persistent industry story is that talent at Intel who designed the 8080 were the same people to design the Z80 device.

If you are familiar with the 8080 device, then making the switchover to Z80 will be very easy. The Z80 instruction set contains all of the 8080 instructions, plus a few more. It is usually claimed that the Z80 device has 158 different instructions, as opposed to only 78 for the 8080. Note that the means for numbering these instructions is a little less obvious, since in Chapter 17 we will introduce you to over 400 Z80 instructions. These "hidden" instructions are merely the expanded list (e.g., BIT, b,r can test any one of eight bits in any of seven different registers—making 56 instructions!)

In general, any program that will run on an 8080 system, with the exception of those dependent upon timing loops, will also run on a Z80 system. There are differences in the clock timing, so those programs that create, or are dependent upon, specific 8080 timing will not usually run properly on the Z80.

Besides the different instruction set sizes, there are other differences between the Z80 and the 8080. The programmer of the Z80 device can use more internal registers and has more addressing modes than does the 8080 programmer.

In addition, there are several hardware differences. For one, the Z80 does away with the two-phase clock of the 8080. In the Z80, then, only a single-phase clock is used. The Z80 clock operates at 2.5 mHz, while the faster Z80A device will accept clock speeds to 4 mHz. The Z80 also differs from the 8080 in that it will operate from a single +5-volt power supply. The 8080 device requires, in addition to the +5-volt supply, a – 5-volt supply and a +12-volt supply.

The Z80 also provides an additional interrupt and the logic required to refresh dynamic memory.

The Z80 uses n-channel MOS technology, so must be handled with care in order to avoid damage from static electricity discharge.

Figure 1-1 shows the block diagram to the internal circuitry of the Z80 device. Note that the Z80 contains the following sections: arithmetic logic unit (ALU), CPU registers, and instruction register, plus sections to decode the instructions received and control the address placed on the address bus.

The Z80 uses an eight-bit data bus and a sixteen-bit address bus. The use of sixteen bits on the address bus means that the Z80 can address up to 65,536 different memory locations.

The internal registers of the Z80 represent 208 bits of read/write memory that can be accessed by the programmer. These bits are arranged in the form of eighteen 8-bit registers, and four 16-bit registers. Figure 1-2 shows the organization of the Z80 register set.

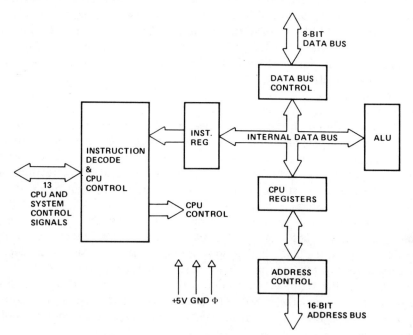

FIG. 1-1   Z80 CPU block diagram.

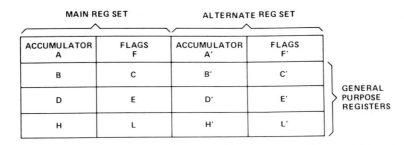

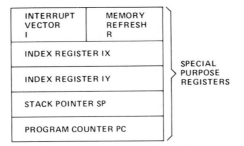

FIG. 1-2   Register organization.

The main register set consists of an accumulator (register **A**) and a flag register (register **F**), plus six general-purpose registers (B, C, D, E, H, and L). An alternate set of registers is provided that duplicates these registers: accumulator (A′) and flag register (F′), plus the general-purpose registers B′, C′, D′, E′, H′, and L′. Only one set of these registers can be active at any one time. One cannot, for example, use the B and B′ registers without first using one of the instructions that interchanges the register sets.

The general-purpose registers can be paired to form three register pairs of 16 bits each: BC, DE, and HL. The alternate registers are also paired to allow 16-bit register pairs BC′, DE′, and HL′.

The Z80 special-purpose registers include interrupt vector I and memory refresh R (both 8-bit registers), and four 16-bit registers: index register IX, index register IY, stack pointer SP, and program counter PC.

Interrupt vector I.   The I register is used to service interrupts originated by a peripheral device. The CPU will jump to a memory location containing the subroutine that services the interrupting device. The device will supply the lower-order eight bits of the 16-bit address, while the I register will contain the high-order eight bits of the address.

Memory refresh R.   This register is used to refresh dynamic memory during the time when the CPU is decoding and executing the instruction fetched from memory. Seven bits of the R register are incremented after each instruction fetch, but the eighth bit remains as programmed through a LD R, A instruction. During refresh, a refresh signal becomes active, the contents of the R register are placed on the lower eight bits of the address bus, and the contents of the I register are placed on the upper eight bits of the address bus.

Index registers IX and IY. These registers are used to point to external memory locations in indirect addressing instructions. The actual memory location addressed will be the sum of the contents of an index register and a displacement integer d (or, alternatively, some instructions use the two's complement of d). Both IX and IY index registers are independent of each other. Note that many microprocessor chips do not have index registers at all.

Stack pointer (SP). The stack pointer is a two-byte register that is used to hold the 16-bit address of a last-in-first-out (LIFO) stack in external memory. The data to and from the memory stack are handled through the PUSH and POP instructions, respectively.

Program counter (PC). The program counter in any computer holds the address of the instruction being fetched from memory. In the Z80, the program counter is a 16-bit register. The PC will be automatically incremented the correct number of digits after each instruction (e.g., one-byte instructions increment PC + 1, two-byte instructions PC + 2, etc.). When a JUMP operation occurs, the program counter will contain the address of the location to which the pro-

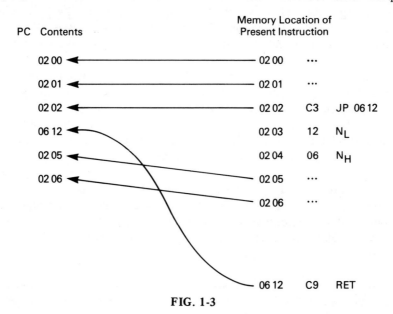

FIG. 1-3

gram jumped. When it is RETurned, the PC will contain the address of the next sequential instruction that would have been fetched if no jump had occurred.

Figure 1-3 shows how the program counter would work on a jump operation. Let us say that we have a program that starts at location 02 00 (hex), and finishes at location 02 06. But when it encounters the instruction at 02 02, it is an unconditional jump to location 06 12. Now, for the purposes of illustration, our subroutine at 06 12 is a RETurn instruction (useless in the real world, perhaps, but useful for illustration). It then jumps back to the next sequential location 02 05. Note that the next sequential location from 02 02 in this case is not 02 03, but 02 05. This is due to the fact that the jump instruction was a three-byte instruction. We had to give it the instruction (02 02), the low-order byte of the memory location to jump to (02 03), and the high-order byte of the memory location (02 04).

ARITHMETIC LOGIC UNIT (ALU)

The heart of any computer or microprocessor, and the factor that distinguishes it from all other digital electronic circuits, is the arithmetic logic unit, or ALU. This circuit performs the data manipulation for the device. The functions possible in the Z80 uP are add, subtract, compare, logical AND, logical OR, logical exclusive-OR (XOR), left shift (logical), left shift (arithmetic), right shift (logical), right shift (arithmetic), increment, decrement, set a bit (i.e., make it 1), reset a bit (make it ∅), and test a bit to see whether it is 1 or ∅.

FLAG REGISTERS (F AND F')

The Z80 provides two status registers; F and F'. Only one is active at any one time, depending upon whether the programmer has selected the main register bank or the alternative register bank. These registers are each eight bits long and each bit is used to denote a different status condition. As a result, these bits of the F and F' register are also called *condition bits*.

The flags in the F and F' register are SET or RESET after certain arithmetic or other operations upon data. The program can then tell something about the result of the operation. The allocations are as follows:

BIT (F/F')	DESIGNATION	MEANING
∅	C	Carry flag. Indicates a carry from the high-order bit of the accumulator (B7).
1	N	Subtraction flag used in BCD subtract operations.

BIT (F/F')	DESIGNATION	MEANING
2	P/V	Parity/overflow
3	X	Undetermined
4	H	BCD *half-carry* flag (bit 4 in BCD operations)
5	X	Undetermined
6	Z	Zero flag is SET if the result of an operation is zero.
7	S	Sign flag is SET if the sign of a result after an operation is negative, RESET if it is zero or positive.

2
Z80 Pin-outs

The Z80 device is constructed in a standard 40-pin DIP integrated circuit package. Since the Z80 uses NMOS technology, one is cautioned to become familiar with the rules for handling such devices before trying to handle the Z80 device. Those rules are actually very simple, so failing to follow them will net you what you deserve—a zapped IC.

Figure 2-1 shows the Z80 pinouts and package configuration. The definitions of the pinputs are given below, and the electrical (ac) specifications of the Z80 are given in Fig. 2-2.

PIN DEFINITIONS FOR THE Z80

A0–A15   Address bus (16 bits). Permits addressing up to 64K (i.e., 65,536 bytes) of memory, plus 256 different I/O ports. The address bus is active when HIGH, and has tri-state outputs. The entire 16 bits are used to address memory, while only the low-order byte (A0–A7) is used to address I/O ports.

D0–D7   Eight-bit data bus terminals. The data bus is, like the address bus, active high and uses tri-state outputs.

$\overline{M1}$ Machine cycle 1. When this terminal is LOW, the CPU is in the op-code fetch portion of the instruction/execution cycle.

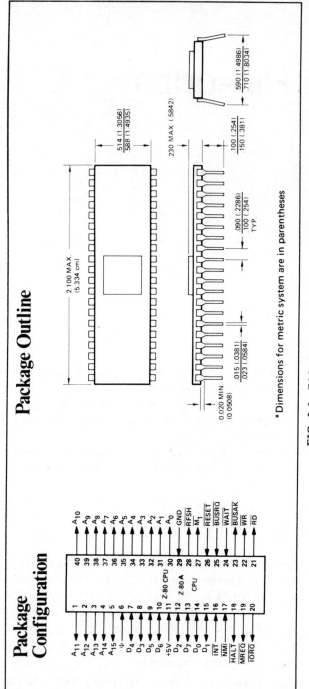

FIG. 2-1 Z80 package and pinouts.

MREQ   Memory request signal. Is active low, and is an active low output. When this terminal goes low, the address on the address bus is valid for a memory operation (read or write).

IORQ   Input/output request. This active low, tri-state output indicates that an I/O operation is to take place. The low-order byte of the address bus (A0–A7) contains the address (0–255) of the selected port. The contents of the accumulator may be placed on the high-order byte of the address bus during this period. The IORQ is also generated to acknowledge an interrupt request, and tells the interrupting device to place the interrupt vector word on the data bus (i.e., low-order byte of the address of the interrupt service program.)

RD   This is an active, low, tri-state output that indicates when a read operation from memory, or an I/O device, to the CPU is taking place.

WR   Tri-state, active, low output that indicates when a write operation from the CPU to a memory location, or I/O device, is taking place. Tells the memory or I/O device that the data on the data bus are currently valid.

RFSH   Refresh signal. This is an active low output that indicates that the lower seven bits of the address bus contain a refresh address for the dynamic memory.

HALT   Active low output that indicates that a halt instruction is being executed. The CPU executes NOPs while in the halt state, and is awaiting the receipt of an interrupt signal.

WAIT   Active low input that indicates that the addressed memory, or I/O device, is not yet ready to transfer data to the data bus.

INT   Active low input that tells the CPU that an external device has requested an interrupt. The CPU will honor the request at the end of the current instruction cycle, if the interrupt flip-flop (software controlled) is SET.

NMI   Active low input for nonmaskable interrupt operation. This line will cause the CPU to honor the interrupt at the end of the current instruction cycle, regardless of the state of the interrupt flip-flop. Forces automatic restart at location 00 66 (hex).

RESET   Active low input that enables the interrupt flip-flop, clears the program counter (i.e., loads PC with 00 00) and clears I and R registers. This terminal can serve as a hardware jump-to-00-00 control.

BUSRQ   Active low input that requests that the CPU address bus, data bus, and the control signals go to the high impedance (tri-state)

A.C. Characteristics   Z80-CPU

$T_A = 0°C$ to $70°C$, $V_{CC} = +5V \pm 5\%$, Unless Otherwise Noted.

Signal	Symbol	Parameter	Min	Max	Unit	Test Condition
Φ	t_c	Clock Period	.4	[12]	μsec	
	$t_w(ΦH)$	Clock Pulse Width, Clock High	180	[E]	nsec	
	$t_w(ΦL)$	Clock Pulse Width, Clock Low	180	2000	nsec	
	$t_{r,f}$	Clock Rise and Fall Time		30	nsec	
A_{0-15}	$t_D(AD)$	Address Output Delay		145	nsec	$C_L = 50pF$
	$t_F(AD)$	Delay to Float		110	nsec	
	t_{acm}	Address Stable Prior to $\overline{MREQ}$ (Memory Cycle)	[1]		nsec	
	t_{aci}	Address Stable Prior to $\overline{IORQ}$, $\overline{RD}$ or $\overline{WR}$ (I/O Cycle)	[2]		nsec	
	t_{ca}	Address Stable from $\overline{RD}$, $\overline{WR}$, $\overline{IORQ}$ or $\overline{MREQ}$	[3]		nsec	
	t_{caf}	Address Stable From $\overline{RD}$ or $\overline{WR}$ During Float	[4]		nsec	
D_{0-7}	$t_D(D)$	Data Output Delay		230	nsec	$C_L = 50pF$
	$t_F(D)$	Delay to Float During Write Cycle		90	nsec	
	$t_{Sφ}(D)$	Data Setup Time to Rising Edge of Clock During M1 Cycle	50		nsec	
	$t_{SΦ}(D)$	Data Setup Time to Falling Edge of Clock During M2 to M5	60		nsec	
	t_{dcm}	Data Stable Prior to $\overline{WR}$ (Memory Cycle)	[5]		nsec	
	t_{dci}	Data Stable Prior to $\overline{WR}$ (I/O Cycle)	[6]		nsec	
	t_{cdf}	Data Stable From $\overline{WR}$	[7]		nsec	
	t_H	Any Hold Time for Setup Time	0		nsec	
$\overline{MREQ}$	$t_{DLΦ}(MR)$	$\overline{MREQ}$ Delay From Falling Edge of Clock, $\overline{MREQ}$ Low		100	nsec	$C_L = 50pF$
	$t_{DHΦ}(MR)$	$\overline{MREQ}$ Delay From Rising Edge of Clock, $\overline{MREQ}$ High		100	nsec	
	$t_{DHΦ}(MR)$	$\overline{MREQ}$ Delay From Falling Edge of Clock, $\overline{MREQ}$ High		100	nsec	
	$t_w(MRL)$	Pulse Width, $\overline{MREQ}$ Low	[8]		nsec	
	$t_w(MRH)$	Pulse Width, $\overline{MREQ}$ High	[9]		nsec	
$\overline{IORQ}$	$t_{DLΦ}(IR)$	$\overline{IORQ}$ Delay From Rising Edge of Clock, $\overline{IORQ}$ Low		90	nsec	$C_L = 50pF$
	$t_{DL\overline{Φ}}(IR)$	$\overline{IORQ}$ Delay From Falling Edge of Clock, $\overline{IORQ}$ Low		110	nsec	
	$t_{DHΦ}(IR)$	$\overline{IORQ}$ Delay From Rising Edge of Clock, $\overline{IORQ}$ High		100	nsec	
	$t_{DH\overline{Φ}}(IR)$	$\overline{IORQ}$ Delay From Falling Edge of Clock, $\overline{IORQ}$ High		110	nsec	
$\overline{RD}$	$t_{DLΦ}(RD)$	$\overline{RD}$ Delay From Rising Edge of Clock, $\overline{RD}$ Low		100	nsec	$C_L = 50pF$
	$t_{DL\overline{Φ}}(RD)$	$\overline{RD}$ Delay From Falling Edge of Clock, $\overline{RD}$ Low		130	nsec	
	$t_{DHΦ}(RD)$	$\overline{RD}$ Delay From Rising Edge of Clock, $\overline{RD}$ High		100	nsec	
	$t_{DH\overline{Φ}}(RD)$	$\overline{RD}$ Delay From Falling Edge of Clock, $\overline{RD}$ High		110	nsec	

[12] $t_c = t_{w(ΦH)} + t_{w(ΦL)} + t_r + t_f$

[1] $t_{acm} = t_{w(ΦH)} + t_f - 75$

[2] $t_{aci} = t_c - 80$

[3] $t_{ca} = t_{w(ΦL)} + t_r - 40$

[4] $t_{caf} = t_{w(ΦL)} + t_r - 60$

[5] $t_{dcm} = t_c - 210$

[6] $t_{dci} = t_{w(ΦL)} + t_r - 210$

[7] $t_{cdf} = t_{w(ΦL)} + t_r - 80$

[8] $t_{w(MRL)} = t_c - 40$

[9] $t_{w(MRH)} = t_{w(ΦH)} + t_f - 30$

$\overline{WR}$	$t_{DL\Phi}$ (WR)	$\overline{WR}$ Delay From Rising Edge of Clock, $\overline{WR}$ Low		80	nsec	
	$t_{DL\overline{\Phi}}$ (WR)	$\overline{WR}$ Delay From Falling Edge of Clock, $\overline{WR}$ Low		90	nsec	$C_L = 50pF$
	$t_{DH\overline{\Phi}}$ (WR)	$\overline{WR}$ Delay From Falling Edge of Clock, $\overline{WR}$ High		100	nsec	
	t_w ($\overline{WRL}$)	Pulse Width, $\overline{WR}$ Low	[10]		nsec	
$\overline{M1}$	t_{DL} (M1)	$\overline{M1}$ Delay From Rising Edge of Clock, $\overline{M1}$ Low		130	nsec	$C_L = 50pF$
	t_{DH} (M1)	$\overline{M1}$ Delay From Rising Edge of Clock, $\overline{M1}$ High		130	nsec	
$\overline{RFSH}$	t_{DL} (RF)	$\overline{RFSH}$ Delay From Rising Edge of Clock, $\overline{RFSH}$ Low		180	nsec	$C_L = 50pF$
	t_{DH} (RF)	$\overline{RFSH}$ Delay From Rising Edge of Clock, $\overline{RFSH}$ High		150	nsec	
$\overline{WAIT}$	t_s (WT)	$\overline{WAIT}$ Setup Time to Falling Edge of Clock	70		nsec	
$\overline{HALT}$	t_D (HT)	$\overline{HALT}$ Delay Time From Falling Edge of Clock		300	nsec	$C_L = 50pF$
$\overline{INT}$	t_s (IT)	$\overline{INT}$ Setup Time to Rising Edge of Clock	80		nsec	
$\overline{NMI}$	t_w ($\overline{NML}$)	Pulse Width, $\overline{NMI}$ Low	80		nsec	
$\overline{BUSRQ}$	t_s (BQ)	$\overline{BUSRQ}$ Setup Time to Rising Edge of Clock	80		nsec	
$\overline{BUSAK}$	t_{DL} (BA)	$\overline{BUSAK}$ Delay From Rising Edge of Clock, $\overline{BUSAK}$ Low		120	nsec	$C_L = 50pF$
	t_{DH} (BA)	$\overline{BUSAK}$ Delay From Falling Edge of Clock, $\overline{BUSAK}$ High		110	nsec	
$\overline{RESET}$	t_s (RS)	$\overline{RESET}$ Setup Time to Rising Edge of Clock	90		nsec	
	t_F (C)	Delay to Float ($\overline{MREQ}$, $\overline{IORQ}$, $\overline{RD}$ and $\overline{WR}$)		100	nsec	
	t_{mr}	$\overline{M1}$ Stable Prior to $\overline{IORQ}$ (Interrupt Ack.)	[11]		nsec	

$$[10] \quad t_w(\overline{WRL}) = t_c - 40$$

$$[11] \quad t_{mr} = 2t_c + t_{w(\Phi H)} + t_f - 80$$

Load circuit for Output

FIG. 2-2 Z80 Electrical (AC) specifications.

NOTES:

A. Data should be enabled onto the CPU data bus when $\overline{RD}$ is active. During interrupt acknowledge data should be enabled when $\overline{M1}$ and $\overline{IORQ}$ are both active.

B. All control signals are internally synchronized, so they may be totally asynchronous with respect to the clock.

C. The $\overline{RESET}$ signal must be active for a minimum of 3 clock cycles.

D. Output Delay vs. Loaded Capacitance.
   $T_A = 70°C \quad V_{cc} = +5V \pm 5\%$
   Add 10nsec delay for each 50pf increase in load up to a maximum of 200pf for the data bus & 100pf for address & control lines

F. Although static by design, testing guarantees $t_{w(\Phi H)}$ of 200 μsec maximum

11

state so that some other device can obtain control of these buses. The $\overline{\text{BUSRQ}}$ has a higher priority than $\overline{\text{NMI}}$, and is always honored at the end of the present instruction.

$\overline{\text{BUSAK}}$ Active low output that is used with the bus request signal, and tells the requesting device that the CPU buses are now in the high impedance state. When $\overline{\text{BUSAK}}$ drops low, then the requesting device may take control of the buses.

Φ   Clock signal input. Wants to see TTL level at 2 mHz or 4 mHz (Z80A) maximum.

GND   DC and signal ground terminal.

+5   Power supply terminal, to which is applied +5 volts dc from a regulated power supply.

3
Z80 Family Support Chips

The Z80 is not a single-chip computer. In order to make the Z80 microprocessor chip think that it is a real live computer we need additional, external circuitry. In some commercial products, this external circuitry takes the form of TTL and/or CMOS devices connected to perform the desired function. But Zilog, Inc. makes it easier to make a computer by using certain external special-function integrated circuits.

Two of the special-function devices are used to provide serial and parallel input/output capability. The Z80-SIO device is a serial I/O chip, while the Z80-PIO is a parallel I/O port. These devices are second-sourced by Mostek under the type numbers MK3884 (Z80-SIO) and MK3881 (Z80-PIO).

There is also a direct memory access device called the Z80-DMA (Mostek MK3883). Direct memory access in a computer allows the external memory to be written to, or read from, by a peripheral device without first going through the CPU. This allows the operation to be performed much more rapidly, and is conservative of CPU time—a precious commodity in some applications.

The Z80-CTC (Mostek MK3882) is a four-channel, multimode counter/ timer circuit. It provides counter and timer capability in Z80-based microcomputer systems.

Z80-PIO

The Zilog Z80-PIO (Mostek MK3881) is used as a parallel I/O port controller. It contains two ports, and is user programmable. The Z80-PIO contains two completely independent, eight-bit, bidirectional ports. Complete handshaking capability is permitted, so the device can be used for synchronous transfers.

The Z80-PIO can be programmed to operate in four different modes: *byte output, byte input, byte bidirectional bus* (port A only), and *bit control*.

The byte output mode, also called mode-$\emptyset$, is used to allow the CPU to write data to the peripheral via the CPU data bus. If mode-$\emptyset$ is selected, a *data write* operation causes a handshake signal (*ready*) to be generated. This signal is used to let the peripheral know that the data are available and valid. Note that the data remain available, and the *ready* signal remains HIGH, until a strobe is received back from the peripheral.

The *byte input mode*, also called mode-1, allows the selected port to behave as an input port only. When a *data read* operation is performed by the CPU, the PIO will issue a *ready* signal to the peripheral. This tells the peripheral that the Z-80 CPU is now in a condition to receive the input data. The peripheral responds by issuing a strobe that causes the data to be transferred to the data input register of the PIO.

The *byte bidirectional mode*, also called mode-2, uses the port as a bidirectional, eight-bit, I/O port. Mode-2 uses all four possible handshake lines. Because of this restriction, only port-A can be used in the bidirectional mode.

The *bit control mode*, also called mode-3, is used for status and control applications. Mode-3 does not make use of the handshake signals. This mode is used to define which port data bus lines will be inputs and which will be outputs. The next word fed to the PIO after mode-3 is selected must define these conditions.

Figure 3-1 shows the pinouts for the Z80-PIO, while below are the definitions of the different types of pins.

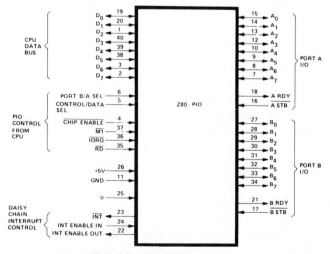

FIG. 3-1   Z80-PIO pinouts.

DØ-D7	These pins connect to the Z80 CPU data bus, and are both bidirectional and tri-state. All command signals and data passed between the CPU and the PIO, in either direction, must be passed over these lines.
B/A SEL	This active-HIGH input will select either port A or port B. A LOW on B/A SEL will select port A, whereas a HIGH will select port A.
C/D SEL	This active-HIGH input selects the type of data transfer to take place between the CPU and PIO. A LOW on this line tells the PIO that the data on the Z80 data bus are I/O data. But a HIGH will tell the PIO that the data being transferred are a command for the port selected by B/A SEL.
$\overline{CE}$	Active-LOW input that acts as a chip enable. A LOW on this terminal allows the PIO to accept command/data inputs from the Z80 CPU during any write cycle, or to send data to the Z80 CPU during and read cycle.
$\overline{M1}$	This terminal synchronizes the PIO to the CPU, and is generally connected to the similarly named terminal on the CPU chip. Indicates that an M1 machine cycle is in progress.
$\overline{IORQ}$	Input/output request line from the Z80 CPU chip that is part of the sync system. Usually connected to the similarly named terminal on the Z80 device.
$\overline{RD}$	Active-low input that detects the read cycle of the Z-80.
IEI	Interrupt Enable Input. This is an active-HIGH input.
A_ϕ-A7	Tri-state, bidirectional address bus for port-A.
$\overline{A\ STB}$	Active-LOW input that strobes port-A from peripheral device.
A RDY	Active-HIGH output signals that the A-register is ready.
B_ϕ-B7	Tri-state, bidirectional, address bus for port-B.
$\overline{B\ STB}$	Active-LOW input that allows peripheral device to strobe port-B.
B RDY	Active-HIGH output that signals that the B-register is ready.

Z80-SIO

The Z80-SIO device is a serial I/O chip that interfaces directly with the Z80 CPU chip. It is similar to the Z80-PIO in that it is a programmable two-channel device. The SIO, however, transmits the data in the *serial* stream, i.e., one bit at a time. Parallel transfer is, of course, faster in most cases. But often a serial transfer is preferred because it reduces the hardware overhead between the computer and the peripheral with which it is communicating. Even when the "run" is only a short distance, it is often much less costly to use a serial data transfer because only one pair of wires, one telephone line, or one radio communications channel is required. The Z80-SIO is designed to handle just about any reasonable serial bit protocol. Like the other chips of the Z80 family, it is operated from a single +5-volt dc supply and uses only a single-phase clock.

The two channels (also labeled A and B, as in the PIO device) are totally independent of each other, except for power supply and CPU bus connections. The SIO channels are full-duplex, so data can be transmitted and received simultaneously. The Z80-SIO allows data rates from zero to 550,000 bits per second.

Both receiver and transmitter registers are fully buffered. But in the case of the transmitter section, the registers are doubly buffered. The receiver registers, on the other hand, are quadruply buffered.

The Z80-SIO is capable of *asynchronous* operation (in which it behaves much like an ordinary UART, but with a Z80-system flavor), *synchronous binary* operation, and HDLC/IBM-SDLC operation. The SIO provides eight MODEM control inputs/outputs, allows daisy chain priority interrupt logic to automatically provide the vector word, and permits both CRC-16 and CRC-CCIT ($-0/-1$).

The SIO looks very much like the ordinary UART in its asynchronous mode. It can be programmed for 5, 6, 7, or 8 eight-bit words. Like the UART, it will provide 1, 1.5, or 2 stop bits at the end of each transmitted word. The CPU, incidentally, need not provide these bits, the SIO adds them to the word received from the CPU before the word is transmitted. Also like the UART, the SIO will provide parity bits (even, odd, none), and detection of parity, framing errors, and overrun. Unlike most UARTs, however, the SIO also provides for the generation and detection of breaks. Clock rates of 1X, 16X, 32X, and 64X the data rate are permitted.

Figure 3-2 shows the organization of the Z80-PIO device. In Fig. 3-2(a) we see the overall block diagram of the device, while Fig. 3-2(b) shows the block diagram for the channels. The input section from the CPU receives eight data bus lines, and six control signal lines. Once inside, the device operates from an internal bus not accessible to the outside world. There are two sections for channels A and B, some internal control logic, the interrupt section, and a discrete control section (used with MODEMs and other controlling devices).

The pinouts for the Z80-SIO are shown in Fig. 3-3, and are listed in detail below:

D∅-D7	Tri-state, bidirectional data bus to/from Z80-CPU and rest of Z80 system.
B/A	Channel A/B select. Channel A is selected when this pin is LOW, and channel B is selected when it is HIGH.
C/D	Control/data select. If this input is HIGH, then the control mode is selected, but if it is LOW, then the data mode is selected.
$\overline{M1}$	Active-LOW input that detects the M1 machine cycle in Z80.

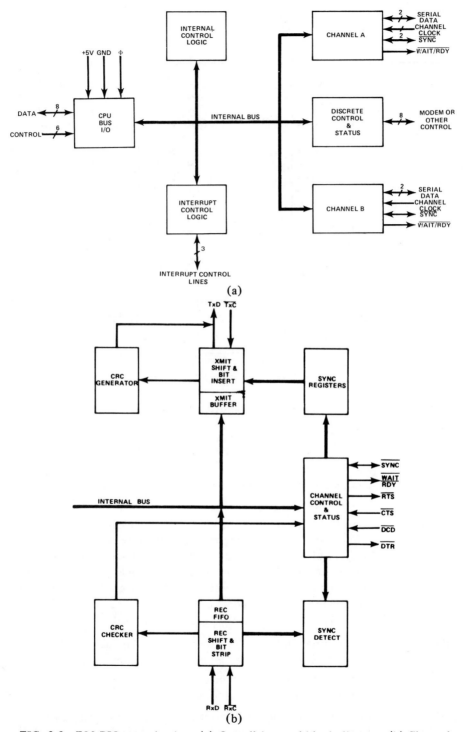

FIG. 3-2 Z80-PIO organization. (a) Overall internal block diagram; (b) Channel block diagram.

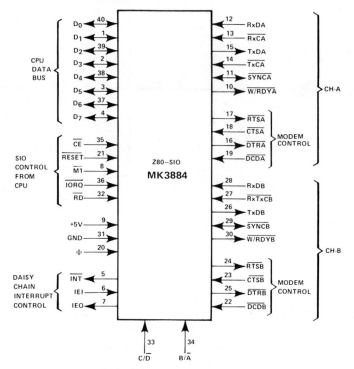

FIG. 3-3 Z80-SIO Pinouts.

$\overline{\text{IORQ}}$	Active-LOW input that detects the Input/Output ReQuest state of the Z80 CPU.
$\overline{\text{RD}}$	Active-LOW input that detects the read cycle of the Z80 CPU.
Ø	Clock terminal.
$\overline{\text{RESET}}$	Active-LOW input that resets the system. Placing a LOW on this terminal has the following results: both receivers and transmitters, are disabled, TDA/TDB are forced marking, modem controls are forced HIGH, and all interrupts are disabled. *Note:* The control registers of the SIO *must* be rewritten from the CPU before the SIO can be again used.
IEI	Active-HIGH interrupt enable input.
IEO	Active-HIGH output. Note that IEI/IEO are used together to form a daisy-chain priority interrupt control function.
$\overline{\text{INT}}$	Active-LOW output to the interrupt request line of the Z80. Note that this terminal is an open-drain type.
WAIT/ READY A	These lines, one of each channel, have two principal functions. In one case, they can be used as ready lines for the Z80 DMA

WAIT/ READY B	(direct memory access) controller. In another, they can be used to synchronize the Z80 CPU to the Z80-SIO (i.e., to sync the data rate between CPU and SIO).
CTSA CTSB	These lines, one for each channel, provide a *clear to send* function. Both are active-LOW inputs. If programmed for *auto enable*, then these pins will act as transmitter enable controls. But when not programmed for auto enable, they can be programmed for general control purposes. *Note:* These pins are buffered through Schmitt-trigger circuits, thereby allowing slow rise-time signals.
DCDA DCDB	Data Carrier Detect. These two active-LOW inputs serve as receiver enable control signals.
RDA/RDB	Active-HIGH receiver data inputs.
TDA/TDB	Active-HIGH transmit data outputs.
RCA/RCB	Schmitt-trigger buffered, active-LOW receiver clock inputs.
TCA/TCB	Same as above, but transmitter clocks.
RTSA/ RTSB	Active-LOW outputs providing *request-to-send* signals.
DTRA/ DTRB	Active-LOW outputs providing *data-terminal-ready* signals.
SYNCA/ SYNCB	Used for synchronization of external characters.

Z80-DMA

The Z80-DMA (Mostek MK3883) is a *direct memory access* controller. This type of operation is very useful in a computer, because it speeds up direct transfers between an external device, or peripheral, and the memory because it allows bypassing of the CPU. Ordinarily, if you wanted to transfer a data word from some peripheral device and a specific memory location, you would have to execute an input instruction to move the data into the accumulator first. Then a second instruction would be required in order to move the data from the CPU to the desired memory location. Unless the data are to be used immediately after input, then such would be a waste of valuable time. DMA allows the data to be placed directly into the desired location from the peripheral.

The DMA chip allows three modes, or classes, of operation: *transfer only*, *search only*, and *search-transfer*. There are also four types of operation: *single byte at a time*, *continuous burst* (as long as ports are ready), *continuous* (CPU locked out), and *transparent* (i.e., it steals time from refresh cycles).

Three types of interrupt are allowed. In one case, it will interrupt the CPU only when a match to a desired word is found. It will also interrupt on *end-of-block* or *ready*. The DMA can be enabled, disabled, or reset totally under software control.

Figure 3-4(a) shows the pinouts for the Z80-DMA, while Fig. 3-4(b) shows the internal block diagram. The pinout functions are discussed below:

A_ϕ-A15   System address bus (from Z80 and memory). This sixteen-bit address bus can, like the Z80 bus, address all 64K of allowed memory.

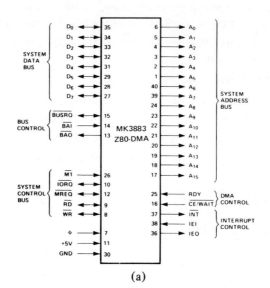

(a)

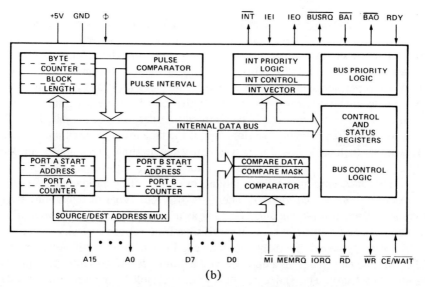

(b)

FIG. 3-4 (a) Z80-DMA pinouts; (b) Z80-DMA block diagram.

D$_\phi$-D7	Data bus from CPU and memory. These tri-state input/output pins carry three types of data: commands from the Z80 CPU, DMA status (from memory/peripherals), and data from the memory/peripherals.
ϕ	System clock.
$\overline{M1}$	Active-LOW input detects the M1 machine cycle in the Z80 CPU.
$\overline{IORQ}$	Used as an input/output request to/from the CPU bus.
$\overline{MREQ}$	Used as a memory request to/from Z80 system bus.
$\overline{RD}$	Read to/from Z80 CPU bus.
$\overline{WR}$	Write signal to/from Z80 CPU bus.
$\overline{CE/WAIT}$	May be used as either chip enable or $\overline{wait}$.
$\overline{BUSRQ}$	Bus request is used to request control of the data bus from the Z80 CPU.
$\overline{BAI}$	Input that tells the Z80-DMA that the CPU has granted it control of the bus. It is a bus acknowledge input.
$\overline{BAO}$	Bus acknowledge output that allows daisy chain connection of DMA-requesting peripherals.
$\overline{INT}$	Active-LOW output that tells the Z80-CPU that an interrupt is requested.
IEI	Active-HIGH interrupt enable input.
IEO	Active-HIGH interrupt enable output. Forms ability to daisy chain, when used in conjunction with IEI.
RDY	Active-HIGH/LOW (i.e., programmable) input that tells the Z80-DMA when a peripheral device is ready for a write/read operation.

Z80-CTC

The Z80-CTC (Mostek MK3882) is a universal counter-timer chip that can provide all of the counter/timer requirements for a Z80-based computer. There are four independent channels in the Z80-CTC. Consistent with the design of the rest of the Z80-family, this device requires only a single +5-volt dc power supply and a single-phase clock. Each of the four channels can operate as either a counter or a timer.

The Z80-CTC pinouts are shown in Fig. 3-5, and their respective descriptions are given below:

D$\emptyset$-D7	Bidirectional tri-state data bus to/from CPU.
CS$\emptyset$-CS1	Active-HIGH channel select inputs.
$\overline{CE}$	Active-LOW chip enable input.

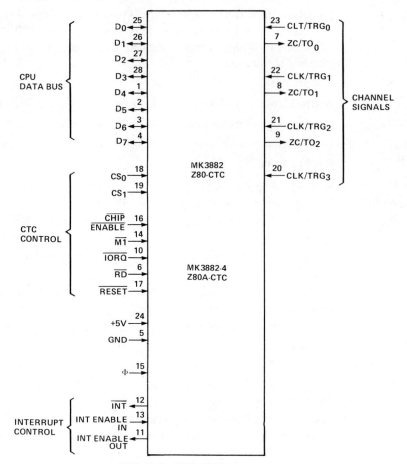

FIG. 3-5 Z80-CTC pinouts.

$\emptyset$	System clock.
$\overline{\text{M1}}$	Active-LOW input from CPU that detects the M1 machine cycle.
$\overline{\text{IORQ}}$	Active-LOW input that detects the input/output request state of the CPU.
$\overline{\text{RD}}$	Active-LOW input that detects the Z80-CPU read cycle.
IEI	Active-HIGH interrupt enable input.
IEO	Active-HIGH interrupt enable output. Used with IEI to permit daisy chaining.
$\overline{\text{INT}}$	Active-LOW, open-drain, output to the Z80-CPU interrupt request input.
$\overline{\text{RESET}}$	Active-LOW, reset input.

4

Z80 Timing and Interface Control Signals

If you are planning to use a ready-built computer containing a Z80 micropro-cessor chip, then it is not likely that you will need to know much about the chip-level interface and timing signals of the chip. Languages like BASIC, and even some assemblers, will not require that you know much at all about these signals. But if you are doing machine level programming, using most assemblers, or are trying to interface some other instrument to the Z80 directly, or to the bus of a Z80 computer, it is then necessary for you to know and understand the timing structure.

In Chapter 2, we discussed the definitions of the Z80 pins. Among the pins discussed were the interface and timing signals. For emphasis, let us reiter-ate these signals here, but grouping them according to use.

DATA/ADDRESS BUSES

There are two buses in the Z80: a 16-bit address bus and an 8-bit data bus. The address bus pinouts are labeled A$\emptyset$–A15, while the data bus terminals are designated B$\emptyset$–B7. In both cases, the $\emptyset$ bit is the least significant bit, while the highest numbered bit (7 on the data bus, 15 on the address bus) is the most significant bit.

Both address and data buses are designed to be tri-state outputs. This means that there are the HIGH and LOW states for logical 1 and $\emptyset$, respectively, plus a third high impedance state which can be used to effectively disconnect the Z80 CPU chip from the external bus lines. In some cases, a bus request signal (discussed below) will cause the data and address buses to go into the tri-state condition, so that an external device can control the buses.

Also, both address and data buses are active when HIGH.

The data bus is used to pass data to, and from, the CPU chip. Unless one knows the status of the control signals, and the word applied to the address bus, however, one does not know what is taking place on the data bus.

The address bus does several things. In the memory address mode, for example, the 16-bit address bus will be capable of designating 2^{16}, or 65,536, different memory locations. This size, incidentally, is usually called "64K," even though 65,000+ locations are addressable. This is due to the fact that a computer "K" is 1024, not 1000 (sigh).

The address bus is also used in the control of input/output operations. When an I/O command is being executed, the lower byte of the address bus holds the address of the I/O port designated in the instruction. The upper byte contains the accumulator data, repeated on the data bus.

The lower byte of the address bus is also used in the memory refresh operation. During the period of the machine cycle in which the refresh operation is to take place, as indicated by a LOW condition on the $\overline{\text{RFSH}}$ output terminal, the lower seven bits (A∅–A6) of the address bus contain the refresh address.

INPUT/OUTPUT (I/O) OPERATIONS

The Z80 design philosophy is a little different from the philosophy of its direct ancestor, the 8080 device. This is especially noticeable in the I/O operations. In the Z80, there is an *input/output request* ($\overline{\text{IORQ}}$) signal available. This is a tri-state, active low output that is used to tell external devices and memory that an input or output operation is taking place.

The $\overline{\text{IORQ}}$ signal will go LOW when (a) an input or output operation is taking place, and (b) when an interrupt is being acknowledged. In the latter case, an $\overline{\text{M1}}$ signal is also generated during interrupts. This combination of signals is used to tell the interrupting device to place the address vector pointing to the interrupt service subroutine. These two types of operation can be distinguished from each other because interrupt acknowledgments always occur during the M1 period (see below), and I/O operations never occur during the M1 period.

It is not possible to use just one signal for I/O control, because there are three possible states: no I/O operation, input, and output. In the first case, the $\overline{\text{IORQ}}$ line would be HIGH, but it will be LOW for both of the other possible conditions. In the Z80 device, the input and output states are distinguished by the condition of the $\overline{\text{WR}}$ and $\overline{\text{RD}}$ control signal. These are also used in memory operations, and are the *write* ($\overline{\text{WR}}$) and *read* ($\overline{\text{RD}}$) signals. If the I/O operation is an input (i.e., read), then the $\overline{RD}$ line goes LOW along with $\overline{IORQ}$. But if the I/O operation is an output, then the $\overline{WR}$ control signal goes LOW along with $\overline{IORQ}$.

MEMORY CONTROL SIGNALS

Control of memory operations requires the same $\overline{WR}$ and $\overline{RD}$ signals as used in the I/O operations. But instead of the $\overline{IORQ}$ signals, a *memory request* $(\overline{MREQ})$ is used. This signal is an active low, tri-state output that is used to indicate that the address bus contains a valid memory location address. Whether the CPU is reading from memory or writing to memory is indicated by the coincidence of the $\overline{MREQ}$ and $\overline{RD}$ (memory read), or $\overline{MREQ}$ and $\overline{WR}$. Address decoders in memory, then, must take note of these signals in order to determine whether a read or write operation is taking place.

There is also a *refresh* $(\overline{RFSH})$ signal used to control dynamic memories. Unlike static memory devices, dynamic memory often requires a refresh operation, or the data stored will be lost. $\overline{RFSH}$ is an active low, tri-state output, and is active once during each instruction fetch operation. When the $\overline{RFSH}$ and $\overline{MREQ}$ are both low, a memory refresh can take place. The contents of the R register are loaded onto the lower seven bits of the address bus to address the memory to be refreshed. The R register is incremented after each operation, so all memory will eventually be refreshed.

CPU CONTROL SIGNALS

There are four basic CPU control signals: $\overline{M1}$, $\overline{RESET}$, $\overline{WAIT}$, and $\overline{HALT}$.

The $\overline{M1}$ signal is used to indicate that an M1 instruction fetch period is in effect. The M1 machine cycle occurs when an instruction is being fetched from memory. If the instruction being fetched is a two-byte instruction, then an $\overline{M1}$ signal is generated as each op-code is being fetched.

The $\overline{M1}$ signal is also generated during interrupt acknowledgments, in conjunction with an $\overline{IORQ}$ signal. This combination allows the interrupting device to place the address vector of the memory location containing the interrupt service subroutine.

The $\overline{RESET}$ signal is an active low input. When this terminal is brought low, the CPU does the following: Disables the interrupt flip-flop; sets the I register to $\emptyset\emptyset$ (hex); sets the R register to $\emptyset\emptyset$ (hex), and sets interrupt mode $\emptyset$. In effect, the $\overline{RESET}$ is a *hardware* jump to $\emptyset\emptyset$ $\emptyset\emptyset$ instruction.

The $\overline{WAIT}$ terminal is an active low input that can be used to tell the CPU that an addressed I/O device is not ready to transfer data. The CPU keeps entering wait states until this signal goes high again. This signal is needed because many types of I/O device are not as fast as the CPU.

The $\overline{\text{HALT}}$ signal is an active low output that indicates that a halt instruction is being executed. The CPU will execute no-ops (NOP) until an interrupt is received.

INTERRUPT SIGNALS

The principal interrupt signals are the $\overline{\text{INT}}$ and $\overline{\text{NMI}}$. The regular *interrupt request* signal is the $\overline{\text{INT}}$. It is an active low input. The interrupt request signal is generated by the interrupting I/O device. The interrupt request will be honored at the end of the present instruction cycle. There are three modes of response by the CPU: mode $\emptyset$, mode 1, and mode 2.

The nonmaskable interrupt ($\overline{\text{NMI}}$) signal is used to allow interrupts that *must* be serviced at the end of the current instruction cycle.

$\overline{\text{BUSRQ}}$ AND $\overline{\text{BUSAK}}$

These signals are used to allow access to the memory by external devices, without the use of the CPU. The $\overline{\text{BUSRQ}}$ is an active low input. When the $\overline{\text{BUSRQ}}$ line goes low, the CPU outputs (address and data buses) go tri-state at the end of the current instruction cycle.

The $\overline{\text{BUSAK}}$ is an active low output that tells the external device that the CPU is in the high impedance tri-state condition. When this signal goes low, the external device knows that it now has control of the data and address buses.

BASIC CPU TIMING

All instructions in any programmable digital computer are merely a series of certain basic operations. In discussing the timing of the CPU, we must determine how these operations occur. The clock produces periods called T-periods (see Fig. 4-1). There are also three different "M-cycles" for each instruction cycle. M cycles are machine cycles, while the T cycles are clock cycles.

Machine cycle M1 is the instruction fetch period, and may be four to six T cycles long. During this period, the CPU is fetching the next instruction from the memory. The other machine cycles (M2 and M3), are used for memory read and memory write, respectively. M2 and M3 are used for memory and I/O operations.

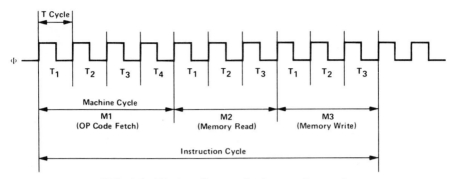

FIG. 4-1 Timing diagram for instruction cycle.

In the paragraphs to follow, we will discuss the *op-code instruction fetch, memory data read/write, I/O read/write, bus request/acknowledge, interrupt request, nonmaskable interrupt request,* and *exit from HALT instruction* cycles.

Op-code instruction fetch. Figure 4-2 shows the CPU timing during the M1 op-code instruction fetch cycle of the Z80 CPU. The program counter (PC) contains the address of the next instruction. The contents of the PC are placed on the address bus (A∅–A15) during the first half of the M1 cycle.

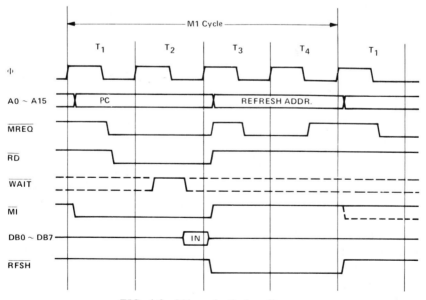

FIG. 4-2 M1 cycle timing diagram.

Since we are trying to fetch, i.e., *read*, an instruction from some location in memory, the $\overline{\text{MREQ}}$ and $\overline{\text{RD}}$ signals are also placed low. This tells the memory that a read operation is taking place from a location whose address is found on the address bus.

The $\overline{\text{WAIT}}$ line is sampled during this period. If the memory device is slow, it may generate a wait signal to slow down the operation. If a wait signal is found during each sample (i.e., once during each T cycle), then the CPU will enter another wait state. When the device is ready to transfer data, the wait signal disappears, and the data bus contains the data from that memory location.

During the last half of the M1 cycle (i.e., T3/T4), the refresh address is placed on the lower seven bits of the address bus, and a $\overline{\text{RFSH}}$ is generated. This will allow the refreshing of dynamic solid-state memories.

During the portion of the M1 cycle that the program counter contents are on the address bus, the $\overline{\text{M1}}$ signal is low.

The M1 machine cycle will lengthen for as long as there is a wait signal present. Using the $\overline{\text{WAIT}}$ line permits us to synchronize the CPU and an external device.

Memory data read/write.   The M2 and M3 machine cycles are used to read to, or write from, memory locations. Figure 4-3 shows the CPU timing during these operations. The principal signals used in this type of operation are the $\overline{\text{MREQ}}$, $\overline{\text{WR}}$, and $\overline{\text{RD}}$.

If a memory read operation is needed, then an address is placed on the address bus (A∅–A15) during the M2 machine cycle. During this period, the $\overline{\text{MREQ}}$ (memory request) and $\overline{\text{RD}}$ lines coincidentally go low. The $\overline{\text{MREQ}}$ signal does not become active until the data on the address bus are stable.

Memory write operations cause data from the CPU to be written into specified locations in memory. This occurs during the M3 machine cycle. In this operation, the $\overline{\text{MREQ}}$ and $\overline{\text{WR}}$ signals become active. The $\overline{\text{MREQ}}$ signal, however, does not become active until the data on the data bus are stable (i.e., valid), so that semiconductor memory can be accommodated. Again, the address of the specified location is applied to the address bus (A∅–A15).

As in the instruction fetch cycle, a wait state can be created. If the $\overline{\text{WAIT}}$ signal is low, then the CPU continues to enter wait states until the signal becomes inactive. The $\overline{\text{WAIT}}$ signal can be used to synchronize the CPU to memory sources.

I/O Read/Write.   Figure 4-4 shows the CPU timing during input and output cycles. During each of these types of operation, the $\overline{\text{IORQ}}$ request line becomes active (i.e., goes low). If the operation is a read cycle, then the $\overline{\text{RD}}$ signal will also go low. But if the operation is a write cycle (i.e., an output), then the $\overline{\text{WR}}$ signal goes low coincidentally with $\overline{\text{IORQ}}$.

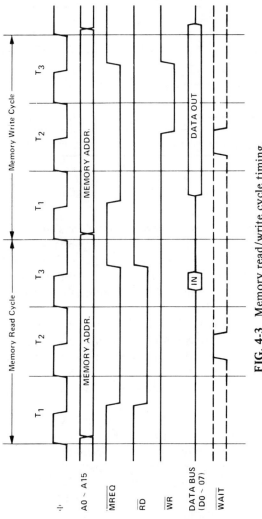

FIG. 4-3 Memory read/write cycle timing.

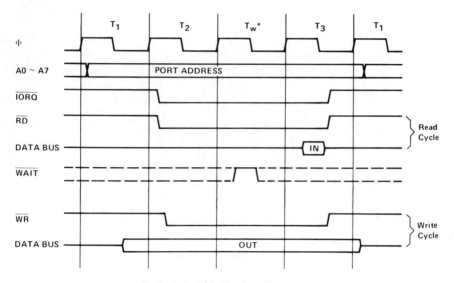

FIG. 4-4 I/O Timing diagram.

In both input and output cycles, the address of the designated port is placed on the lower byte of the address bus (A∅–A7). Since this is an eight-bit address, we can specify up to 256 different addresses from ∅∅∅–255 (decimal).

During an input (i.e., I/O read) operation, the $\overline{\text{IORQ}}$ and $\overline{\text{RD}}$ signals are low during T2 and T3, and data from the input port are passed along the data bus.

During an output (i.e., I/O write) operation, the $\overline{\text{IORQ}}$ and $\overline{\text{WR}}$ signals are low during T2 and T3. Data from the accumulator are passed over the data bus to the output port whose address is contained on the lower byte of the address bus. But note that the $\overline{\text{IORQ}}$ signal does not become active immediately, allowing the data on the data bus to stabilize before the operation is consummated.

Bus request/acknowledge. The bus request signal ($\overline{\text{BUSRQ}}$) is used to allow external devices to gain control of the CPU control lines, the address bus and the data bus. This allows direct access to memory for the external device.

The CPU samples the $\overline{\text{BUSRQ}}$ input during the last T cycle of any given M cycle. If the bus request is active, the CPU will complete the current instruction, and then service the request. Following the last T cycle of the last M cycle, the CPU will go into a high impedance state. The address bus lines, the data bus lines, and the control lines ($\overline{\text{MREQ}}$, $\overline{\text{RD}}$, $\overline{\text{WR}}$, $\overline{\text{IORQ}}$, $\overline{\text{RFSH}}$) are placed in the high impedance condition, effectively disconnecting them from the external circuits. This will allow the external device to gain control of the lines, to directly input data to memory locations without going through the CPU. When the CPU lines are in the high impedance state, the CPU generates a $\overline{\text{BUSAK}}$ (bus acknowl-

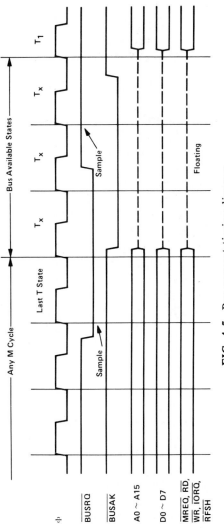

FIG. 4-5 Bus request timing diagram.

edge) signal that tells the requesting device that the buses are available to its use. The timing for this type of operation is shown in Fig. 4-5.

When the external device is finished with the memory, it will deactivate (i.e., make high) the $\overline{BUSRQ}$ signal, telling the CPU that it can have control again.

Interrupt request.   The ability to service interrupts allows the CPU to use certain types of external device more efficiently. The CPU can do other chores while the slower external device is working, or it may perform other chores while awaiting rarely occurring situations to develop. The $\overline{INT}$ signal is the interrupt request. This line is sampled by the CPU on the rising edge of the last T state of each M cycle. See Fig. 4-6.

These interrupts can be masked in software because the CPU will not accept the request unless an internal CPU flip-flop is set. This interrupt flip-flop is controlled by software commands. Interrupts are also ignored if the bus request ($\overline{BUSRQ}$) line is active (i.e., low).

If the CPU accepts the interrupt request, then a special M1 state is generated, so the $\overline{M1}$ line goes low. The address bus receives the contents of the program counter (PC), so that the CPU can return to the original program after the interrupt is serviced. The address of the next instruction, to be executed following termination of the interrupt, is stored on an external memory stack.

Once the PC contents are stored, the $\overline{IORQ}$ line goes low, telling the interrupting device that it can place an address vector on the data bus, which tells the CPU where the program that services the interrupt is located.

As in the previous conditions, the $\overline{WAIT}$ signal can be used to lengthen the timing by causing the CPU to enter wait states. If the $\overline{WAIT}$ line is active when sampled, the CPU enters the wait state. If the signal is inactive, then no wait state is generated, and the CPU continues.

Nonmaskable interrupts.   Certain types of interrupt situations cannot wait for the software being executed by the CPU to set an internal flip-flop. Such interrupts might be an alarm condition in the process or factory, or in a medical computer. These situations require a nonmaskable interrupt. Figure 4-7 shows the CPU timing for the nonmaskable interrupt in the Z80.

This type of interrupt cycle is very similar to the regular interrupt, except that it is not dependent upon the software-controlled interrupt flip-flop. This type of interrupt will be serviced as soon as the present instruction cycle is completed. The contents of the program counter are stored in an external memory stack, and the CPU jumps automatically to location $\emptyset\emptyset$ 66 (hex) to find the interrupt service program.

Exit from a HALT.   If a software HALT instruction is encountered, the CPU will sit there executing no-ops (NOP) until one of two situations occurs:

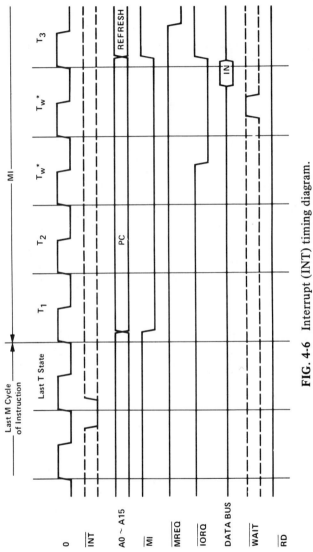

FIG. 4-6 Interrupt (INT) timing diagram.

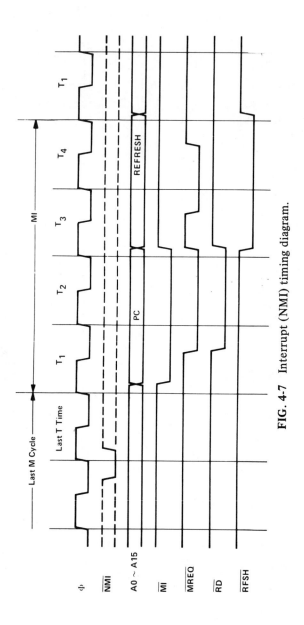

FIG. 4-7 Interrupt (NMI) timing diagram.

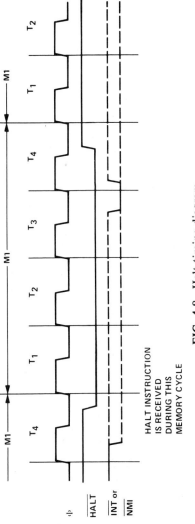

FIG. 4-8 Halt timing diagram.

(a) a nonmaskable interrupt is received, or (b) a maskable interrupt is received, and the internal interrupt flip-flop is SET.

If the Interrupt lines ($\overline{\text{INT}}$ or $\overline{\text{NMI}}$) are active when sampled during the T4 portion of the M1 cycle, then the HALT condition is terminated following T4. The $\overline{\text{HALT}}$ line then goes inactive (high). The CPU timing for the exit from halt operation is shown in Fig. 4-8.

5

Z80 Addressing Modes

The many different instructions offered by the Z80 microprocessor reflect, in part, a number of different addressing modes for the same basic operations. In all cases, the Z80 instructions pertain to operations on data between internal registers, in the external RAM or ROM memory, or input and output ports. It is, perhaps, easier to realize just where such a large, magnificient instruction set comes from when you consider that there are several different forms of operation, on data in up to eighteen 8-bit registers, and four 16-bit registers. And since the Z80 uses a 16-bit address bus, it can accommodate a mix of *random access memory* (RAM) and *read only memory* (ROM) up to 2^{16} (65,536, or so-called, "64K") one-byte locations. There are also up to 256 input and 256 output port selections possible.

One of the advantages of the Z80 is the large number of addressing modes, taking it out of the simple process controller stage and making it a real live computer. The modes of addressing offered by the Z80 device include:

Immediate addressing
Immediate extended addressing
Modified page-zero addressing
Relative addressing
Extended addressing
Indexed addressing
Register addressing

Implied register addressing
Register indirect addressing
Bit addressing

In this chapter we will discuss the various different types of addressing, and then deal with sample instructions (enumerated more fully in Chapter 17), using examples.

Immediate addressing. In the immediate addressing mode, the operand follows the op-code in sequential locations, and the operand is loaded into the selected location immediately. A prime example of the immediate addressing mode is the ADD A,n and Sub A,n instructions. In these instructions, the operand n is added (or subtracted if SUB A,n) to the contents of the accumulator, and the result is then stored in the accumulator.

The format for the immediate addressing type of instruction is shown below:

byte 1   op-code
byte 2   (n)

Example

The op-code for the ADD A,n instruction is 11000110 in binary or C6 in hexadecimal. Let us say that the accumulator contains A7 (hex) before the following code is encountered:

memory location	code	
06 00	C6	byte 1
06 01	Ø7	byte 2

This means that the instruction fetched (C6) is the ADD A,n instruction, and that operand n (the next sequential memory location) is Ø7 (hex). After the execution of this two-byte instruction, therefore, the contents of the accumulator will be

A   A + n
A   A7 + Ø7
A contains AE

The main utility of the immediate addressing mode is to load data into specific registers or locations or to perform arithmetic operations using constants.

Immediate extended addressing. This form of addressing is merely immediate addressing extended so as to accommodate 16-bit data transfers. While the immediate addressing type of instruction can be only two bytes (e.g., the op-code and operand n), the extended immediate type of instruction requires three bytes of data (op-code and two following n bytes). The format of this type of instruction is

byte 1	op-code
byte 2	(n1)
byte 3	(n2)

An example is the load HL instruction that causes two operands to be loaded into the 16-bit HL register pair. LD HL,nn would look like:

byte 1	21	op-code for LD HL,nn
byte 2	n	low-order byte for HL
byte 3	n	high-order byte for HL

There are also similar instructions for the other 16-bit register pairs, namely, LD, BC,nn; LD DE,nn; and LD SP,nn.

Example

Suppose we wanted to load the HL register pair with the 16-bit binary word 00111101 01101111 (3D 6F in hex). The program would look like

byte 1	21	op-code for LD HL,nn
byte 2	6F	data for low-order byte of HL
byte 3	3D	data for high-order byte of HL

Following the execution of this instruction, the the low-order (L) side of the HL register pair would contain 6F (hex) and the high-order side (H) would contain 3D. Taken together, these data form the 16-bit word 3D6F (hex).

Modified page-zero addressing. This type of instruction allows the programmer to call any of eight memory locations on page zero (i.e., first 256 addresses, starting at ∅∅ hex). The example of this type of addressing is the RST p instruction which, depending upon operand p, will reset the program counter to any one of the following addresses on page zero of memory: ∅∅∅∅, ∅∅1∅, ∅∅1∅, ∅∅18, ∅∅2∅, ∅∅28, ∅∅3∅, ∅∅38. In this instruction, the current contents of the program counter are pushed onto an external memory stack. The high-order byte of the program counter is loaded with ∅∅ (hex), while the low-order byte is loaded with a word that selects any of the eight locations called out above. For example, loading the low-order byte of the program counter with CF (hex) would cause the instruction to be RST,∅8.

The main use of the modified page-zero addressing is to allow servicing of subroutines with a single-byte call instruction. Consider Fig. 5-1. We are executing a program in page 1∅, and at location 1∅B2 encounter a CF during an instruction fetch cycle. This tells the Z80 that it is a modified page-zero call to a subroutine at location ∅∅ ∅8, so program control jumps to location ∅∅ ∅8. Note that the program counter (PC) contained 1∅ B2 when the RST,∅8 instruction was encountered. The high-order byte of the PC is pushed into stack

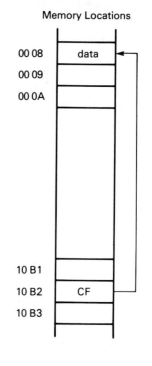

Memory Locations

00 08	data
00 09	
00 0A	

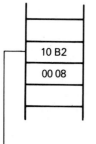

Program Counter

	10 B2
	00 08

10 B1	
10 B2	CF
10 B3	

Stack Pointer

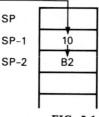

SP	
SP–1	10
SP–2	B2

FIG. 5-1

pointer location SP-1, while the low-order byte is in location SP-2. When program control returns from the subroutine, then the program counter would reclaim the data in the stack, and increment appropriately to pick up the next instruction at 1∅ B3.

Relative addressing. The relative addressing mode allows jump instructions in two bytes that cause program control to shift by a displacement integer e. The jump will occur to a memory location that is -126 to $+129$ locations away from the current address. These instructions are two-byte instructions, so the value of e would be -128_{10} to $+127_{10}$. The displacement integer e is always represented as a signed two's complement number, so these values in binary would be 10000000 to 01111111 (8∅ to 7F in hex). Since this is a two-byte instruction, and the jump cannot occur until the instruction is finished, the program counter will increment *twice* before the jump occurs. This accounts for the difference in the two ranges of decimal numbers given above. The format for this type of instruction is

byte 1   op-code

byte 2   displacement integer (-128_{10} to $+127_{10}$)

Figure 5-2 shows a typical example, using the unconditional jump instruction JR,e. This instruction will cause an unconditional branch to a subroutine located at a displacement e from the op-code. The value of the second byte will be a e-2. Note that we encounter the op-code 18 (hex) at location ∅∅ ∅9 and displacement integer FA (two's complement for -6) at location ∅∅ ∅A. After the execution of this instruction, the program counter will contain the new address, ∅∅ ∅4 (hex).

LOCATION	DATA	
∅∅ ∅∅		
∅∅ ∅1		
∅∅ ∅2		
∅∅ ∅3		
∅∅ ∅4	PC after execution	
∅∅ ∅5		
∅∅ ∅6		
∅∅ ∅7		
∅∅ ∅8		
∅∅ ∅9	18	op-code for JR,e
∅∅ ∅A	FA	2's complement for -6
∅∅ ∅B		
(etc.)		

FIG. 5-2

Extended addressing. In extended addressing, we are allowed to use two 8-bit integers nn to create a 16-bit address. In the typical extended addressing scheme, there will be a one- or two-byte op-code, followed by two address bytes or operands. In either case, the first n byte is the lower-order byte, while the second is the high-order byte. The format would be

byte 1   op-code
byte 2   (possible additional op-code)
byte 3   n1
byte 4   n2

Example

LD A, (nn) is an extended addressing instruction that tells us to load the accumulator (i.e., A register) with the byte located at a memory location given by two-byte operand nn. Note that the use of parentheses around the operand tells us that we mean the "contents of location nn," rather than the value nn. The code for this is

byte 1   3A   op-code for Ld A, (nn)
byte 2   n1   low-order byte of address
byte 3   n2   high-order byte of address

Indexed Addressing. This type of addressing uses the two 16-bit index registers (IX and IY), plus a displacement value following the op-code, to compute the effective address of a jump. In a typical indexed addressing instruction, there will be a two-byte op-code, followed by the displacement integer d. The format of indexed addressing instruction is given below.

byte 1   (op-code)
byte 2   (op-code)
byte 3   (d)

Consider, for example, the LD (IX+d),A instruction. This instruction causes the memory location pointed to by the contents of the IX index register and displacement integer d to be loaded with the contents of the accumulator. The code would be as follows.

byte 1   DD   (op-code for LD (IX+d),A)
byte 2   77   (op-code for LD (IX+d),A)
byte 3   d   displacement integer d

Example

The accumulator contains 3F (hex), and the IX index register contains 44 00 (hex). The code DD 77 05 is encountered on an instruction fetch. This indicates a LD (IX+d),A instruction, in which d is 05 (hex). The memory location 44 00 + 05 = 44 05 will contain 3F (hex) after the execution of this instruction.

Register addressing. This addressing mode allows us to transfer data between different registers of the Z80. An example is the LD r,r' instruction. Registers, A, B, C, D, E, H, and L can be used for either r or r'. We make up the one-byte op-code using the register codes in appropriate spots in the op-code, using the format as shown below:

$$0 \ 1 \ | \leftarrow \underline{r} \rightarrow | \leftarrow \underline{r'} \rightarrow |$$

Example

The register code for the D register is 010, and the regiser code for the E register is 011. Since the operation of the LD r,r' instruction is r - -r', if we want to load the D register with the contents of the E register, we would use the op-code 01010011.

Implied addressing. In the implied addressing mode we use special instructions that always use the same CPU register to contain the operands. An example of this type of instruction is the LD R,A instruction, which will load the R (refresh memory) register with the contents of the accumulator.

Register indirect addressing. This powerful type of instruction causes the transfer of data between the CPU and a memory location pointed to by the contents of one of the 16-bit register pairs. An example of this type of instruction is the LD (DE),A. This mnemonic is read, "Load the memory location pointed to by the contents of the DE register pair with the contents of the accumulator."

Example

The accumulator contains 9D (hex), and the DE register pair contains 65 08 (hex). If the following is encountered,

    00010010   (op-code for LD (DE),A)

then memory location 65 08 will contain the byte 9D (hex) after the execution of this instruction.

Bit addressing. One of the principal advantages of the Z80 in many types of programming is the ability to set, reset, or test the condition of any single bit in any register. The op-code will be of the form

byte 1   (op-code)
byte 2   0 1 _ b _ _ r _

Example

The bit code (b) for bit 5 is 101, and the register code for the D register is 010. In order to test the condition of bit 5 in the D register, we would use the Bit 5,D instruction with the op-code

byte 1   1 1 0 0 1 0 1 1
byte 2   0 1 1 0 1 0 1 0

In this particular case, the Z flag in the F register would be SET if the tested bit is ∅ and RESET if the bit is 1.

6

The Z80 Instruction Set (General)

There are 158 instructions that can be executed by the Z80. Actually, when they are broken down into their various forms, counting the various modes of instruction, we count over *400* Z80 instructions. In a previous chapter we classified these instructions according to the addressing mode used. But in this chapter, we will classify the instructions in their respective groups. The groups are

Load and exchange
Block transfer and search
Arithmetic and logical instructions
Rotate and shift
Bit manipulation
Jump, Call, and Return
Input/Output
CPU control

LOAD INSTRUCTIONS

The load instructions are used to move data from one location to another. More specifically, there are two basic types of LOAD instruction: (a) move data from one internal register to another internal register, and (b) move data from CPU registers to/from external memory locations.

There are two basic groups of LOAD instructions: the 8-bit and the 16-bit LOAD instructions. These instructions move single bytes of data, and use the 8-bit registers and 8-bit memory locations (sometimes pointed to by 16-bit index registers).

The 16-bit LOAD instructions use the register pairs AF, BC, DE, HL, SP, IX, and IY. They also use two-byte memory addresses to specify the locations of two bytes of data to be moved into the CPU, or from the CPU.

In all of the LOAD instructions, there must be specified both a source of the data and a destination. These may be an internal register or a memory location.

EXCHANGE INSTRUCTIONS

The exchange instructions are used to exchange the contents of any two specified registers. These are the instructions that are represented by the mnemonics EX and EXX.

BLOCK TRANSFER AND BLOCK SEARCH

One of the nicest things about the Z80 is the block search and transfer instructions. The transfer instructions include LDI, LDIR, LDD, and LDDR. The search instructions are CPI, CPIR, CPD, and CPDR.

The block instructions use three 16-bit register pairs in their execution:

HL   Address of source location
DE   Address of destination location
BC   Byte counter

In any program using these instructions, it is necessary for these registers (HL, DE, BC) to be initialized to the value required. When the block instructions are executed, these registers are automatically incremented to point to the next location.

The block transfer instructions are defined as follows:

LDI   Load and increment. This instruction moves one byte of date from the location pointed to by the HL register pair to the location pointed to by the DE register pair. After the execution of an LDI instruction, the HL and DE registers are incremented (pointing to the next sequential location), and the BC register is decremented.

LDIR   This is the same as the load and increment instruction class, but will *load-increment-repeat*. The same operation is repeated until the contents of BC are zero. If the BC register is initialized to a specified value, then this one instruction will be used to move an entire block of data from one location to another.

LDD
LDDR
The LDD and LDDR instructions are analogous to LDI and LDIR instructions, respectively. The difference is that the HL and DE register pairs are decremented, instead of incremented, after each execution. The BC register decrements, as in the other group. These instructions transfer data from the highest location to the lowest, while the opposite takes place in the LDI and LDIR instructions.

The block search instructions are as follows:

CPI
Compare and increment. This type of instruction will compare the contents of the accumulator with the contents of the memory location pointed to by the contents of the HL register pair. The result of the comparison is reflected by the condition of the flag register bits. After the execution of this instruction, the HL register pair contents are incremented, and the BC register pair contents of HL point to an address in memory, while BC is a byte counter.

CPIR
In this type of instruction, a CPI operation is performed and repeated, until either of two conditions are found: (a) the byte counter (BC) is zero, or (b) the data in the addressed memory location matches the data in the accumulator.

CPD
CPDR
These are the *compare and decrement* and *compare, decrement, and repeat* instructions. They are analogous to the CPI and CPIR instructions, respectively, but the HL register pair is decremented after execution, instead of incrementing.

ARITHMETIC AND LOGICAL INSTRUCTIONS

There are two groups of arithmetic and logical instructions: 8-bit and 16-bit. In the 8-bit arithmetic group are the *addition* (ADD), *add with carry* (ADC), *subtract* (SUB), and *subtract with carry* (SBC). The 8-bit logical group consists of AND, OR, or XOR instructions.

Also included in this 8-bit classification are *compare* (CP), *increment* (INC), and *decrement* (DEC) instructions.

The same basic set of ADD, ADC, SBC, INC, and DEC instructions are used in the 16-bit arithmetic/logical group, but instead of the 8-bit registers (A, B, C, D, E, H, and L), and single memory locations, they use the register pairs (HL, IX, IY, BC, DE, and SP).

There is also a series of instructions that decimal adjust the accumulator data (DAA). These can be used to allow multiprecision BCD numbers, signed or unsigned binary numbers, or two's complement signed numbers.

There are four additional instructions in the arithmetic/logic group: *complement accumulator* (CPL), *negate accumulator* (NEG), *complement carry flag* (CCF), and *set carry flag* (SCF). The CPL instruction causes the number in the accumulator to be complemented. This means that the 1's become 0's and the 0's become 1's. The NEG instruction causes the contents of the accumulator to be expressed in two's complement form. The CCF instruction causes the carry flag to be complemented. If the carry flag is 1, then it will become 0, and if it is 0 it will become 1. The SCF instruction will cause the carry flag to be set (i.e., made 1).

ROTATE AND SHIFT INSTRUCTIONS

The rotate and shift group instructions include RLC, RRC, RL, RR, SLA, SRA, SRL, RLD, RRD, RLCA, RRCA, RLA, and RRA. These instructions move specified bits left or right, according to rules given in Chapter 17.

BIT MANIPULATION INSTRUCTIONS

One of the things that make the Z80 one of the better uP chips is the existence of the bit manipulation instructions. We can test a bit for 1 or 0, we can reset a bit (RES), and we can set (SET) a bit. The particular bit tested, set, or reset can be in any specified register (A, B, C, D, E, H, and L), or any memory location. In the latter case, we may use either indexed or register indirect addressing of the selected memory location. There are quite a large number of individual instructions in this group, because we can select any of eight bits (0-7), seven different registers, or memory locations specified by HL, IX, or IY register pairs.

JUMP, CALL, AND RETURN INSTRUCTIONS

A digital computer executes instructions in a sequential manner. In the ordinary course of events, the program counter is incremented one to several counts every time an instruction is executed. The number of counts incremented is determined by the number of bytes required for the particular type of instruction. Although this sequential execution is one of the powerful aspects of digital computers, it would also limit the range of possible problems that could be solved to those amenable to direct sequential processing. It would be impossible to perform most operations requiring even the simplest decision. Even the simple matter of inputting data would become impossible. In those operations, an input port is connected to a keyboard. We create a loop, using a JUMP instruction that tests the strobe bit (usually B7), and if none is found, jumps back to the beginning of the loop. If a strobe is found, on the other hand, the program is allowed to fall through to the next instruction (usually an input instruction). But this is merely a trivial example. Most problems requiring decision logic on the part of the computer could not be performed without the use of the JUMP, CALL, and RETURN instructions. The instructions in this group include JP, JR, CALL, DJNZ, RET, and RETN.

A JUMP (JP mnemonic) instruction is a branch to a subroutine at some address other than the next address in sequence. The address at which the next instruction (i.e., the first instruction of the subroutine) is to be found is loaded into the program counter (PC). We may use either of three addressing modes: immediate extended, register indirect, and relative.

Each of the different types of JUMP instruction are keyed to certain conditions that are reflected by the status bits of the flag (F) register. The conditions that may be specified by the selection of the op-code include carry, noncarry, zero, nonzero, parity even, parity odd, sign negative, sign positive, and unconditional.

The conditional jump instructions look for the status of the appropriate bit of the flag register. If the condition is met, then the jump operation occurs.

In immediate extended addressing, the jump occurs to a 16-bit memory address specified by the two bytes following the jump instruction. If the condition called for is met, then the program control will be shifted to the location specified by the following two bytes.

Register indirect addressing allows us to store the 16-bit address of the first instruction in the subroutine we wish to execute in one of the three double registers. Either the HL, IX, or IY register pairs can be specified by appropriate selection of the op-code. The register indirect jump instructions are all unconditional.

A relative addressing JUMP (JR mnemonic) instruction exists for each of the following conditions: carry, noncarry, zero, nonzero, and unconditional. In this type of jump instruction the next instruction for the program to execute (i.e., the first instruction op-code in the subroutine) is specified by the current contents of the PC added to a displacement integer e. The value of e can be anything in the range -126 to $+129$, as measured from the address of the instruction op-code (rather than the location of the displacement integer.)

In the case of one of the unconditional jump instructions (all forms of jump used in the Z80 will recognize an unconditional "condition"), the program counter is loaded immediately with the two bytes immediately following the op-code for the jump. The second byte of these three-byte instructions becomes the low-order byte of the PC address, while the third byte of the instruction becomes the high-order byte of the PC address. Since the contents of the PC are now changed, program control is transferred to the instruction located at a memory location specified by the PC.

There is also one special form of jump instruction that is very useful: DJNZ. This stands for decrement register B and jump if it is nonzero. This instruction allows us to use the B register as a byte counter. We load register B with an integer equal to the number of times that we wish to execute a subroutine. The program control will transfer to the subroutine specified by a displacement integer e (this is relative addressing) as soon as the DJNZ is encountered. When the program control returns, the B register is decremented. If this operation does not bring the contents of B to zero, then the jump occurs again. This will continue until B counts down to zero. If B was preloaded with zero, then the program will jump and loop through all 256 bytes before terminating when zero is again encountered.

An example of a possible application of this type of instruction is in signal averaging. If we want to average 100 data points, then we can nest an input instruction inside a DJNZ loop. The B register is loaded with 100, and is decremented with each execution. When all 100 data points are input, then the B register decrements one more time to zero, terminating the operation. The program then falls through to the next instruction in sequence. Note that the relative displacement integer e is expressed in the form of a two's complement number.

The CALL instruction is a special case of the JUMP instruction. If the CALL is used, then the address of the memory location immediately following the CALL instruction is loaded into an external memory stack (pointed to by the SP register contents). This allows us to branch to a subroutine, and then return to the main program sequence.

The return (RET) instruction is a reverse call instruction, and is used to return to the main program once the subroutine jumped to by the CALL instruction is finished. The RET instruction is usually the last instruction in the subroutine. When this instruction is encountered, the program counter is loaded with the contents of the external memory stack (again, pointed to by SP). This will be the address of the first instruction following the CALL instruction that instigated the subroutine branch.

There are two specialized return instructions, RETI and RETN. These are for returning to main program control after the servicing of an interrupt and a nonmaskable interrupt, respectively.

INPUT/OUTPUT INSTRUCTIONS

Input/output instructions cause data to be input to, or output from the CPU. The Z80 uses several different registers, and has I/O instructions allowing direct use of these registers without first requiring the programmer to transfer the contents of the accumulator. In addition, there are several block I/O instructions.

Immediate addressing is available to the accumulator (i.e., register **A**), while the B, C, D, E, H, and L registers use register indirect addressing. The block I/O instructions are also register indirect.

Perhaps the most common I/O instructions are the immediate input and immediate output instructions (IN A, n and OUT A,n). In these instructions, the operand n is the eight-bit address of one of 256 (000-255) possible ports. This address will appear on the lower eight bits (A∅-A7) of the address bus, while the contents of the accumulator appear on the upper eight bits of the address bus (A8-A15). The input or output data are passed over the eight-bit data bus to, or from, the accumulator, respectively.

In the case of register indirect addressing, the contents of the C register specify the eight-bit address of the selected port. This address (i.e., contents of C) are passed over the lower byte of the address bus to signal the device being selected. Also at this time, the contents of the B register are passed over the high-order byte of the address bus. This is analogous to the immediate I/O instructions, except that the sources of the data passed to the address bus are different.

The block input instructions include INI, INIR, IND, and INDR. The block output instructions include OUTI, OTIR, OUTD, and OTDR. They are analogous to the memory block transfer instructions, except that they use the contents of register pair HL to point to an eight-bit I/O address at an external memory location. In these instructions, register B is used as a byte counter. As in the register indirect case above, the contents of the C register hold the address of the I/O port. Note that this means that the contents of register pair HL point to a location in external memory. The contents of this location are then loaded into register C. When the actual transfer takes place, the contents of C are then placed on the low-order byte of the two-byte address bus. Also, as in other register indirect I/O instructions, the contents of the B register (i.e., byte counter) are placed on the high-order byte of the address bus.

CPU CONTROL INSTRUCTIONS

There are seven instructions in the Z80 set that are used exclusively for the control of the CPU: NOP, HALT, DI, EI, IM0, IM1, IM2.

The NOP instruction is a "no operation" instruction. During the execution of the NOP, the CPU will do absolutely nothing.

The HALT instruction causes the CPU to cease operations until an interrupt is received. The DI instruction disables the interrupts, while EI enables interrupts.

The IM0, IM1, and IM2 instructions allow the programmer to set any of three interrupt modes. The zero-mode (IM0) causes the Z80 to think that it is an 8080A. The IM1 causes program control to transfer automatically to location 00 38 (hex) when an interrupt is received. Interrupt mode 2 (IM2) allows indirect call to an interrupt service subroutine at a location specified by two bytes: the contents of the I register and the 8-bit word received from the interrupting device. This feature allows vectored interrupts serving several peripheral devices whose subroutines may be different.

7
Z80 Flags

The F and F' registers in the Z80 CPU chip are used as condition flags. Six of the eight bits in each register are SET (i.e., made equal to 1) or RESET (i.e., made equal to 0), depending upon the conditions resulting from various CPU operations. The flag register contents are available to the programmer. The bits of the flag registers are assigned as follows:

BIT NO.	DEFINITION
0	C
1	N
2	P/V
3	(undefined)
4	H
5	(undefined)
6	Z
7	S

The C (carry) flag tells us if there was a carry bit from the highest-order bit in the accumulator. The flag will be set if there is a *carry* from an addition operation, or *borrow* during a subtraction operation, or in certain cases, during the execution of the shift and rotate instructions.

The Z (zero) flag will be set if the operation performed results in a zero's

53

(i.e., 00000000_2) being loaded into the accumulator. If any number other than zero results from the operation, then the Z flag is reset (i.e., made 0).

The S (sign) flag stores the state of bit 7 in the accumulator (i.e., 1 or 0). This results from the fact that bit 7 represents the sign of the number. If the number is negative, then bit 7 is a 1, but if it is zero or positive, then bit 7 is 0.

The P/V (parity/overflow) flag has two purposes. When logical operations (AND, OR, XOR) are performed, the P/V flag indicates the parity of the contents of the accumulator (odd or even). When two's complement operations are being performed, the P/V flag indicates whether or not an overflow occurs. An overflow condition indicates that the answer in the accumulator is in error, because it has exceeded the maximum permissible range of numbers (-128 to +127). The P/V will be set if the overflow occurs, but there is no carry (C flag).

In the case of logical operations, the P/V flag will be set for even parity of the result in the accumulator, and reset for odd parity.

The H (half-carry) flag is a BCD borrow or carry from the least significant half-byte (½-byte = nybble?) of the accumulator contents. Similarly, the subtract flag (N) is used for correcting (decimal adjusting) BCD subtract operations.

8

Interfacing Memory to the Z80

The Z80 microprocessor chip uses a 16-bit address bus, so it is able to directly address up to 2^{16}, or 65,536 memory locations. Note that this upper limit is usually written "64K" rather than "65K" because a "computer-K" is 1024 instead of 1000. The Z80 data bus uses one byte (eight bits), so each memory location can store a single eight-bit word.

The mixture of possible memory devices used with the Z80 includes static random access memory (RAM), dynamic RAM, read only memory (ROM), programmable read only memory (PROM), erasable PROM (EPROM), plus a number of devices such as analog-to-digital converters (ADC), and digital-to-analog converters (DAC), which are sometimes treated as memory. This technique, called *memory mapping*, makes some data acquisition chores easier (or at least faster).

CONTROL SIGNALS FOR MEMORY OPERATIONS

We must be cognizant of the basic Z80 control signals that apply to memory operations: $\overline{\text{MREQ}}$, $\overline{\text{WR}}$, and $\overline{\text{RD}}$. These signals are the memory request, write, and read, respectively. The memory request signal will drop LOW whenever the CPU is executing either a memory read or memory write operation. It tells the system that the data on the bus are memory data. If a memory write operation is taking place, then the *write* ($\overline{\text{WR}}$) signal will also go LOW. If, on the other hand, it is a memory read, then the *read* ($\overline{\text{RD}}$) signal will go LOW. All memory operations, therefore, will generate a LOW on two control pins of the Z80: $\overline{\text{MREQ}}/\overline{\text{WR}}$ for memory write operations and $\overline{\text{MREQ}}/\overline{\text{RD}}$ for memory read operations.

Most integrated circuit memory devices have at least one chip enable (CE) pin, and some have two chip enable pins (labelled CE1 and CE2). There also may be a *read/write* (W/R) pin to instruct the device whether the desired operation is a memory read or a memory write.

One of the simplest cases is shown in Fig. 8-1. Here we see 1024 bytes of *read only memory* (ROM) interfaced directly to the Z80. In this case, we have assigned the ROM to the lower 1K of the memory address range. The locations available, then, are 00 00 (H) to 03 FF (H). Since we are dealing with the lower 1K, we need only the lower-order byte of the address bus, A∅–A7, plus the two least significant bits of the upper-order byte (A8 and A9).

Two chip enable (CE) terminals are available. We use one of them (CE2) to make sure that the ROM will respond only to addresses in the lower 1K of memory. Address bus bit A10 will always remain LOW when the CPU is address-ing a location in the lower 1K, but will go HIGH when an address greater than 03 FF (H) is selected. The ROM, therefore, is enabled only when the address on the address bus is less than 03 FF (H).

The second chip enable pin (CE1) is used to turn on the ROM only when the memory read operation is taking place. This CE pin wants to see a HIGH for turn-on of the ROM. Recall that a NOR gate will output a HIGH only when both inputs are LOW. We can, therefore, create a device select command for CE1 by applying the $\overline{\text{MREQ}}$ and $\overline{\text{RD}}$ control signals from the CPU to the inputs of a NOR gate. CE1 will go HIGH, then, only when a memory read operation takes place.

At least two of the more popular ROM chips require only a single chip enable command. In the example shown in Fig. 8-2(a), the chip enable is an

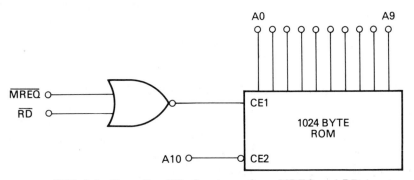

FIG. 8-1 Operating CE of memory from MREQ and RD.

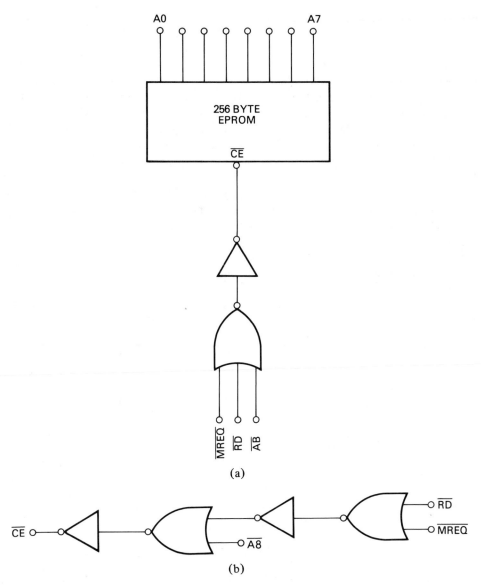

FIG. 8-2 (a) Enabling EPROM from MREQ/RD/A8; (b) Same function accomplished with two-input gates.

active-LOW input (so is designated $\overline{CE}$). This terminal is brought LOW whenever we want to read the contents of one of the locations in the chip.

The example shown in Fig. 8-2(a) is a 256-byte ROM, with a single $\overline{CE}$ terminal. We must, therefore, construct external circuitry that will bring the chip enable terminal LOW when we want to perform the read operation. The simplest way is to use a three-input NOR gate and an inverter. The output of the NOR gate will go HIGH only when all three of the inputs are LOW. We connect the $\overline{MREQ}$, $\overline{RD}$, and bit A8 of the address bus to the respective inputs of the NOR gate. When the conditions are met, then the output of the gate snaps HIGH, and is then inverted to become the $\overline{CE}$ signal required by the EPROM chip.

An alternative method is shown in Fig. 8-2(b). Here we are using two inverters and a pair of NOR gates to form the $\overline{CE}$ signal. The idea is to cause $\overline{CE}$ to go LOW when the three conditions are met. To do this, we must see both inputs of NOR gate G2 LOW simultaneously. One of the inputs is connected to bit A8 of the address bus, while the other is connected to the inverted output of NOR gate G1. The inputs of G1 are, in turn, connected to the $\overline{MREQ}$ and $\overline{RD}$ signals.

A situation that is a little more complicated is shown in Fig. 8-3. Here

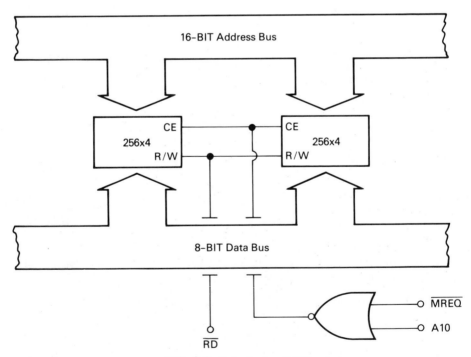

FIG. 8-3 Interfacing RAM.

we are interfacing static RAM devices that have a chip enable and a $\overline{R}/W$ terminal. This latter terminal will cause the device to read out data when LOW, and allow writing in data when HIGH. We connect the $\overline{R}/W$ terminal, then, to the $\overline{RD}$ signal of the Z80 CPU.

The chip enable in this example wants to see a HIGH in order to turn on the device. We can, then correct CE to the output of a NOR gate. The $\overline{MREQ}$ and $\overline{A8}$ signals are connected to the two inputs of the NOR gate. If both of these signals go LOW simultaneously, and the $\overline{RD}$ is also LOW, a memory read operation takes place from the location addressed by A∅-A7. Alternatively, if the $\overline{MREQ}$ and $\overline{A7}$ signals are LOW, and the $\overline{RD}$ signal is HIGH, then a memory write operation will take place.

Note in Fig. 8-3 that two chips are used to form a 256-byte static RAM memory. Most memories require more than a single chip in order to form a complete byte-array. In this case, each memory chip contains a 256×4-bit array, so two connected together will form a 256×8-bit array (i.e., 256 bytes of memory). The popular 2102 device is listed as a 1024×1-bit device. Connecting eight of these devices into an array will result in a 1024-byte memory.

ADDRESS DECODING

In most microcomputers more than 1K of memory is used. But many of the memory chips available are only 1024-byte (with some being 256-byte). Although there are more modern devices capable of very large byte arrays, many users still prefer the older, smaller devices. The question arises, "How does the memory device allocated to a location greater than the maximum address in each individual chip know when it is being addressed?" The solution seems to be ordering of the memory in 1K blocks, and then the use of some form of address decoding to tell which 1K block is being designated.

Figure 8-4 shows a selection scheme used by several manufacturers of 8K memory banks. Each block of this memory is an array of 1024 bytes, so every location can be addressed by bits A∅-A9 of the address bus. The address pins for all devices are connected together to form the address bus (A∅-A9). We must, however, select which of the eight blocks is addressed at any given time. One way to do this is to use a data selector IC. The 7442 device shown in Fig. 8-4 is a BCD-to-one-of-ten decoder. It will examine a four-bit binary (i.e., BCD) input word, and issue an output condition that indicates the value of that word. In this simplified example, we are going to limit the memory size to 8K, so only the 1, 2, and 4 inputs of the 7442 are needed. The input weighted 8 is grounded (i.e., set = ∅). The 7442 indicates the active output by going LOW, exactly the right condition for the RAM devices in the memory blocks. The table below shows the code that will exist on the A1∅-A12 bits of the address bus for the various memory addresses in the range 0-8K.

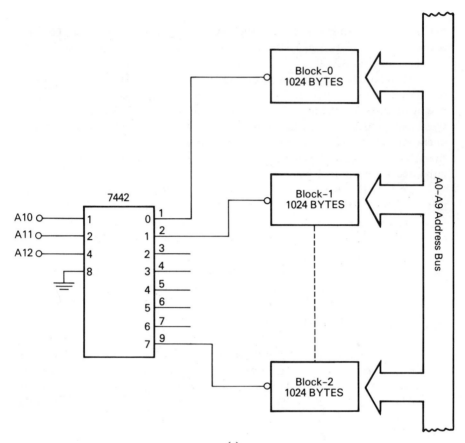

(a)

		A13	A12	A11	A10
Block-Ø	0–1K	Ø	Ø	Ø	Ø
	1K–2K	Ø	Ø	Ø	1
	2K–3K	Ø	Ø	1	Ø
	3K–4K	Ø	Ø	1	1
	4K–5K	Ø	1	Ø	Ø
	5K–6K	Ø	1	Ø	1
	6K–7K	Ø	1	1	Ø
	7K–8K	Ø	1	1	1

(b)

FIG. 8-4 (a) Using 7442 in bank selection of memory; (b) Code for above.

MEMORY LOCS.	A13	A12	A11	A1∅	BLOCK NO.	7442 OUTPUT	7442 PIN
0K–1K	0	0	0	0	0	0	1
1K–2K	0	0	0	1	1	1	2
2K–3K	0	0	1	0	2	2	3
3K–4K	0	0	1	1	3	3	4
4K–5K	0	1	0	0	4	4	5
5K–6K	0	1	0	1	5	5	6
6K–7K	0	1	1	0	6	6	7
7K–8K	0	1	1	1	7	7	9

For an 8K memory, then, the lower 10 bits of the address bus (A∅–A9) select which location in the individual chips is wanted, and A10–A12 select which block of 1024 bytes contains the address.

In the example of Fig. 8-4 we limited the memory size to a mere 8K. This was done intentionally to keep the circuit simple. But how do we select memory in ranges higher than 8K? The answer is to use the 7442 input weighted "8" as a bank select control. Recall from Fig. 8-4 that this input was kept grounded. If it is HIGH, then none of the eight outputs of the 7442 will go LOW. But if it is LOW, then the circuit will work. Figure 8-5 shows a simplified selection scheme for all 65K addressable by the Z80, using the "8" weighted inputs of the 7442 block selectors as a *bank select* terminal. Each bank of 8K contains its own block select 7442, and one additonal 7442 is used to select the bank of 8K that will become active. The table below shows the codes existing on address lines A13–A15 for each 8K bank of locations:

MEMORY LOCS.	BANK NO.	A15	A14	A13	7442 OUTPUT	7442 PIN LOW
0K–8K	∅	∅	∅	∅	∅	1
8K–16K	1	∅	∅	1	1	2
16K–24K	2	∅	1	∅	2	3
24K–32K	3	∅	1	1	3	4
32K–40K	4	1	∅	∅	4	5
40K–48K	5	1	∅	1	5	6
48K–56K	6	1	1	∅	6	7
56K–64K	7	1	1	1	7	9

Figure 8-6 shows an alternate bank selection circuit that is based on a three-input NAND gate (i.e., one section of a 7410 TTL I.C. device). The properties of a NAND gate are

1. If any input is LOW, the output is HIGH.
2. If *all* inputs are HIGH, then the output is LOW.

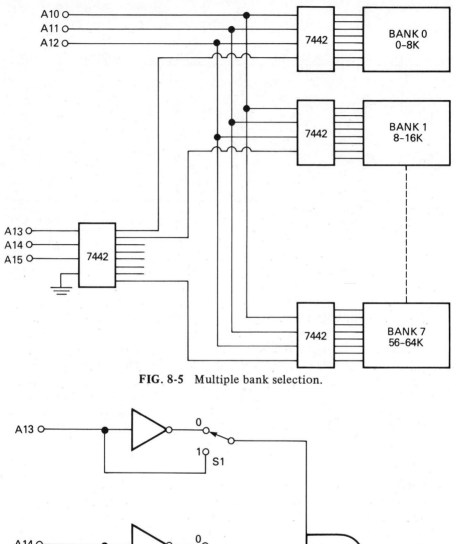

FIG. 8-5 Multiple bank selection.

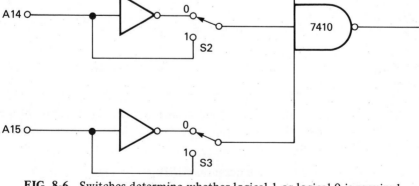

FIG. 8-6 Switches determine whether logical-1 or logical-0 is required.

In this case, then, all three of the inputs must be HIGH for the output to drop LOW. If the output of the NAND gate is used to drive the "8" input of the 7442, then the particular bank served by that 7442 will be selected only when all three inputs are HIGH.

How do we contrive the circuit to force all inputs HIGH only when the correct bit pattern is seen on lines A13–A15? The solution is the inverters and switches shown in Fig. 8-6. Each switch selects either the inverted (i.e., "∅" position) or noninverted (i.e., "1" position) versions of each address bus signal. We set the three switches according to our bank selection format, using the codes from the table given previously. Each switch is to be set to the position corresponding to the digit expected at that input when the address bus code is correct. For bank ∅, for example, the code is ∅∅∅. If S1–S3 are set to "∅" position, then the NAND gate sees the inverted address line signals. When ∅∅∅ appears on A13–A15, the NAND gate sees 111. Since this is the condition required, the output drops LOW and turns on the selected bank.

Note that Intel manufactures a 1-of-8 decoder intended specifically for bank selection in the 8080A device. It should also work nicely with the Z80.

DYNAMIC MEMORY

Dynamic memory (RAM) will not hold its data for an indefinite length of time, unless a refresh operation is performed. The refresh operation is a function of the CPU in most cases, although some non-CPU examples exist. Although the use of static RAM will eliminate this problem, it is only at the cost of a higher power consumption. The Z80A device provides for refresh of the dynamic memory by adding a refresh segment to the M1 (instruction fetch) machine cycle.

During clock periods T3 and T4 of the M1 cycle, used by the Z-80 for the decoding of the instructions fetched in the earlier T-periods a refresh signal is generated. The $\overline{\text{RFSH}}$ terminal (pin 28) of the Z80 will go LOW during this period. Note that this signal must be used in conjunction with the $\overline{\text{MREQ}}$ (memory request) signal, because the $\overline{\text{RFSH}}$ is guaranteed to be stable only when the $\overline{\text{MREQ}}$ is also active.

During the refresh period the lower portion of the address of a refresh location is placed on the lower seven bits (A∅–A6) of the address bus (A7 is ∅). The data on A∅–A6 are from the R register in the Z80, which is incremented after each instruction fetch. The upper eight bits of the address bus carry the contents of the I register. Figure 8-7 shows an example of an 8K dynamic RAM interfaced to a Z80. In this particular case, 4K × 8-bit dynamic RAMs are used. If no other RAM is used, we may use bit A12 of the address bus as a chip-select line.

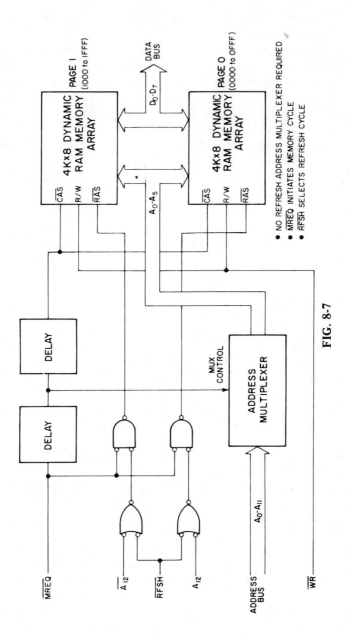

FIG. 8-7

- NO REFRESH ADDRESS MULTIPLEXER REQUIRED
- MREQ INITIATES MEMORY CYCLE
- RFSH SELECTS REFRESH CYCLE

64

ADDING WAIT STATES

All solid-state memory chips require a certain minimum period of time to write data into, or read data from, any given location. Many such devices are graded (and priced!) according to memory speed. The popular 2102 device, a 1K × 1-bit IC, is available in 250-nanosecond, 400-nanosecond, and 500-nanosecond versions. Of course, the cost per chip rises with the speed.

Since the Z80A can operate at speeds up to 4 mHz, we sometimes find the cycle (M1 or memory) over before the data have settled to, or from, memory.

This problem can be overcome by adding the circuitry shown in Fig. 8-8. Both of these circuits generate a $\overline{WAIT}$ input (pin 24 of the Z80) equal to the period of one clock pulse.

The circuit in Fig. 8-8(a) uses both sections of a TTL 7474 dual Type-D flip-flop. The 7474 is a positive-edge triggered device, meaning that data on the D-input are transferred to the Q output *only* during the positive-going transitions of the clock pulse.

Immediately after the onset of clock pulse T1, the $\overline{M1}$ line goes LOW, forcing the D input of FF1 LOW. When clock pulse T2 snaps HIGH, then, this LOW is transferred to the Q output of FF1. This signal becomes the $\overline{WAIT}$ signal for the CPU, and inserts one additional clock period (T_w) into the M1 cycle.

At the onset of clock period T_w, then, FF2 sees a LOW (i.e., the $\overline{WAIT}$ signal) on its D input. This LOW is transferred to the Q output of FF2. The Q_2 terminal (FF2) is connected to the *set* input of FF1, so this condition forces the Q_1 (FF1) HIGH again, thereby terminating the action.

A similar circuit, shown in Fig. 8-8(b), is used to add a wait state to any memory cycle. When the first clock pulse (T1) arrives, the $\overline{MREQ}$ line goes LOW, forcing the D-input of FF1 LOW. At the onset of clock pulse T2, then, this LOW is transferred to the Q output of FF1. At this time $\overline{Q_1}$ is HIGH and Q_2 is HIGH, so the output of the NAND gate drops LOW. (Both NAND inputs must be HIGH for the output to be LOW.) This causes the $\overline{WAIT}$ input of the CPU to become active. But at the onset of T_w, the added clock period, the LOW on Q_1 is transferred to Q_2. This forces one input of the NAND gate HIGH, thereby cancelling the $\overline{WAIT}$ signal.

MEMORY MAPPED DEVICES

Some peripheral devices used with microcomputers can be more efficiently employed if they are treated as a memory location, instead of an I/O device. An example might be a *digital-to-analog converter* (DAC), which is a device that creates an analog output voltage (or current) that is proportional to a binary digital word applied to its input.

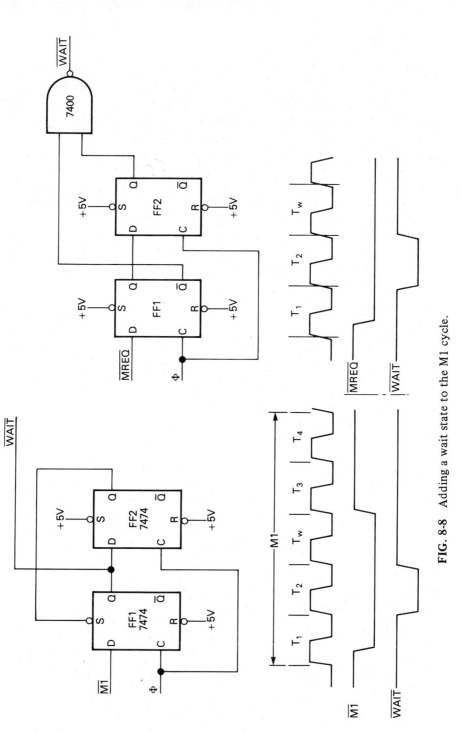

FIG. 8-8 Adding a wait state to the M1 cycle.

Figure 8-9 shows how an 8-bit DAC can be interfaced with a Z80 *as if the DAC were a memory location*. The DAC requires stable input data, but the data on the bus are transitory. Therefore, we need a *data latch* between the 8-bit data bus and the DAC inputs. There are a number of interface chips that will perform this job, but most of those special-purpose devices are costly. A low-cost solution, which works just as well, is to use a 74100 TTL dual quad-latch. The two four-bit sections of the 74100 become an eight-bit latch when the *strobe* terminals are tied together.

The 74100 latch transfers the information on the data bus to the DAC when the strobe line is HIGH. The 74100 outputs, connected to the DAC inputs, will retain these data when the strobe line again goes LOW. The idea, then, is to make the 74100 strobe line HIGH during the period when the desired DAC input data are present on the data bus.

Three criteria must be met before the data on the bus can be input to the DAC: (1) The write signal ($\overline{WR}$) must be active; (2) the memory request ($\overline{MREQ}$) must be active; (3) the correct address (the address of the location assigned to the DAC) must be present on the address bus. The first two criteria are examined by a single NOR gate. When both $\overline{WR}$ and $\overline{MREQ}$ are LOW (i.e., active), we are producing a memory write operation. This will cause point "A" to go HIGH, and point "B" to go LOW. We do not want the DAC to respond, however, unless point "C" is LOW at the same time. When point "C" is LOW, we know that the address for the DAC is being sent over the address bus.

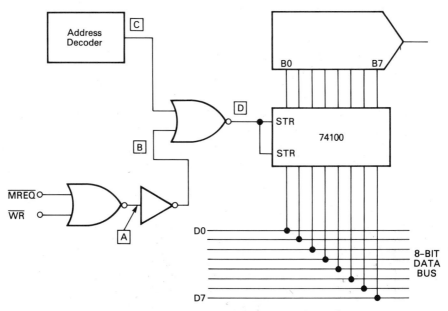

FIG. 8-9   Using a device such as a DAC as a piece of memory.

When all three criteria are met, the strobe input of the 74100 (point "D") will go HIGH. This will allow transfer of data from the data bus into the DAC.

Most microcomputers have less than the full 64K complement of memory. This is the reason why most memory-mapped devices tend to be allocated addresses in the upper 32K of memory. This, incidentally, allows us to use bit A15 of the address bus to discriminate between the various addresses.

9

Z80 I/O

Input/output (I/O) devices may include such apparatus as keyboards, teletype-writers, printers, digital displays analog-to-digital converters (ADC), digital-to-analog converters (DAC), or mass memory storage devices such as disc drives or cassette drives (e.g., Phi-Decks). The Z80 uses the lower-order byte of the address bus to address I/O ports. We may, therefore, address 2^8, or 256 different ports, which are given numerical assignments in the range $\emptyset\emptyset\emptyset$ to 255. If port $\emptyset\emptyset6$ is addressed, for example, the address will be $\emptyset6$ (hex), or $\emptyset\emptyset\emptyset\emptyset\emptyset11\emptyset$ in binary.

Z80 I/O CONTROL SIGNALS

In Chapter 4 we defined the various control signals generated and/or recognized by the Z80 microprocessor chip. Here we will review those that are relevant to the I/O functions. The $\overline{\text{IORQ}}$ (i.e., input/output request) signal is an active LOW, tri-state output. When this terminal (Z80 pin 20) goes LOW, the outside world knows that the lower byte of the address bus contains a valid input or output port address. There is also one additional use of the $\overline{\text{IORQ}}$ signal. It will go LOW during the M1 machine cycle when an interrupt is being acknowledged, so that external I/O devices will know to place an interrupt response vector (i.e., the lower-order byte of the address at which the interrupt service subroutine may be located) on the data bus.

The $\overline{\text{IORQ}}$ signal occurs for both input and output operations. This could cause some confusion, so the Z80 designers, in their infinite wisdom, elected to also provide a read ($\overline{\text{RD}}$) and a write ($\overline{\text{WR}}$) signal. These signals occur for both memory and I/O operations, and allow the external circuitry or devices to determine whether we are reading to or from the CPU. When the $\overline{\text{RD}}$ and $\overline{\text{IORQ}}$ control lines are simultaneously LOW, the external world knows that the command being executed is an *I/O read* (i.e., an input) operation. Similarly, if the $\overline{\text{IORQ}}$ and the $\overline{\text{WR}}$ are simultaneously LOW, then the external world knows that an *I/O write* (i.e., an output) operation is to take place.

Interrupts are also sometimes classified as an I/O function, but they are sufficiently different as to warrant separate treatment in Chapter 11.

Z80 I/O INSTRUCTIONS

The Z80 I/O instructions are a powerful group that allows both block and direct commands. The accumulator (i.e., A register) can be used in either input or output immediate commands. Both types are two-byte instructions in which the accumulator either inputs from, or outputs to, the port whose address is given by the byte following the op-code. The other registers, however, use register indirect instructions, in which the address of the input or output port is given by the contents of the C register. *IN B,C*, for example, loads register B with the binary word at an input port whose address is given by the contents of the C register.

The block transfer instructions allow us to transfer whole blocks of sequentially stored data using but one instruction. These instructions are INI, INIR, IND, INDR, OUTI, OTIR, OUTD, and OTDR. Many programmers feel that these are among the most powerful of the Z80 instructions.

I/O PORT ADDRESS DECODERS

Address decoders for I/O ports are very similar to those used for memory ports, with the exception that only eight-bit addresses are anticipated (as opposed to 65,536 memory addresses!) This will simplify the design process, but keep in mind that the same circuits as were used for the memory address can be pressed into service for decoding I/O addresses.

The problem is this: The $\overline{\text{IORQ}}$, in conjunction with $\overline{\text{RD}}$ and $\overline{\text{WR}}$, tells the I/O devices that an I/O operation is to take place. But just which I/O port is being designated? The address passed over the lower eight bits (A∅–A7) of the address bus must be decoded. Each I/O device, or I/O port, will contain its own address decoder circuit. This circuit will tell the device to respond (as appropriate) to the $\overline{\text{IORQ}}/\overline{\text{WR}}$ or $\overline{\text{IORQ}}/\overline{\text{RD}}$ conditions.

The first address decoder is shown in Fig. 9-1, and is one of the most popular circuits used. The 7430 IC is a TTL eight-input NAND gate. Its output will remain HIGH as long as any one of the eight inputs is LOW. The output terminal of the 7430 will go LOW only if all eight inputs are HIGH. The trick is to make the entire set of inputs HIGH when the correct address is present on the lower eight bits of the address bus. Of course, if the address is FF (hex) (11111111 in binary), then we have no problem. Connecting one each of the 7430 inputs to one of the lower-order bits of the address bus will automatically

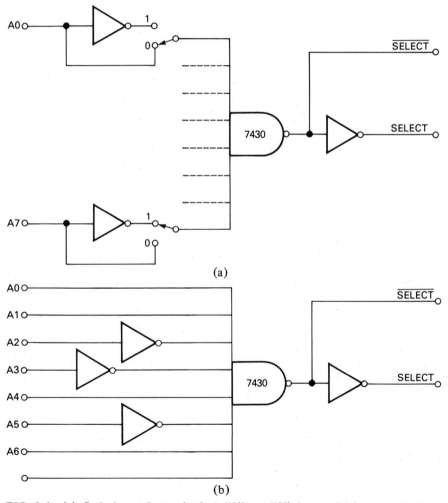

FIG. 9-1 (a) Switches select whether "1" or "0" is required to generate a SELECT pulse. Only the LSB and MSB positions are shown in detail; (b) Decoder for address selected.

give us our decoder. But all other addresses will require one or more inverters between the address bus lines and the inputs of the 7430. If you want maximum flexibility, then one inverter may be dedicated to each 7430 input. But this is a terrible waste of inverters, because there is only one address in which all of the inverters are required: 0̸0̸0̸0̸0̸0̸0̸0̸ (binary)! All other addresses will use fewer than eight inverters. As a practical matter, most commercially available I/O printed circuit boards have but three or four inverters. The user is then asked to carefully select I/O port addresses such that no more than three or four zeroes occur. It is rare, indeed, that all 256 possible I/O ports would be required, so this is not the sacrifice that it might appear. In the example of Fig. 9-1 we have shown inverters only on the A0̸ and A7 lines, with those for the other lines implied. In actual practice, most designers have the inverters wired in with small jumpers, rather than formal switches, so that they may be dedicated to *any* 7430 input as might be required.

By way of illustration, let us assign the address 11010011 (D3 in hex) to an I/O port. We see by inspection that all but three of the bits in this address are ones, so no inverters will be needed for them. Only the zero bits (i.e., A2, A3, and A5) will require inverters. The decoder for this address is shown in Fig. 9-1(b). Notice that the A0̸, A1, A4, A6, and A7 lines are connected directly to 7430 inputs, while the A1, A2, and A5 address lines are passed through inverters before being applied to the 7430 inputs. When the address 11010011 appears on the bus, then, all of the 7430 inputs will see ones, and the 7430 can drop LOW. This creates a $\overline{\text{SELECT}}$ signal for use by the I/O circuitry. An optional inverter will turn this signal upside down, creating a SELECT signal, for those cases where a positive-going transition is needed.

Another form of address decoder is shown in Fig. 9-2. This circuit is based on the TTL-type 7485 comparator IC. This device will compare two four-bit words ("A" and "B") and issue an output that indicates whether A is equal to,

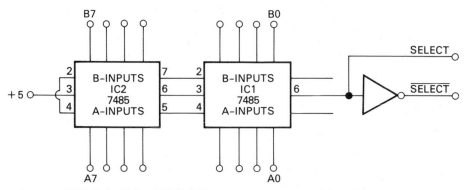

FIG. 9-2 Using 7485 TTL comparators as an address decoder.

greater than, or less than, B. Of these, we are interested in the A = B output
(pin 6). The 7485 has cascading inputs that sense the status of a lower-order
four bits. We need two 7485 devices connected in this cascade manner in order
to use it to decode an eight-bit address bus.

We connect the bits of the address bus to the A-inputs of the 7485's. The
B-inputs are used to program the device with the address of the port to be
selected. In the previous case, we selected port D3 (hex), i.e., 11Ø1ØØ11 in
binary and 211 in decimal, using a 7430. If we wanted to use the 7485's as
shown in Fig. 9-2, we would program IC1 with the binary word ØØ11 (i.e.,
3 hex), and IC2 with 11Ø1 (i.e., D hex). When this address appears on the address bus, then the A = B output of IC1 will go HIGH, forming a SELECT signal.
An inverter is needed if a $\overline{\text{SELECT}}$ is desired instead.

We can also use any of the various "1-of-N" decoder ICs as address selectors. the 7442 is a 1-of-10 decoder, while the 74154 device is a 1-of-16 device.
Each of these has a four-bit binary input to determine which output line (Ø
through 9, or Ø through 15) will go LOW. Figure 9-3 shows the use of the 7442
1-of-10 decoder. Two 7442 devices are needed. A NOR gate is connected so
that one input of the NOR gate is driven by one of the outputs of each 7442.

As an example, let us say that we want to use the circuit of Fig. 9-3 to
decode address 115 (decimal), which is 73 in hex. The binary code for "7" is
0111, and the code for "3" is 0011. We want, then, to see binary code 01110011
on the AØ-A7 lines. We connect the four-bit inputs of IC1 to the lower-order
four bytes of the address line (AØ-A3), and the high-order four-bits (A4-A7)
to the four-bit inputs of IC2. One input of the NOR gate is then connected to
the "3" output of IC1, and the other input is connected to the "7" output of
IC2. When the correct address appears, both of these outputs will drop LOW,
causing the output of the NOR gate to snap HIGH. This signal then becomes
our SELECT signal. Again, an inverter is used to form a $\overline{\text{SELECT}}$ signal where
required.

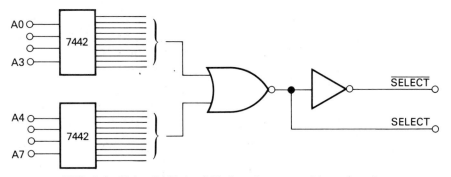

FIG. 9-3 Using 7442 1-of-10 decoder as an address decoder.

USING THE ADDRESS DECODERS

The address decoder performs just one of the functions necessary for I/O operations: it decodes the correct address for the specified port. But there are two other functions that need to be recognized in each case, $\overline{\text{IORQ}}$ and either $\overline{\text{WR}}$ or $\overline{\text{RD}}$. Figure 9-4 shows how these functions, along with the $\overline{\text{SELECT}}$ function, can be combined to form an I/O control circuit. In this case, we are assuming that the I/O devices want to see positive-going pulses in order to operate. Gates G1 through G3 are used in the output operations, while gates G4 through G6 are used for input operations.

Output operations. Here we use G1–G3 in Fig. 9-4. Gate G1 is a NOR gate and is controlled by the $\overline{\text{SELECT}}$ output of the address decoder and by the $\overline{\text{WR}}$ control signal generated by the Z80 CPU. G3, which creates the actual OUT signal, is controlled by the $\overline{\text{IORQ}}$ Z80 control signal and the inverted output of G1 (note that gate G2 is an inverter, i.e., a NOT gate). We require three simultaneous conditions for the output to occur: The $\overline{\text{WR}}$ and $\overline{\text{IORQ}}$ must be active (i.e., LOW), and the correct address must be present on the address bus. The latter condition is indicated by the $\overline{\text{SELECT}}$ output of the address decoder circuit going LOW. If $\overline{\text{WR}}$ and $\overline{\text{SELECT}}$ are active, indicating a *possible* output operation, then the output of gate G1 will go HIGH. This signal is inverted, and applied to one input of gate G3. If the command is a *genuine* output operation for this port, then the $\overline{\text{IORQ}}$, applied to the alternate input of NOR gate G3, will also be active (i.e., LOW). The three conditions, being met, allow an OUT signal to be generated. This signal is used to tell the output device whose address was called to accept the data currently on the data bus.

A similar action occurs on the input operation, except that $\overline{\text{RD}}$ must be sensed instead of $\overline{\text{WR}}$. Note that the IN circuit is substantially the same as the OUT circuit, except for the use of $\overline{\text{RD}}$ on NOR gate G4.

Another, and simpler, circuit that performs essentially the same job is shown in Fig. 9-5. Here we are using the familiar 7442 (TTL 1-of-10 decoder). This circuit has proven popular, and is used by such manufacturers as The Digital Group, Inc. The 7442 A, B, and C inputs are connected to the $\overline{\text{IORQ}}$, $\overline{\text{RD}}$, and $\overline{\text{WR}}$ outputs of the 7442, respectively. The D-input of the 7442 is permanently connected to ground, so always sees a zero input. If an input operation is commanded, then the four-bit word applied to the 7442 inputs is 0100 (decimal 4). But if an output operation occurs, then the word applied to the 7442 inputs is 0010 (decimal 2). In the case of an input operation, then, the "4" output of the 7442 will drop LOW. If an output operation is taking place, then the "2" output of the 7442 drops LOW. These 7442 terminals are applied to the inputs of a pair of NOR gates. The other input of each NOR gate is connected to the $\overline{\text{SELECT}}$ output of the address decoder. This line will be LOW for both input and output operations, depending only upon the address bus lower byte.

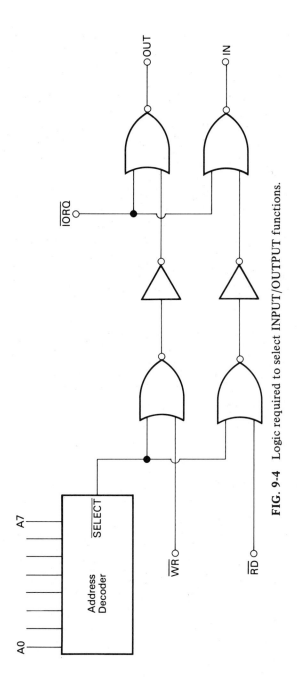

FIG. 9-4 Logic required to select INPUT/OUTPUT functions.

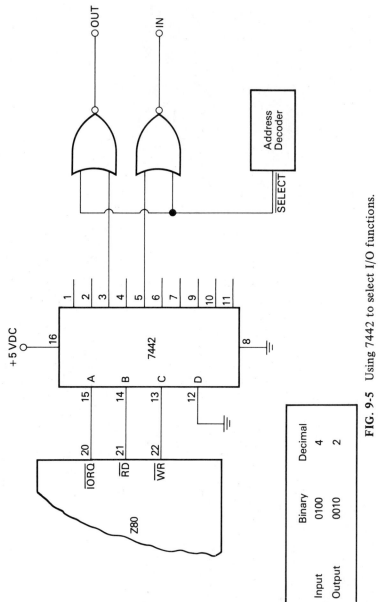

FIG. 9-5 Using 7442 to select I/O functions.

	Binary	Decimal
Input	0100	4
Output	0010	2

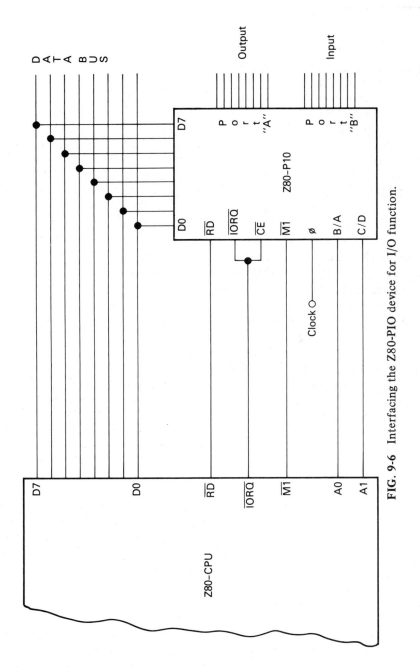

FIG. 9-6 Interfacing the Z80-PIO device for I/O function.

Z80-PIO

The Z80-PIO Zilog IC (also called the Mostek MK3881) is a special parallel I/O controller. It is a programmable, two-port I/O device. It contains two independent, bidirectional, eight-bit ports for data transfer between the Z80 CPU chip and external devices. Complete "handshake" capability is permitted. There are four distinct modes of operation in the Z80-PIO: *byte output*, *byte input*, *byte bidirectional bus* (port A only), and *bit control*. Only a single +5-volt dc power supply and a single-phase clock are required.

One of the more powerful aspects of the Z80-PIO is that it permits use of the interrupt modes of the Z80 CPU chip. The Z80-PIO is semi-intelligent, in that it can be programmed to recognize specific interrupts (i.e., alarms) from external devices. Zilog bills this feature as allowing the CPU to spend time on chores other than polling the external device for an interrupt condition.

Figure 9-6 shows a simple I/O port using the Z80-PIO IC. The DØ–D7 inputs of the PIO are connected to their respective lines on the data bus. Similarly, the $\overline{IORQ}$ and $\overline{M1}$ inputs on the PIO are connected to their respective outputs on the Z80 IC. The $\overline{IORQ}$ and $\overline{CE}$ (i.e., chip enable) inputs of the PIO are connected to the $\overline{IORQ}$ output on the Z80. In this example, we have designated PIO port-A as the output port, and PIO port-B as the input port. In more sophisticated systems, however, we can use both A and B as bidirectional I/O ports by appropriate programming of the B/A pin.

The Z80-SIO is a serial communications controller that can be directly interfaced with the Z80 CPU chip. This device is very similar to the UART IC, except that it permits both synchronous and asynchronous communications, and has two channels (A and B).

10
Interfacing Peripherals

Most microcomputers require additional peripheral devices to make them useful: teletypewriters, printers, video terminals, keyboards, etc. These devices allow the input or output of data, or provide a "hard copy" readout for the end user.

Any number of schemes have been used to connect such devices to the microcomputer, but only a few are described here. Before one goes to a lot of trouble on any one device, it is wise to see if a special-purpose integrated circuit, or a small printed circuit board kit, has been developed to make the interfacing chore a bit easier. New interface chips are being developed all of the time, so check the catalogs of the IC manufacturers. A large number of "basement laboratories" businesses advertise in the hobby computer magazines, and many of these offer kits of parts or printed circuit boards for projects that aid interfacing chores. Most of these are well designed, or are so simple that anybody could do a good job. The prices asked are often small enough to attract even the wisened professional.

STRAIGHT I/O METHODS

Some peripherals can be interfaced to the Z80 directly through an ordinary I/O port. Most such ports (see Chapter 9) offer eight parallel, TTL-compatible bits. These can be interfaced directly to any other eight-bit, TTL-compatible device.

79

An example might be certain types of printer. Among several options available at the time that you order the printer is the input format. Some will allow you to select TTL-compatible parallel ASCII input format. The ASCII code is a seven-bit code, so the eighth bit can be used as a strobe. Such a machine can be connected directly to a Z80 I/O port, any of which from Chapter 9 will suffice. It is necessary only that a length of multiconductor cable be provided. The cable must be fitted with the appropriate connectors (usually DB-25 family) so that it can be connected directly.

To make the beast work, you must load the accumulator of the Z80 with the binary code whose bit pattern represents the ASCII character that you wish to print. The contents of the accumulator are then output to the port assigned to the printer. Ordinarily, printers are a lot slower than CPUs, so one has to place a timing loop, or series of no-ops (NOP instruction in Z80 language) between character prints. This scheme will give the printer time to catch up with the speedy CPU.

The standard ASCII code is shown in Table 10-1. From this table, we see that the ASCII code for the character "?" is the binary bit pattern 0111111. If we use the most significant bit (not needed in ASCII) to strobe the printer, then the code will be 10111111, or BF in hexadecimal. To print the question mark ("?") symbol we load the accumulator of the Z80 with BF hex and then output it to the proper port. Suppose, for example, that we wanted to use port 175_{10} for the printer. Such a program might look like:

```
    .            .
    .            .
    .            .
3E          LD A,N
BF          N (i.e., ASCII "?")
D3          OUT 175₁₀, A
AF          175₁₀ in hex
```

Of course, with a "dumb printer," you would have to send it a character, and then waste a lot of time in a loop until you were sure that it has time to print the character and advance a space before sending it another character. But if the machine were a little smarter, it could do some "handshaking." This means that the printer could send a bit back to the CPU to tell it when the next character could be sent. We would loop, or do other chores (interrupts are handy here!), until the strobe is received back from the printer. A typical program might be

```
00 01      DB      IN 175₁₀
00 02      AF      175₁₀ in hex
```

00 03	CB	Test Bit-7 of accumulator
00 04	7F	
00 05	20	JR NZ
00 06	86	(Jump − 4)
00 07	3E	LD A,N
00 08	BF	N (ASCII for "?")
00 09	D3	OUT 175_{10}
00 0A	AF	175_{10} in hex
00 0B	C3	JP 00 01
00 0C	01	N (L byte)
00 0D	00	N (H byte)

Again, we are using port 175_{10}. The handshaking strobe pulse from the printer is applied to bit-7 (i.e., MSB) of the input port 175_{10}. The output data to the printer are applied to the output side of port 175_{10}. We are assuming that the strobe will go HIGH (i.e., logical-1) when active. Instructions 1-6 are a test and loop program that seeks the condition of the strobe bit. We first input the contents of 175_{10} (instructions 1-2), and then test bit-7 of the input data (instructions 3-4). If this bit is 0, indicating that the printer is not yet ready, the program counter (PC) is told to pick up the instruction four locations back from JR NZ (i.e., location 00 01). These instructions cause the Z80 to continuously input data from the printer, and test to see if the strobe is active. If the strobe is not active, the program loops back to the input, and starts over again.

When the condition is met (i.e., bit-7 is 1), then the program will fall through and output the ASCII character.

Following the output operation, the program control is transferred back to 00 01 by a JP NN instruction.

We could also write a similar program to input data from a keyboard. Again, let us assume that the strobe is active HIGH (in real life, do not *assume;* examine that strobe. Many are active LOW, especially on keyboard units), and that it is applied to the MSB of port 175_{10}. We will continue to loop until a HIGH is received at bit-7 of port 175_{10}:

00 01	DB	IN 175_{10}
00 02	AF	175_{10} in hex
00 03	CB	Test bit-7
00 04	7F	
00 05	20	JR NZ
00 06	86	(Jump − 4)
00 07		(program to do something with

```
ØØ xx      .         input data)
ØØ xx      .
ØØ xx      C3        JP ØØ Ø1
ØØ xx      Ø1        N (L byte)
ØØ xx      ØØ        N (H byte)
```

As in the previous example, the CPU inputs from port 175_{10} and tests bit-7. If bit-7 is LOW, program control jumps back to ØØ Ø1, and the loop is repeated. But if bit-7 is HIGH, the program continues on to location ØØ Ø7. The instruction in this location must *do something* with the data input from port 175_{10} in instruction step ØØ Ø1. Since it is a keyboard routine, we usually PUSH A onto an external memory stack.

Following the portion of the program that "does something" with the ASCII character input in ØØ Ø1, we jump immediately back to ØØ Ø1 to repeat the routine.

TELETYPEWRITERS

Teletypewriters have been around for several decades, and form one of the lowest-cost hard-copy devices used in computer work. Most machines are manufactured by the Teletype Corporation, of Skokie, Illinois. The word *Teletype* is a registered trademark of that company, while the word *teletypewriter* is a generic term.

Most of the older model Teletypes[R] (i.e., models 15, 19, 28, etc.) are encoded in the Baudot code system, a five-bit code. The newest models (33 and 43) are encoded in the ASCII code system (see Table 10-1).

The popularity of teletypewriters is due to their low initial cost and relatively good reliability. For hobbiests, they are popular because they are available at relatively low cost on the government and commercial surplus market. For most hobby applications, and for many commercial, scientific, or engineering applications, the Model 33 Teletype[R] is a best bet (around $500 used and in good condition). This machine is encoded in ASCII, so it is compatible with most microcomputers, and is easy to maintain.

Like most electric typewriters, teletypewriters use electrical solenoids to pull in the selector arms that actually determine which character is printed. For ASCII (a 7-bit code), seven selector magnets and seven solenoids are used.

The basis for selection is to pull in those selectors (each selector represents one bit) common to the desired character. This is done by series-connecting the solenoids together in a circuit called a *current loop*. Older machines used a 60-milliampere current loop, while the 33 and 43 use 20-milliampere current loops.

Figure 10-1 shows the circuit for interfacing a 60-mA machine to a micro-

Table 10-1   **ASCII Code**

	000	001	010	011	100	101	110	111
0000	NULL	① DC_0	b	0	@	P		
0001	SOM	DC_1	!	1	A	Q		
0010	EOA	DC_2	''	2	B	R		
0011	EOM	DC_3	#	3	C	S		
0100	EOT	DC_4 (stop)	$	4	D	T		
0101	WRU	ERR	%	5	E	U		
0110	RU	SYNC	&	6	F	V		
0111	BELL	LEM	'	7	G	W	Unassigned	
1000	FE_0	S_0	(	8	H	X		
1001	HT / SK	S_1	)	9	I	Y		
1010	LF	S_2	*	:	J	Z		
1011	V_{TAB}	S_3	+	;	K	[		
1100	FF	S_4	(comma) ,	<	L	\		ACK
1101	CR	S_5	—	=	M	]		②
1110	SO	S_6	.	>	N	↑		ESC
1111	SI	S_7	/	?	O	←		DEL

Example: | 100 | 0001 | = A

b_7 ——————b_1

The abbreviations used in the figure mean:

NULL	Null Idle	CR	Carriage return
SOM	Start of message	SO	Shift out
EOA	End of address	SI	Shift in
EOM	End of message	DC_0	Device control ①
			Reserved for data
			Link escape
EOT	End of transmission	$DC_1 - DC_3$	Device control
WRU	"Who are you?"	ERR	Error
RU	"Are you . . . . ?"	SYNC	Synchronous idle
BELL	Audible signal	LEM	Logical end of media
FE	Format effector	$SO_0 - SO_7$	Separator (information)
HT	Horizontal tabulation		Word separator (blank, normally non-printing)
SK	Skip (punched card)	ACK	Acknowledge
LF	Line feed	②	Unassigned control
V/TAB	Vertical tabulation	ESC	Escape
FF	Form feed	DEL	Delete Idle

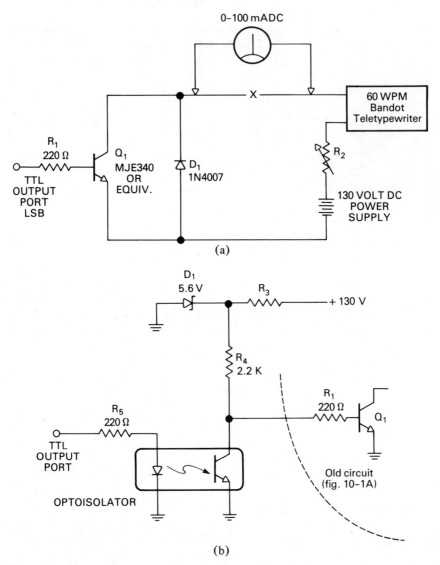

FIG. 10-1 (a) Simple circuit to interface old-style Baudot teletypewriters. Adjust R2 for 60 mA in the loop; (b) Circuit above modified to isolate the teletypewriter from the computer output circuitry.

computer, while Fig. 10-2 shows the circuit for a 20-mA machine. In both cases, we use one bit of a TTL-compatible output port (see Chapter 9) for drive to the teletypewriter.

Figure 10-1(a) shows the most basic circuit for a 60-mA machine. An external 130-volt dc power supply is needed. The current loop circuit consists of the dc supply, resistor R2, the teletypewriter machine, and *c-e* path of transistor Q1.

Diode D1 is used as a spike suppressor. The solenoid coils will produce a spike-like pulse (i.e., high amplitude, short duration) every time the current flow in one of the coils is interrupted. Diode D1 is connected to suppress these spikes, and is used mainly to protect transistor Q1.

Transistor Q1 can be any high-voltage power transistor that is capable of handling a 60-mA collector current. Q1 acts as a switch to turn the loop on and off.

If a HIGH appears on the LSB of the selected output port, then Q1 is forward-biased. Its *c-e* path conducts current, closing the loop. When the LSB of the output port is LOW, then Q1 is reverse-biased. Under this condition, its *c-e* path is turned off, so the loop is open.

It is best to adjust resistor R2 to obtain a loop current of 60 mA. Place a HIGH on the LSB of the selected port, and press one of the teletypewriter keys. A millammeter placed at the point indicated in Fig. 10-1(a) will show the current. Adjust the resistor (R2) for a flow of 60 mA.

It is probably best if all high-voltage circuits are isolated from your computer's output. A fault in transistor Q1 could otherwise cause damage to the output port circuits. An appropriate circuit for this is shown in Fig. 10-1(b). The secret is to use an optoisolator device. On the computer side of the device is an LED, while on the teletypewriter side is an optotransistor. The transistor will be turned off unless the LED is turned on. The collector of the optoisolator transistor is connected to the point in the previous circuit that connected to the computer. This collector is also connected to a 5.6-volt dc power supply that is derived from the +130-volt dc power supply used in the current loop. On the computer side, the LED is connected, through a current-limiting resistor (R5), to the LSB of the selected port.

When the LSB of the output port is HIGH, then the LED is turned on. This turns on the transistor in the optoisolator, shorting out the bias to the current loop transistor. This action turns off the loop. Similarly, the LOW on the LSB of the port turns off the transistor, so Q1 is turned on, closing the loop. The action in this circuit is inverted, so it is necessary to complement the Z80 accumulator before outputting data. Alternatively, you could use one other transistor inverter, between the isolator and Q1, to invert the output of the isolator.

Figure 10-2 shows a circuit that is used to interface the model 33 to a Z80 output port. Looking from the front panel, there is a terminal strip on the right-rear side of the Model 33. This terminal strip, shown schematically in Fig. 10-2(a), contains the send/receive connections for the teletypewriter.

The *receive* side of the machine (terminals 6 and 7) contains the loop, so that the solenoids can be pulled in. The *send* side is merely a set of contact

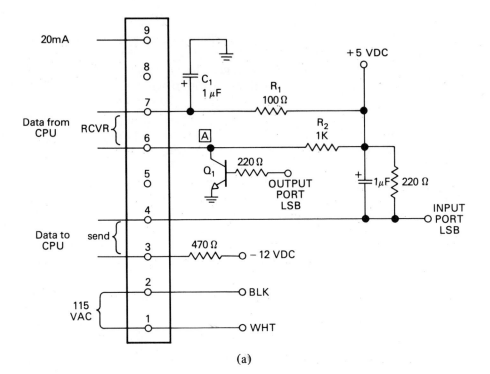

(a)

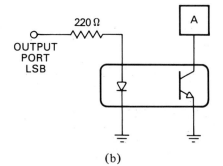

(b)

FIG. 10-2 (a) Circuit to connect computer output port to the Model 33 tele-typewriter. Terminal block shown is found under the top cover of the Md1. 33, on the right rear when viewed from the front of the keyboard. Use separate +5 volt dc power supplies for best results; (b) Modification of the standard circuit to allow isolation of the computer from the teletypewriter.

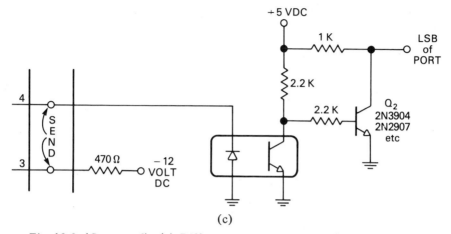

Fig. 10-2 (*Continued*) (c) Different circuit to accomplish the same job.

closures. In my own experience, this circuit has produced some problems. If the loop is turned on after the microcomputer is loaded and ready to work, a random pulse seems to change a few (important) bits in a few memory locations. The problem is partially relieved by using +5-volt and −12-volt power supplies that are completely divorced from the computer power supply. But I like the approach shown in Figs. 10-2(b) and 10-2(c). We would use R1, R2, and C1 [from Fig. 10-2(a)], but replace Q1 with the transistor from the optoisolator (connect the collector to point "A"). The LED is connected, again through a current-limiting resistor, to the LSB of the selected output port.

We can use the −12-volt supply to drive the LED, or the +5-volt supply (in which case, the polarity is reversed). The isolator transistor (Q1) drives an inverter stage (Q2). When the LED is turned on, Q2 is turned off, so the LSB of the selected input port is HIGH. But if the LED is off, then Q2 is turned on, dropping the LSB of the input port to zero.

Quite a number of small companies that advertise in the hobby computer magazines offer optoisolator, 20-mA current loop kits as add-ons for many computers. Take advantage of them; they are low in cost.

RS-232 INTERFACING

The Electronic Industries Association (EIA) standard RS-232 pertains to a standardized serial data transmission scheme. The idea is to use the same connector (i.e., the DB-25 family), wired in the same manner all of the time, and to use the same voltage levels. Supposedly, one could connect together any two devices that provide RS-232 I/O without any problem (it usually works).

Modems, CRT terminals, printers (i.e., Model 43 Teletypewriter), and other devices will be fitted with RS-232 connectors. Some computers provide RS-232 I/O, and this feature can be added by using a set of Motorola ICs called RS-232 drivers/receivers. An RS-232 driver IC accepts TTL outputs from a computer or other device, and produces RS-232 voltage levels at its output. The RS-232 receiver does just the opposite. It takes RS-232 levels from the communications/interface and produces TTL outputs.

Unfortunately, the RS-232 is a very old standard, and it predates even the TTL standard. That is why it uses such odd voltage levels for logical-1 and logical-$\emptyset$.

Besides voltage levels, the standard also fixes the load impedances and the output impedances of the drivers.

There are actually two RS-232 standards—the older RS-232B and the current RS-232C (see Fig. 10-3). In the older version, RS-232B, logical-1 is any potential in the -5- to -25-volt range, and logical-$\emptyset$ is anything between +5 and +25 volts. The voltages in the range -3 to +3 are a transition state, while +3 to +5 and -3 to -5 are undefined.

The speedier RS-232C standard narrows the limits to ±15 volts. In addition, the standard fixes the load resistance to the range 3000 to 7000 ohms, and the driver output impedance that is low. The driver must provide a slew rate of 30 volts/microsecond. The Motorola MC1488 driver and MC1489 receiver ICs meet these specifications.

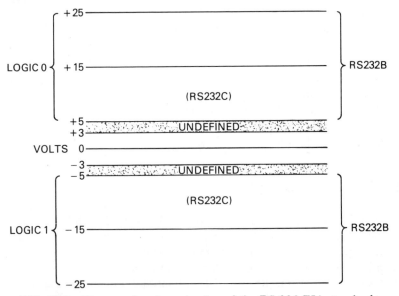

FIG. 10-3 Diagram showing meaning of the RS-232 EIA standards.

The standard wiring for the 25-pin DB-25 connector used in RS-232 ports is shown in Table 10-2.

Table 10-2   **EIA RS-232 Pin-outs for Standard DB-25 connecta**

PIN NO.	RS232 NAME	FUNCTION
1	AA	Chassis ground
2	BA	Data from terminal
3	BB	Data received from modem
4	CA	Request to send
5	CB	Clear to send
6	CC	Data set ready
7	AB	Signal ground
8	CF	Carrier detection
9	undef	
10	undef	
11	undef	
12	undef	
13	undef	
14	undef	
15	DB	Transmitted bit clock, internal
16	undef	
17	DD	Received bit clock
18	undef	
19	undef	
20	CD	Data terminal ready
21	undef	
22	CE	Ring indicator
23	undef	
24	DA	Transmitted bit clock, external
25	undef	

11
Interrupts

WHAT IS AN INTERRUPT?

An *interrupt* is a process in which your computer stops executing the main program, and begins executing another program located somewhere else in memory. This is not a mere "jump" or "call" operation, but a response to an external stimulus.

There are several reasons why an interrupt capability may be required. One of these is the case of an *alarm* condition. We could, for example, use a computer in an environmental control system, and use the interrupt capability to allow response to alarm situations (e.g., smoke detector, liquid level, burglar alarm, over-temperature, etc.). The computer would ordinarily go about some other chore, perhaps the business of controlling the system. But once during the execution of each instruction of the program, the CPU will interrogate the interrupt system. It is, then, monitoring the alarm status while executing some unrelated program. When an interrupt is received, indicating an alarm status, the computer would jump immediately to the program that *services* the interrupt (see Chapter 12)—rings a bell, calls the fire department, turns on a light, sighs heavily, etc.

Another application is to input data that occurs only occasionally, or whose periodicity is so long as to force the computer to do nothing for an inordinate amount of time. A real-time clock, or timer, for example, might want to update its input to the computer only once per second or once per minute.

An analog-to-digital converter (ADC) might have a 20-millisecond conversion time. Even the slower version of the Z80 CPU chip (using a 2.5-mHz clock) can perform hundreds of thousands of operations while waiting for that ADC to complete its conversion job. Since the ADC will not provide valid data until after the conversion time expires, waiting for those data would be a tremendous waste of CPU time.

Another use is to input, or output, data to/from a peripheral device such as a line printer, teletypewriter, keyboard, terminal, etc. Those electromechanical devices are notoriously slow to operate. Even so-called "high-speed" line printers are considerably slower than the Z80 CPU. A classic example is the "standard" 100-word-per-minute teletypewriter. A "word," in this case, is five ASCII characters, so we have to output 500 characters per minute to operate at top speed. This is a rate of 8 characters per second, so each character requires 1/8 of a second, or 125 milliseconds, to print. The CPU, on the other hand, is a trifle faster. It can output the character to the input buffer of the teletypewriter in something like 3 *microseconds*. The Z80 can execute almost 42,000 outputs in the time it takes the teletypewriter to print just one character.

There are at least two ways to handle this situation, and both involve having the peripheral device signal the CPU when it is ready to accept another character. This is done by using a strobe pulse from the peripheral, issued when it is ready to receive (or deliver) another data byte. One way to handle this problem is to have the programmer write in a periodic poll of the peripheral. The strobe pulse is applied to one bit of an input port. A program is written that periodically examines that bit to see if it is HIGH. If it is found to be HIGH, then the program control will jump to a subroutine that services the peripheral. But this approach is still wasteful of CPU time, and places undue constraints on the programmer's freedom.

A superior method is to use the computer's interrupt capability. The peripheral strobe pulse becomes an *interrupt request*. When the CPU recognizes the interrupt request, it transfers program control to an interrupt service subroutine (i.e., a program that performs some function required for the operation of the peripheral that generates the interrupt). When the service program is completed, then control is transferred back to the main program at the point where it left off. Note that the CPU does not recognize an interrupt request until after it has finished executing the current instruction. Program control then returns to the *next* instruction in the main program that would have been executed had no interrupt occurred.

TYPES OF Z80 INTERRUPT

There are two basic types of interrupt recognized by the Z80 CPU: *nonmaskable* and *maskable*. The nonmaskable interrupt is executed next in sequence regardless of any other considerations. The maskable interrupts, however, depend upon the condition of an interrupt flip-flop inside of the Z80. If the programmer wishes to mask, i.e., ignore, an interrupt, then the appropriate flip-flop is turned off.

There are three distinct forms of maskable interrupt in the Z80, and these take the designations *mode-∅*, *mode-1*, and *mode-2*.

There are two interrupt input terminals on the Z80 chip. The $\overline{\text{NMI}}$ (pin 17) is for the nonmaskable interrupt, while the $\overline{\text{INT}}$ is for the maskable interrupts.

The nonmaskable interrupt ($\overline{\text{NMI}}$) is much like a *restart* instruction, except that it automatically causes program control to jump to memory location ∅∅ 66 (hex), instead of to one of the eight standard restart addresses. Location ∅∅ 66 (hex) must be reserved by the programmer for some instruction in the interrupt service program, very often an unconditional jump to some other location higher in memory (see Chapter 12).

The mode-∅ maskable interrupt causes the Z80 to pretend that it is an 8080A, preserving some of the software compatibility between the two CPUs. During a mode-∅ interrupt, the interrupting device places any valid instruction on the CPU data bus, and the CPU executes this instruction. The time of execution will be the normal time period for that type of instruction, plus two clock pulses. In most cases, the interrupting device will place a *restart* instruction on the data bus, because all of these are one-byte instructions. The restart instructions transfer program control to one of eight page-∅ locations.

Any time that a $\overline{\text{RESET}}$ pulse is applied (i.e., pin 26 of the Z80 is brought LOW), the CPU automatically goes to the mode-∅ condition. This interrupt mode, like the other two maskable interrupt modes, can be set from software by executing the appropriate instruction (in this case, an IM ∅ instruction).

The mode-1 interrupt is selected by execution of an IM1 instruction. Mode-1 is totally under software control, and cannot be accessed by using a hardware action. Once set, the mode-1 interrupt is actuated by bringing the $\overline{\text{INT}}$ line LOW momentarily. In mode-1, the Z80 will execute a restart to location ∅∅ 38 (hex).

The mode-2 interrupt is, perhaps, the most powerful of the Z80 interrupts. It allows an *indirect* call to any location in memory. The 8080A device (and the Z80 operating in mode-∅) permits only eight interrupt lines. But in mode-2, the Z80 can respond to as many as 128 different interrupt lines.

Mode-2 interrupts are said to be *vectored*, because they can be made to jump to any location in the 65,536 bytes of memory. In Chapter 12 we will discuss this mode more fully.

INTERRUPT HARDWARE

In this section we will discuss some of the circuitry needed to support the Z80 interrupt capability. Note that the primary emphasis in this chapter will be low-cost circuits not necessarily intended originally for use with the Z80. Keep in mind, however, that Zilog, Mostek, and others manufacture some sophisticated interrupt controller devices, or build into PIO and SIO chips the ability to control interrupts.

INTERRUPT REQUESTS

In the simplest cases, interrupt request lines can be built simply by extending the $\overline{INT}$ and/or $\overline{NMI}$ lines to the peripheral device. This assumes a very simple arrangement, in which only one peripheral is to be serviced. Figure 11-1 shows how this might be accomplished. The $\overline{NMI}$ line (pin 17) is brought out as a nonmaskable interrupt line. The optional pull-up resistor (R1) is used to insure that pin 17 remains at the HIGH condition, and thereby helps reduce noise response.

The $\overline{INT}$ line can be treated in exactly the same manner if there is to be but one interrupting peripheral. But in this case, we have demonstrated how the same pin might be used to recognize up to eight interrupts. This arrangement can be used if only mode-∅ is anticipated. The peripheral that generates the interrupt then places the correct restart instruction on the data bus. The specific restart instruction received tells the CPU which peripheral initiated the interrupt.

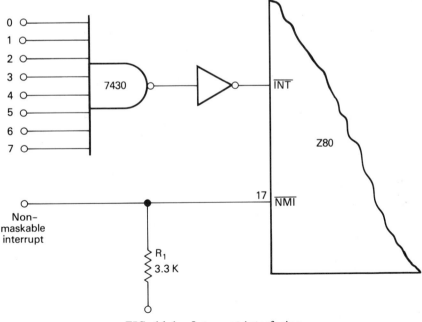

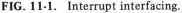
FIG. 11-1. Interrupt interfacing.

The key to this $\overline{\text{INT}}$ circuit is the eight-input TTL NAND gate (i.e., a 7430 IC). If any one of its inputs, which form $\overline{\text{INTERRUPT REQUEST}}$ lines, goes LOW, then the 7430 output goes HIGH. This forces the output of the inverter LOW, creating the needed $\overline{\text{INT}}$ signal at pin 16 of the Z80.

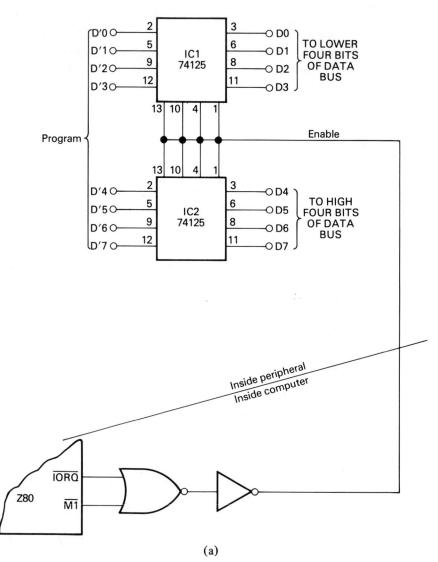

(a)

FIG. 11-2 (a) Interrupt acknowledge circuit.

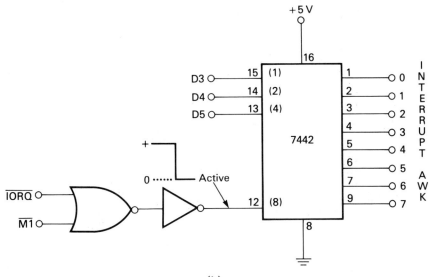

(b)

FIG. 11-2 (*Continued*) (b) Interrupt acknowledge for more than one device.

INTERRUPT ACKNOWLEDGE

The CPU will always finish executing the current instruction before recognizing an interrupt request. There is, therefore, a slight delay between the initial request and the time when the CPU is ready to process that request. We need some type of signal to tell the peripheral that generated the interrupt request when the CPU is ready to do business. The Z80 samples the $\overline{\text{INT}}$ line on the rising edge of the last clock pulse of the current instruction. If the $\overline{\text{INT}}$ line is LOW, then the CPU responds by generating an $\overline{\text{IORQ}}$ (input/output request) signal during the next M1 machine cycle. We can, then, accept simultaneous existence of LOW conditions on $\overline{\text{IORQ}}$ and $\overline{\text{M1}}$ to form the interrupt acknowledge signal.

Figure 11-2(a) shows an interrupt acknowledge scheme that works for a single interrupt line. We assume that one of the interrupt request schemes of Fig. 11-1 is also used. The 74125 (IC1/IC2) is a quad, tri-state, TTL buffer. Each 74125 contains four noninverting buffer amplifiers that accept TTL inputs, and provide TTL outputs. When a control line is HIGH, the associated buffer output will "float" in the high-impedance "tri-state" mode. But if the control line is brought LOW, the buffer turns on and operates like any other TTL buffer. The control lines for all eight tri-state buffers (four from each 74125) are tied together to form a single *enable* line. The 74125 devices are located inside the peripheral device.

The particular restart instruction designated to service that particular peripheral must be programmed onto the inputs of the 74125s. For example, if we want the peripheral to cause a jump to the RST 10 location (i.e., memory location $\emptyset\emptyset$ 1$\emptyset$), then we must place D7 (hex), or 11010111 (binary), on the data bus following the acknowledgment of the interrupt request. We program this value by setting the D$\emptyset$, D1, D2, D4, D6, and D7 inputs of IC1/IC2 to HIGH (binary 1), and the D3 and D5 inputs to LOW (binary $\emptyset$). This enable line is connected to the inverted output of the NOR gate that detects the interrupt acknowledge condition (i.e., the simultaneous LOW on $\overline{\text{IORQ}}$ and $\overline{\text{M1}}$). The enable line ordinarily remains HIGH, causing the 74125 outputs to float at high impedance. When the brief interrupt acknowledge pulse comes along, this line momentarily drops LOW, thereby transferring the word (D7 hex) at the 74125 inputs to the data bus. The CPU will decode this instruction, and perform a restart jump to $\emptyset\emptyset$ 1$\emptyset$ (hex).

Although there is a practical limit to how many tri-state outputs one can easily float across the data bus, we find it quite easy to connect all eight allowed in mode-$\emptyset$, and a few more. But how do we differentiate between the peripherals? All will generate the same interrupt request, and these can be handled by using a multi-input NAND gate (see Fig. 11-1 again). But how do we decode the restart instruction given and then send the interrupt acknowledgment to only the *correct* peripheral? Chaos would result if we sent the signal to all eight (or more!) peripherals at the same time. It is very often useful to examine the range of *possible* binary words that are to be used in any given situation. For the mode-$\emptyset$ interrupt, we are going to use one of eight restart locations, each having its own unique RST op-code. These are listed in Table 11-1. Note that, for all possible states, only three bits change: D3, D4, and D5. The other bits (D$\emptyset$, D1, D2, D6, and D7) remain constant in all cases (in this particular example, they are all HIGH, but the *important* thing is that they remain at one level in all cases). We can, then, press the 7442 one-of-10 decoder into service once again [see Fig. 11-2(b)]. Recall that the 7442 is a four-bit (BCD) to one-of-10 decoder. The BCD inputs are weighted 1-2-4-8. The 1-2-4 inputs are connected to

Table 11-1   RST n Codes for Interrupts 0–7

INTERRUPT	RST n	HEXADECIMAL	BINARY
$\emptyset$	$\emptyset\emptyset$	C7	11000111
1	$\emptyset$8	CF	11001111
2	1$\emptyset$	D7	11010111
3	18	DF	11011111
4	2$\emptyset$	E7	11100111
5	28	EF	11101111
6	3$\emptyset$	F7	11110111
7	38	FF	11111111

the D3-D4-D5 lines of the data bus. The 8 line of the 7442 is used as the control line, and is connected to the interrupt acknowledge signal.

In normal, noninterrupt operation, the 8-input of the 7442 is kept HIGH, so the lower eight outputs can never be LOW (when 8 is HIGH, only the 8 and 9 outputs can be active). But when the interrupt acknowledge signal is generated, the 7442 detects the condition of the D3-D5 lines of the data bus, and issues the appropriate signal. The only problem that must be considered is the possibility that more than one peripheral will attempt to interrupt at one time. This could cause confusion, to say the least. In a moment we will consider methods for prioritizing the interrupts.

Figure 11-3 shows a decoding scheme that can be used inside the computer, and will allow single line selection for up to eight interrupt lines in mode-$\emptyset$. We are using 74125 quad, tri-state buffers in the same manner as in Fig. 11-2. But notice in Table 11-1 that the least significant four bits of each restart instruction op-code is always either a 7 or F (both hex). Furthermore, the most significant four bits will be one of four possible states C, D, E, or F. We can, then, create all eight possible op-codes by using only six 74125s and some gates, instead of 16 (as would be required if Fig. 11-2 were implemented for all eight!). The inputs of the 74125s are programmed as follows:

IC1	7
IC2	F
IC3	C
IC4	D
IC5	E
IC6	F

The key to our decoding scheme is to gate on the enable lines of only the appropriate 74125s. IC1 and IC2 form the code for the least significant half-byte of the op-code. There are four interrupt lines that should turn on IC1, and the other four should turn on IC2. We may use a 7420 four-input NAND gate to select which is turned on. If any input of a NAND gate goes LOW, then its output is HIGH. We connect the respective inputs of gate G1 to those interrupt lines that want a "7" in the least significant spot; i.e., $\emptyset$, 2, 4, and 6 (see Table 11-1). If any of these four interrupt lines goes LOW, then IC1 is turned on, and a hex 7 is output to the lower-order half-byte of the data bus. Similarly, gate G2 controls IC2. Its inputs are connected to the 1, 3, 5, and 7 interrupt lines. If any of these lines goes LOW, then a hex F is output to the lower-order half-byte of the data bus.

A similar scheme is used to control the higher-order half-byte of the op-code. But in this case, we have four possibilities, each affecting two interrupt lines. IC3–IC6 form the high-order half-byte of the op-code. Since each of these

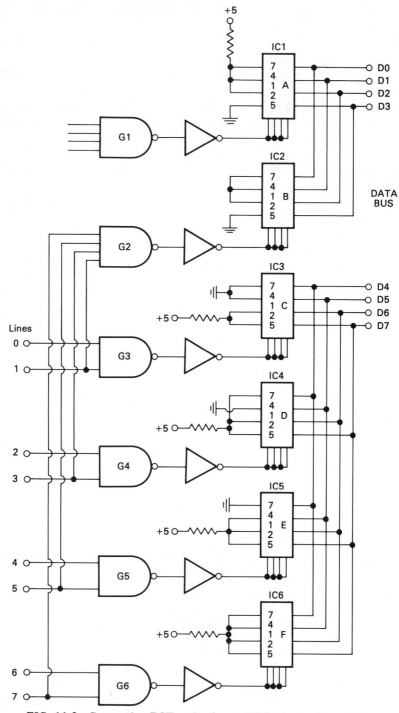

FIG. 11-3 Generating RST codes for multiple-device interrupts.

ICs affects only two interrupt lines, gates G3–G6 need only two inputs. These are connected as follows:

GATE	INTERRUPT LINES
G3	Ø,1
G4	2,3
G5	4,5
G6	6,7

If either interrupt Ø or interrupt 1 becomes active, that line will go LOW, causing the output of G3 to go HIGH. This signal is inverted and applied to IC3, which outputs a hex C onto the data bus. Similarly, G4–G6 will cause the appropriate 74125 to output the correct op-code when their interrupts become active.

The schemes above are all relatively simple, and involve the use of ordinary TTL support integrated circuits. But they all also suffer from a common malady. If more than one peripheral device decides to issue an interrupt request, then chaos reigns! The logic to prioritize the interrupt response sequence is much more complex than the circuits shown thus far. Fortunately, there are special-purpose integrated circuits, designed for direct interfacing with microprocessor chips, that will allow programming to prioritize and control the interrupts.

In their famous *Bugbook* series, Larsen, Titus, and Rony used a 74148 priority encoder and an Intel 8212 (see *The 8080A Bugbook*, by Rony, et al., Howard W. Sams & Co., Inc., 21447) to prioritize interrupts for the 8080A. With little modification the same scheme should work on the Z80 in mode-Ø.

You are also permitted to use the Intel 8214 interrupt controller IC (with a little extra logic), even though it was designed for use with the 8080A. Both 8255 and 8257 devices are also useful in Z80 circuits.

Zilog and Mostek, the sources for the Z80, make a Z80-PIO device. This IC is an I/O controller that can handle interrupts. The Z80-PIO was covered in Chapter 8 and Chapter 3.

12
Servicing Interrupts

Interrupts are a powerful tool on any programmable digital computer. The designers of the Z80 microprocessor chip, probably well aware of this fact, built into the device four ways to interrupt the CPU: nonmaskable, maskable mode-∅, maskable mode-1, and maskable mode-2. In Chapter 11 we briefly discussed these interrupts, and then concerned ourselves with the hardware aspects of the Z80 interrupt system. In this chapter, we will expand the topic of interrupts by considering the programming aspects of servicing the interrupt request.

NONMASKABLE INTERRUPTS

The nonmaskable interrupt is always recognized by the CPU, regardless of the programming being executed. The nonmaskable interrupt goes into effect following the completion of the instruction currently being executed, and is initiated by bringing the $\overline{NMI}$ terminal of the Z80 (i.e., pin 17) LOW. This terminal is sampled by the CPU during the last clock pulse (i.e., T-period) of each machine cycle. If $\overline{NMI}$ is found to be LOW when this sample is taken, then the CPU will automatically begin the interrupt sequence on the next clock pulse.

One principal difference between the nonmaskable interrupt and the maskable interrupts is that the maskables must be enabled by turning on the interrupt flip-flop (IFF1). The nonmaskable does not need to see IFF1 in a SET condition, and, in fact, will cause IFF1 to RESET in order to lock out the maskable interrupts ($\overline{\text{INT}}$).

One principal difference between the nonmaskable interrupt and the maskable interrupts is that the maskables must be enabled by turning on the interrupt flip-flop (IFF1). The nonmaskable does not need to see IFF1 in a SET condition, and, in fact, will cause IFF1 to RESET in order to lock out the maskable interrupts ($\overline{\text{INT}}$).

The nonmaskable interrupt is very much like a "hardware restart" instruction. In fact, it is an RST 66 instruction (meaning that it will cause a restart instruction to be executed to location $\emptyset\emptyset$ 66 hex). The nonmaskable interrupt cannot be disabled by software, and is always recognized by bringing $\overline{\text{NMI}}$ LOW. Recall that the restart instructions caused program control to be transferred to one of eight locations in page zero. The principal difference between the eight software restart instructions and the nonmaskable interrupt are (1) $\overline{\text{NMI}}$ to a fixed location (address $\emptyset\emptyset$ 66 hex), and (2) $\overline{\text{NMI}}$ is *hardware* implemented.

$\overline{\text{NMI}}$ is used in those situations where it is not prudent to ignore the interrupt. It may be that critical, but transitory, data may be ready to input. Or it may be an alarm condition. A program used to control the environment in a building, for example, probably would want to see no priority higher than the automatic fire alarm. One common application of $\overline{\text{NMI}}$ when the Z80 is used in a microcomputer is to guard against the problems consequent to a loss of ac mains power. A circuit is built that monitors the ac mains at the primary of the computer's dc power supply. If the ac power drops out for even a few cycles, the circuit generates an $\overline{\text{NMI}}$ signal to the CPU. The CPU will immediately honor the request, and transfer program control to a power loss subroutine. This program is used to transfer all of the data in the volatile (i.e., solid-state) memory, and the CPU registers/flags, into some form of nonvolatile memory (i.e., disc, magnetic tape, etc.). Computers that require this ability must have sufficient back-up power stored in batteries, of even the massive filter capacitors of the dc power supply, to execute the power loss subroutine before the energy gives out.

Figure 12-1 shows an example of a typical program sequence for the non-maskable interrupt. We are executing a program in page-6 (i.e., locations from $6\emptyset\ \emptyset\emptyset$ hex). The interrupt service subroutine is stored in locations beginning at $8\emptyset\ \emptyset\emptyset$ hex. An interrupt occurs while the instruction at location $6\emptyset\ \emptyset3$ is being executed. The sequence of events is given below:

1. $\overline{\text{NMI}}$ occurs while the CPU is executing the instruction located at $6\emptyset\ \emptyset3$.
2. Program counter (PC) is incremented from $6\emptyset\ \emptyset3$ to $6\emptyset\ \emptyset4$, and then its contents are pushed onto the external memory stack.

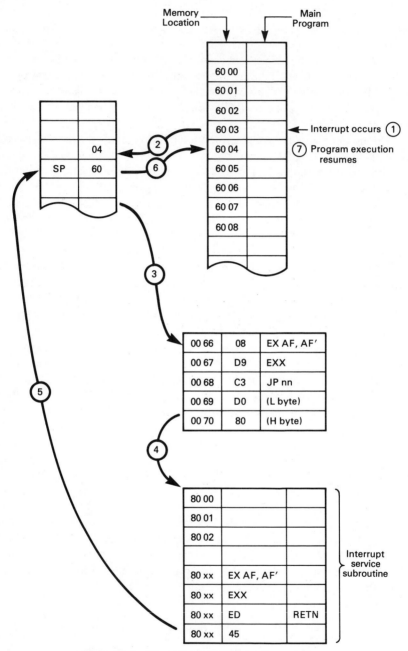

FIG. 12-1 Operations in interrupt servicing.

3. PC is then loaded with ∅∅ 66 hex, transferring program control to ∅∅ 66 hex.

   Before we can service the interrupt, however, we must tend to some housekeeping chores that will allow us to reenter the main program at the point left off, and with no problems. We will want the main program to begin executing at the location that would have been called if the interrupt had not occurred (i.e., 6∅ ∅4). The *address* of this next location was saved automatically in an external memory stack, but nothing has been done for the flags and other CPU registers. In order to save this environment for use when program control is returned to the main program, we must execute the two exchange instructions (EX and EXX). These are the instructions located at the restart location (∅∅66 and ∅∅ 67 hex). The EX instructions exchanges the contents of the AF and A′F′ registers, while the EXX instruction causes the other CPU registers to exchange with their alternates. (A′, F′, B′, C′, D′, E′, H′, and L′ are the alternate bank of CPU registers in the Z80). The environment, i.e., the contents of the main registers, is now saved in the alternate registers. This will free the main registers for use in the interrupt subroutine, and will permit the main program to come back unscratched from the interrupt. Trying to figure out where the CPU was otherwise, without EX and EXX, is a lot like trying to nail jello to the wall.

   In some cases, the interrupt service program is short enough that it can be located in the page-∅ locations following ∅∅ 66 hex. We could, for example, make the first instruction of the service routine at ∅∅ 68 hex. But we usually want to save that part of memory for other housekeeping chores (i.e., other restart instructions). In the example shown in Fig. 12-1, we execute EX and EXX to save the environment, and then jump immediately to location 8∅ ∅∅.

4. The interrupt service program is located higher in memory. In this example we have located it at 8∅ ∅∅. This program is not shown in detail, because its nature would depend on the type of interrupt being serviced.

   The last instruction in any nonmaskable interrupt service program *must* be RETN (return from nonmaskable interrupt). This instruction tells the CPU to return control to the main program.

5. RETN returns the contents of the external memory stack to the program counter. Since the PC now contains 6∅ ∅4 hex, the program resumes at that location. This is the location immediately following the location that was executing when the $\overline{\text{NMI}}$ signal occurred.

   Note that, prior to the RETN instruction, we had to re-exchange the registers by executing once again the EX and EXX instructions. This will regain the environment lost when the restart-66 occurred.

The nonmaskable interrupt is a hardware function of the Z80 CPU chip. It *cannot* be overridden by the programmer. The maskable interrupt, on the other hand, is designed so that it *can* be overridden by the programmer.

The Z80 contains two interrupt flip-flops, labelled IFF1 and IFF2. The first of these, IFF1, is the main interrupt flip-flop, whereas IFF2 is a secondary interrupt flip-flop used to store the condition of IFF1 when a nonmaskable interrupt occurs. We want the CPU restored to its previous state when the nonmaskable interrupt has been serviced. The contents of IFF1 are copied into IFF2 automatically when $\overline{NMI}$ is recognized. When RETN is executed, the contents of IFF2 are copied back to IFF1, restoring the condition of IFF1 to that existing when the interrupt occurred. This action completes the restoration of the CPU.

The $\overline{NMI}$ will automatically cause the state of IFF1 to be stored in IFF2, and then cause IFF1 to be RESET. This is done to prohibit any additional maskable interrupts during the period that $\overline{NMI}$ is being serviced.

MASKABLE INTERRUPTS

Maskable interrupts can be software-controlled through the use of EI, DI, IMØ, IM1, and IM2 instructions. The maskable interrupt is initiated by bringing the $\overline{INT}$ terminal on the Z80 (pin 16) LOW momentarily. This action is necessary, but not sufficient, to turn on the interrupt. Recall that IFF1 must be SET before a maskable interrupt is recognized by the CPU. If IFF1 is RESET, then the $\overline{INT}$ command is masked; i.e., it is not seen by the CPU—it is ignored. IFF1 is SET by executing IMØ, IM1, IM2, or EI instructions. It can RESET by applying a $\overline{RESET}$ pulse to pin 16 of the Z80, or by executing a DI (disable interrupt) instruction. There are, then, two ways to turn off the maskable interrupt capability of the CPU.

There are three types of maskable interrupts, designated mode-Ø, mode-1, and mode-2.

Mode-Ø is the "default" mode. Unless the programmer demands another mode, by causing the IM1 or IM2 instructions to be executed, mode-Ø will be assumed. The CPU is placed in mode-Ø as soon as a $\overline{RESET}$ signal is received at pin 26 of the Z80. It is usually the practice of designers to automatically apply a *power-on* $\overline{RESET}$ as soon as dc power is applied to the Z80.

Of course, setting any given interrupt mode does not allow the CPU to respond to interrupts. An EI (enable interrupt) instruction must be executed first. Once EI is executed, the interrupt flip-flop (IFF1) is SET, so the CPU will respond to $\overline{INT}$ requests (regardless of mode selected).

MODE-Ø

Mode-Ø is used to make the Z80 think that it is an 8080A microprocessor. This was probably done because one of the objectives of Z80 design was to maintain as much software compatibility between Z80 and the older 8080A as possible. Although there are some differences where timing becomes important, it is a general rule of thumb that 8080A programs will execute on Z80 systems, but the reverse is not true; many Z80 instructions have no 8080A counterparts.

Mode-∅ is automatically selected as soon as a $\overline{\text{RESET}}$ pulse is received. Mode-∅ can also be selected through software. The IM∅ instruction will cause the CPU to enter mode-∅, and is used when the programmer has previously selected one of the other interrupt modes, and then wants to return to mode-∅ without resetting the CPU.

Like all of the maskable interrupts, mode-∅ cannot be recognized by the CPU unless the interrupt flip-flop is SET. This flip-flop will be set only if the enable interrupt (EI) instruction is executed. When this is done, then the CPU will be ready to respond to maskable interrupt requests.

The mode-∅ interrupt requires that the interrupting device place a valid Z80 instruction onto the eight-bit data bus as soon as the interrupt acknowledge signal is generated (see Chapter 11). In most cases, the instruction used is the one-byte restart instruction. There are eight unique restart instructions in the Z80 instruction repertoire, and these cause immediate jumps in program control to eight different locations in page zero.

The interrupt service routine should be located at the location in memory where the restart transfers control. For example, if a keyboard causes an interrupt and then jams a restart-10 instruction onto the data bus, the CPU will transfer control to the instruction located at ∅∅ 1∅. If the interrupt service routine is short enough, then it might be located in the memory spots immediately following ∅∅ 1∅ (as well might be the case in a simple keyboard input subroutine), or the instruction may be a jump immediate to some location higher in memory. It is very common for programmers to locate these service programs in the top end of the memory available in that particular computer.

Figure 12-2 shows a typical mode-∅ response. For the sake of continuity, we are using the same locations as in the nonmaskable interrupt discussion earlier. The program is executing the instruction at location 6∅ ∅3 when the $\overline{\text{INT}}$ signal is received by the CPU. The interrupt request is recognized following the completion of the instruction at 6∅ ∅3, provided that IFF1 is SET. The sequence is as follows:

1. $\overline{\text{INT}}$ occurs during the execution of the instruction at location 6∅ ∅3. This is recognized by the CPU during the last clock cycle of that instruction.
2. On the next clock pulse, the CPU acknowledges the interrupt request by causing $\overline{\text{IORQ}}$ and $\overline{\text{M1}}$ to go LOW immediately.
3. When the interrupt acknowledge signal is received, the interrupting device places an RST 10 code on the CPU data bus.
4. The CPU executes the RST 1∅ by incrementing the PC to 6∅ ∅4, stor-

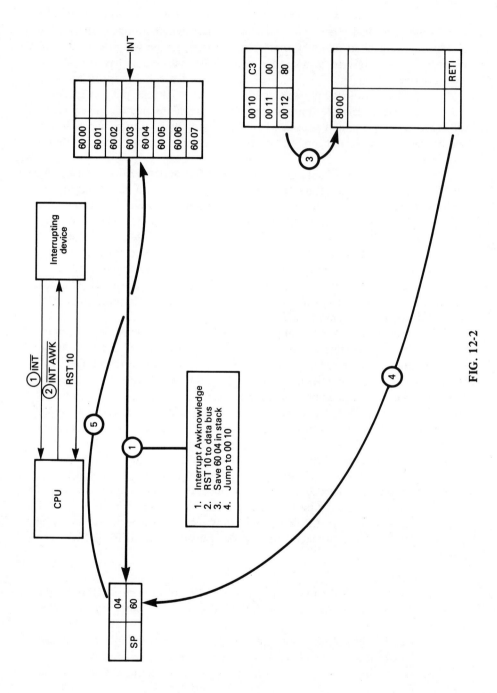

FIG. 12-2

ing the incremented contents in the external memory stack, and then jumping immediately to location ∅∅ 1∅.

5. At location ∅∅ 1∅ the instruction is an immediate jump to location 8∅ ∅∅, where the interrupt service program is found.

6. Again, the environment must be saved. There are two ways in which this can be done. One is to use the EX and EXX instructions of the previous example. Another is to use the PUSH instructions:

8∅ ∅∅	PUSH AF
8∅ ∅1	PUSH BC
8∅ ∅2	PUSH DE
8∅ ∅3	PUSH HL
8∅ ∅4	PUSH IY
8∅ ∅5	PUSH IX

The next instructions would then be instructions of the interrupt service subroutine. When this program is completed, we must execute all of the POP instructions, to bring the contents of the registers back from the memory stack, and an RETI (return from maskable interrupt) instruction:

8∅ xx	POP AF
8∅ xx	POP BC
8∅ xx	POP DE
8∅ xx	POP HL
8∅ xx	POP IY
8∅ xx	POP IX
8∅ xx	RETI

7. After the RETN instruction, the CPU will replace the contents of PC with the data stored in the external stack (6∅ ∅4). This is the address of the instruction in the main program that would have been executed *next* if the interrupt had not occurred.

8. Program execution resumes at location 6∅ ∅4.

The mode-∅ interrupt preserves some of the compatibility of the Z80 with the Intel 8080A microprocessor. But there is a limitation in this mode. The device will allow only eight interrupt devices, one for each of the eight restart locations.

Interrupt priority encoding is possible by using a priority controller, such as the Intel 8214 (or one of the related devices), or one of the Zilog Z80 peripheral chips.

MODE-1

Mode-1 is not similar to any function of the 8080A device, so it is unique to the Z80, in this respect. It is almost identical to the nonmaskable interrupt, except: (1) it is maskable, and (2) it causes a restart jump to location $\emptyset\emptyset$ 38 instead of $\emptyset\emptyset$ 66.

The mode-1 interrupt is dependent upon the programmer's setting mode-1 by enabling interrupt flip-flop IFF1 (the EI instruction), and setting mode-1 by executing an IM1 instruction.

The use of mode-1 is similar to the nonmaskable interrupt, except that the priority would be lower than that of a nonmaskable interrupt. It has the advantage that no external logic is needed to cause the restart instruction. It is, then, somewhat faster than the mode-$\emptyset$ operation.

Refer back to the discussion of the nonmaskable interrupt for a discussion of how this interrupt is serviced. Just be sure to replace in your mind the location $\emptyset\emptyset$ 66 with $\emptyset\emptyset$ 38.

MODE-2

The mode-2 interrupt is one of the most powerful microcomputer interrupts. It allows vectored interrupts of up to 128 levels, as opposed to only eight levels in mode-$\emptyset$ and one level in mode-1 and the nonmaskable interrupt.

Zilog has conveniently caused the Z80 peripheral control chips (Z80-PIO, Z80-SIO, and Z80-CTC) to allow prioritizing of the interrupts through a daisy-chaining scheme.

The key to the versatility of the mode-2 interrupt is that it is *vectored*. That is, it can use a single eight-bit word to point to any location in memory! The 16-bit address of the interrupt service program is stored in a table of interrupt addresses located somewhere in memory. The location of this table is pointed to by a two-byte digital word formed from the contents of the Interrupt (I) register, and the one-byte word supplied by the interrupting device. The upper eight bits of this 16-bit pointer is supplied by the I register, and must be preloaded by the program. The lower-order eight bits of the pointer is supplied by the interrupting device.

There is one restriction on the addresses of the table, and that is that they must begin on an even-numbered memory location. All of the entries in this table will be two bytes in adjacent locations. The first byte of each entry in the table is the low-order byte of the desired address, while the second entry is the high-order byte. One consequence of this constraint is that the least significant bit of the eight-bit word supplied by the interrupting device must be $\emptyset$.

Figure 12-3 shows an example of such a table. In this case, the programmer elected to locate the table in page-8, and it commences at 8$\emptyset$ $\emptyset\emptyset$ hex. The

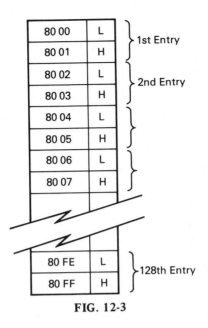

80 00	L	} 1st Entry
80 01	H	
80 02	L	} 2nd Entry
80 03	H	
80 04	L	}
80 05	H	
80 06	L	}
80 07	H	
80 FE	L	} 128th Entry
80 FF	H	

FIG. 12-3

first entry is found at 8∅ ∅∅ and 8∅ ∅1. These locations contain the low, and high, order bytes of the address where the first interrupt service program is located. The first part of this address (8∅ hex) is stored in the I register. The second part is supplied by the interrupting device. Notice that the binary equivalent of ∅∅ ends in a ∅.

Similarly, the other entries are found beginning at 8∅ ∅2, 8∅ ∅4, 8∅ ∅6, etc. all the way up to 8∅ FE (if 128 levels are required). Each of these table addresses contains the address of a location in memory where the CPU will find the program that serves that particular interrupting device.

Figure 12-4 shows a typical mode-2 interrupt sequence. In this program, the main program is located in page-4 (i.e., beginning at 4∅ ∅∅), the vector table is located in page-8, and the interrupt subroutine for the device shown is in page-6 (begins at 6∅ 5∅ hex). The I register contains 8∅ hex, and the interrupting device is programmed to enter ∅4 hex on the data bus when the interrupt acknowledge signal is received. The interrupt flip-flop IFF1 must be SET, and the bus request $\overline{BUSRQ}$ must be HIGH. The sequence of events is as follows:

1. The interrupting peripheral issues an $\overline{INT}$ signal to the CPU.
2. When the interrupt acknowledge signal is received, the peripheral jams 04 hex onto the data bus. This is merged with the 8∅ from the I register to form the address 8∅ ∅4 hex. This address in memory will contain the address of the actual interrupt service program required by this peripheral.

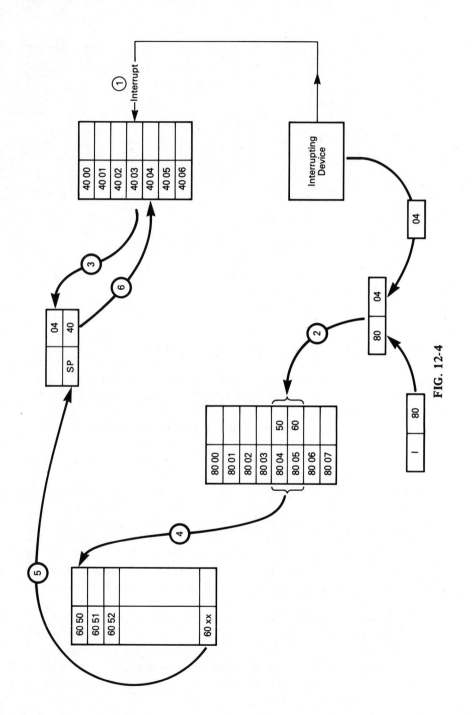

FIG. 12-4

3. The PC is incremented, and then its contents are pushed onto an external memory stack.

4. The PC is loaded with the address found at location 8∅ ∅4. This address is 6∅ 5∅ hex, so program control jumps to this location.

5. After the last instruction (RETI) of the service program, the PC data saved in the external stack are loaded back into the PC.

6. The main program resumes at location 4∅ ∅4.

It is necessary to save the environment when the jump occurs, or the CPU will not necessarily be in the same state as before the interrupt occurred. These techniques were discussed earlier in this chapter.

13

Arithmetic Operations

The arithmetic instructions permit direct addition and subtraction operations by the Z80 CPU. By using one of the standard algorithms we are also able to provide multiplication and division operations. Note, however, that many computer users prefer to use *hardware* multiplication/division in order to gain much in the speed department. This is true of all microcomputers and most minicomputers, not just the Z80 device. The Z80 instruction set also includes a *decimal adjust* (DAA) that permits BCD arithmetic operations.

The Z80 arithmetic instructions are divided into eight- and sixteen-bit groups. Additionally, some of the control group instructions also pertain to arithmetic operations.

The eight-bit group contains the following type of instructions:

ADD	(addition)
ADC	(addition-with-carry)
SUB	(subtraction)
SBC	(subtraction with carry)

Also parts of this eight-bit group are the logical instructions AND, OR, XOR, CP (compare), INC (increment), and DEC (decrement). Although these are covered elsewhere in this book, they do form a very necessary part of some arithmetic operations.

In all of the eight-bit arithmetic instructions it is assumed that the accumulator and one other operand are used. The second operand may be *immediate* (i.e., ADD A,N), the contents of one of the Z80 registers (directly or indirectly addressed), or the contents of an external memory location.

The sixteen-bit arithmetic group uses register pairs (i.e., HL, IX, BC, DE, SP) in order to perform operations with longer data words. The sixteen-bit group contains ADD, ADC, and SBC instructions. It also contains INC (increment) and DEC (decrement) instructions. There are, however, no logical instructions in this group.

ADD INSTRUCTIONS

The ADD instructions permit addition between the accumulator and data obtained from another location. The result of the addition is stored in the accumulator, and certain condition flags are set to denote the nature of the result.

ADD A,A. This is a single-byte instruction that adds the contents of the accumulator to the contents of the accumulator (i.e., the contents of the accumulator are added to themselves). The result is stored in the accumulator. The op-code is 87 (hex).

Example

The contents of the accumulator are 3F (hex). If an ADD A,A instruction is encountered:

$$3F + 3F = 7E$$

The result (7E) is stored in accumulator after the execution of this instruction.

ADD A,r. This series of instructions is also single-byte. There is a separate op-code for each register of the Set B, C, D, E, H, and L. The format for these instructions op-codes is

$$1\ 0\ 0\ 0\ 0\ \_\ r\ \_$$

The most significant four-bits form the hex digit "8." The second hex digit required for the op-code is determined by the particular "r" selected from the table on the next page.

REGISTER	r
B	000
C	001
D	010
E	011
H	100
L	101

The op-codes for ADD A,r are, therefore,

B	80
C	81
D	82
E	83
H	84
L	85

When one of these instructions is encountered, then the contents of the specified register are added to the contents of the accumulator, and the result is stored in the accumulator.

ADD A, (HL). This is a register-indirect method of locating a given byte in the external memory. In this instruction, the contents of the external memory location whose address is given by the contents of the HL register pair are added to the contents of the accumulator. The result is stored in the accumulator.

Example

Consider Fig. 13-1. The contents of the accumulator are 3D (hex) when the ADD A, (HL) instruction is encountered. At that same time the contents of the HL register pair are 8Ø Ø3 (pointing to location 8Ø Ø3 in external memory). The contents of the accumulator (3D) are added to the contents of 80 03 (2B), and the result 3D + 2B, or 68 (hex), is stored in the accumulator. At the end of the execution of the ADD A, (HL) instruction the contents of the accumulator are 68.

ADD A,n. This is a two-byte instruction where the first byte is the op-code (C6) and the second byte of the value "n" to be added to the contents of the accumulator. This is an example of an immediate instruction.

Example

The contents of the accumulator are 1F when the following code is encountered:

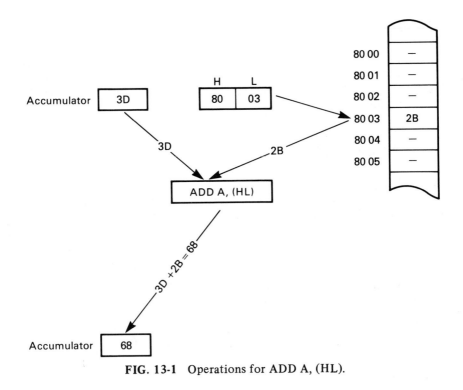

FIG. 13-1   Operations for ADD A, (HL).

C6   (op-code for ADD A, n)
3∅   ("n")

This tells the Z80 to add the contents of the accumulator (1F) to "n" (3∅). The operation carried out will be 1F + 3∅ = 4F. The value stored in the accumulator at the end of this instruction is 4F.

ADD A, (IX+d) and ADD A, (IY+d).   These addition instruction add together the contents of the accumulator and the contents of an external memory location that is specified by the contents of either the IY or IX index registers and a displacement integer d. Both of these are three-byte instructions:

IX + d	IY + d
DD	FD
86	86
d	d

ADC INSTRUCTIONS

These instructions are similar to the ADD instructions, with the exception that they take into account any carry bits generated from previous operations. The C-flag of the F register determines whether there has been a carry on any given operation.

SUB INSTRUCTIONS

The SUB instructions are analogous to the ADD instructions, and the SBC instructions are analogous to the ADC instructions. The difference, of course, is that the operation performed is subtraction instead of addition. The same range of instruction types is available as in the ADD/ADC group. Only SBC is available, however, in the sixteen-bit arithmetic group. The operations are as follows:

SBC	SUB
A ← A-s-cy	A ← A-s

14

Logic Operations

The Z80 instruction set contains certain logical and compare instructions. A logical instruction is one that performs the binary logic operations of AND, OR, or Exclusive-OR (XOR). With some exceptions, the compare instructions are functionally much like the subtraction operations.

Binary logic operations are used in digital electronics, and are similar to logic taught as philosophy in college (if P then Q). The AND function compares two inputs (i.e., bits), and issues a HIGH output (i.e., a logical-1) only if both inputs are also at a logical-1 (HIGH) level. The rules for AND are

```
Ø AND Ø = Ø
Ø AND 1 = Ø
1 AND Ø = Ø
1 AND 1 = 1
```

The OR function compares two inputs, or bits in the case of a microcomputer instruction, and issues a HIGH (logical-1) output if *either* input bit is HIGH. The rules are as follows:

```
Ø OR Ø = Ø
Ø OR 1 = 1
1 OR Ø = 1
1 OR 1 = 1
```

The Exclusive-OR, or XOR, logical function is a little different. This instruction will produce a HIGH output if either input is HIGH, but not if *both* inputs are HIGH. The rules for XOR are

```
Ø XOR Ø = Ø
Ø XOR 1 = 1
1 XOR Ø = 1
1 XOR 1 = Ø
```

Note that both cases where the output is HIGH (perhaps we should say the *result*) are when the two bits (inputs) are the *same*. In the case of $Ø$ XOR $Ø$ and 1 XOR 1, the output is LOW (logical-$Ø$).

The Z80 microprocessor provides all three types of logical operation (AND, OR, XOR). All of these are actually multi-instruction functions AND s, OR s, and XOR s.

The AND s instructions include AND R, AND N, AND (HL), AND (IX+d), and AND (IY+d). Like the other forms of Z80 logical instruction, AND s performs a *bit-by-bit* comparison between the specified data and the contents of the accumulator. The result is stored in the accumulator.

The AND R instruction performs an AND operation between the accumulator and the register specified by a three-bit field in the op-code. The op-code is of the form 10100---, where the last three bits specify the register from the set $ØØØ$ (B), $ØØ1$ (C), $Ø1Ø$ (D), $Ø11$ (E), $1ØØ$ (H), $1Ø1$ (L), and 111 (A, or accumulator).

The AND N instruction is an immediate type in which the AND operation is performed between the accumulator and the byte following the op-code. The op-code is 11100110 (E6 hex), while the word to be compared with the accumulator is the following byte. For example, suppose the accumulator contains the byte 5F hex, and the following code is encountered:

E6   op-code for AND N
D7   data (hex for 215_{10})

This means that we want to perform an AND operation between 5F hex and D7 hex. On a bit-for-bit basis this is

```
       Ø 1 Ø 1 1 1 1 1    (5F hex)
AND    1 1 0 1 0 1 1 1    (D7 hex)
       ─────────────────
       0 1 0 1 0 1 1 1    (57 hex)
```

(see the rules given earlier, and apply them on a bit-by-bit basis without any carries or borrows).

This means that 5F hex AND D7 hex, when compared in an AND instruction, produce a result of 57 hex, and this result is left in the accumulator at the end of the instruction's execution.

The AND instruction is used to mask out any unwanted bits in the eight-bit data word stored in the accumulator. We might, for example, make use of bit-packing to make more efficient use of the field. We might, for example, want to see only bits 3, 4, and 5 (i.e., bits 3-5 out of the field $\emptyset$-7). This means that we will need to mask out bits $\emptyset$, 1, 2, 6, and 7. By placing a 1 at all bits that we want to keep, and a $\emptyset$ at all other bit positions, the desired bits will be passed. Recall the rules for AND. We will compare the desired bits with a 1. If the input bit is 1, then we have a 1 AND 1 = 1 situation. But if we input a $\emptyset$, then we have a $\emptyset$ AND 1 = $\emptyset$ situation. This means that the sense of the input bit is retained, while all others are masked out.

For example, in the situation given above, we wanted to mask out all bits except bits 3-5, so we would want to compare the contents input to the accumulator with $\emptyset\emptyset$111$\emptyset\emptyset\emptyset$. All bits except 3, 4, and 5 are zero, so will be masked out regardless of the input word. Suppose that the contents of the accumulator are 1$\emptyset$1$\emptyset$1$\emptyset$1$\emptyset$, and we want to retain only bits 3-5. We would use the AND N instruction as follows:

        1 1 1 $\emptyset$ $\emptyset$ 1 1 $\emptyset$ (E6 hex)
        $\emptyset$ $\emptyset$ 1 1 1 $\emptyset$ $\emptyset$ $\emptyset$ (N)

The AND comparison performed by this, when the contents of the accumulator are 10101010, will be:

$$
\begin{array}{r}
\emptyset\ \emptyset\ 1\ 1\ 1\ \emptyset\ \emptyset\ \emptyset \\
\text{AND} \quad 1\ \emptyset\ 1\ \emptyset\ 1\ \emptyset\ 1\ \emptyset \\
\hline
\emptyset\ \emptyset\ 1\ \emptyset\ 1\ \emptyset\ \emptyset\ \emptyset
\end{array}
$$

Note that in the Z80 some of the bit-test instructions can also be used to strip the field of the desired bits.

The other AND instructions use memory locations pointed to by the contents of certain registers. AND (HL), for example, compares the contents of the accumulator with the contents of an external memory location pointed to by the contents of the HL register pair. The AND (IY+d) and AND (IX+d) instructions perform the comparison between the accumulator and external memory locations pointed to by a displacement integer d, which is part of the instruction, and either the IY or IX index registers.

The OR instruction is also of the OR s format, similar to the AND s instructions discussed above. The same different types of OR instruction are allowed: OR R, OR N, OR (HL), OR (IY+d), and OR (IX+d). We use the OR s instructions to merge data, or to set certain bits.

Recall that the OR rules require a 1 result if *either* "input" is 1. For example, let us compare B3 hex with C9 hex in an OR instruction:

```
       1 0 1 1 0 0 1 1    (B3 hex)
OR     1 1 0 0 1 0 0 1    (C9 hex)
       1 1 1 1 1 0 1 1    (FB hex)
```

Let us consider an example of the case where we want to set bit-7 to 1 unconditionally. We would OR the contents of the accumulator with 1∅∅∅∅∅∅∅. This would make bit 7 a 1 regardless of the data:

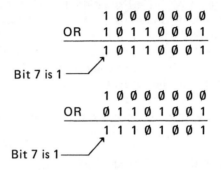

The XOR s instruction performs a bit-by-bit Exclusive-OR operation between the contents of the accumulator and the contents of the source, *s*. We have XOR R, XOR N, XOR (HL), XOR (IY+d), and XOR (IX+d) instructions in the Z80 set.

Recall the rules for the XOR operation. We will create a 1 result only if both inputs are different from each other (i.e., ∅ XOR 1, or 1 XOR ∅). An example of an XOR operation using the XOR N instruction follows.

Suppose the accumulator contains B2 hex, and we encounter the following XOR N instruction:

```
1 1 1 ∅ 1 1 1 ∅    (EE hex—op-code for XOR N)
∅ ∅ 1 ∅ 1 ∅ 1 ∅    (2A hex—N)
```

The operation that the Z80 will perform is

```
       ∅ ∅ 1 ∅ 1 ∅ 1 ∅    (2A hex)
XOR    1 ∅ 1 1 ∅ ∅ 1 ∅    (B2 hex)
       1 ∅ ∅ 1 1 ∅ ∅ ∅    (98 hex)
```

When we compare 2A hex with B2 hex in an XOR instruction, the result is 98 hex, and this is stored in the accumulator at the end of the execution of the XOR N instruction.

15
Miscellaneous Z80 Information

The instruction set (and certain other information) is rarely given in easily available form. Programmers often have to look up certain information in several different books. In this chapter, we are going to help you by offering certain information that has proved useful in programming any computer. Included is the Z80 instruction set sorted (a) by op-code, and (b) by mnemonic. The former will help you especially when you are trying to decode a program, whereas the latter is of use most often when one is trying to originate a new program.

ASCII (AMERICAN STANDARD CODE FOR INFORMATION INTERCHANGE) CODE

This code is used on most modern printers and is commonly employed in many peripheral devices. It is a seven-bit code, so in eight-bit systems one additional bit is available. On keyboards, and certain other peripherals, the eighth bit is used to strobe the computer. The computer will continuously loop, polling the input, to determine the state of the eighth bit (usually designated B7). It will branch to an input instruction only if the strobe bit indicates that the data are valid. Typically, B7 is made HIGH-active. When B7 goes HIGH, therefore, the computer knows that the data are valid, so an input operation is executed. But when B7 is LOW, it is assumed that the data are invalid (i.e., garbage).

FIG. 15-1 Z-80 CPU Instructions Sorted by Op-code

OBJ CODE	SOURCE STATEMENT	OBJ CODE	SOURCE STATEMENT	OBJ CODE	SOURCE STATEMENT
00	NOP	282E	JR Z, DIS	50	LD D, B
018405	LD BC, NN	29	ADD HL, HL	51	LD D, C
02	LD (BC), A	2A8405	LD (HL), (NN)	52	LD D, D
03	INC BC	2B	DEC HL	53	LD D, E
04	INC B	2C	INC L	54	LD D, H
05	DEC B	2D	DEC L	55	LD D, L
0620	LD B, N	2E20	LD L, N	56	LD D, (HL)
07	RLCA	2F	CPL	57	LD D, A
08	EX AF, AF'	302E	JR NC, DIS	58	LD E, B
09	ADD HL, BC	318405	LD SP, NN	59	LD E, C
0A	LD A,(BC)	328405	LD (NN), A	5A	LD E, D
0B	DEC BC	33	INC SP	5B	LD E, E
0C	INC C	34	INC (HL)	5C	LD E, H
0D	DEC C	35	DEC (HL)	5D	LD E, L
0E20	LD C, N	3620	LD (HL), N	5E	LD E, (HL)
0F	RRCA	37	SCF	5F	LD E, A
102E	DJNZ DIS	382E	JR C, DIS	60	LD H, B
118405	LD DE, NN	39	ADD HL, SP	61	LD H, C
12	LD (DE), A	3A8405	LD A, (NN)	62	LD H, D
13	INC DE	3B	DEC SP	63	LD H, E
14	INC D	3C	INC A	64	LD H, H
15	DEC D	3D	DEC A	65	LD H, L
1620	LD D, N	3E20	LD A, N	66	LD H, (HL)
17	RLA	3F	CCF	67	LD H, A
182E	JR DIS	40	LD B, B	68	LD L, B
19	ADD HL, DE	41	LD B, C	69	LD L, C
1A	LD A,(DE)	42	LD B, D	6A	LD L, D
1B	DEC DE	43	LD B, E	6B	LD L, E
1C	INC E	44	LD B, H, NN	6C	LD L, H
1D	DEC E	45	LD B, L	6D	LD L, L
1E20	LD E, N	46	LD B, (HL)	6E	LD L, (HL)
1F	RRA	47	LD B, A	6F	LD L, A
202E	JR NZ, DIS	48	LD C, B	70	LD (HL), B
218405	LD HL, NN	49	LD C, C	71	LD (HL), C
228405	LD (NN), HL	4A	LD C, D	72	LD (HL), D
23	INC HL	4B	LD C, E	73	LD (HL), E
24	INC H	4C	LD C, H	74	LD (HL), H
25	DEC H	4D	LD C, L	75	LD (HL), L
2620	LD H, N	4E	LD C, (HL)	76	HALT
27	DAA	4F	LD C, A	77	LD (HL), A

FIG. 15-1 (cont'd.)

OBJ CODE	SOURCE STATEMENT	OBJ CODE	SOURCE STATEMENT	OBJ CODE	SOURCE STATEMENT
78	LD A, B	A0	AND B	C8	RET Z
79	LD A, C	A1	AND C	C9	RET
7A	LD A, D	A2	AND D	CA8405	JP Z, NN
7B	LD A, E	A3	AND E	CC8405	CALL Z, NN
7C	LD A, H	A4	AND H	CD8405	CALL NN
7D	LD A, L	A5	AND L	CE20	ADC A, N
7E	LD A, (HL)	A6	AND (HL)	CF	RST 8
7F	LD A, A	A7	AND A	D0	RET NC
80	ADD A, B	A8	XOR B	D1	POP DE
81	ADD A, C	A9	XOR C	D28405	JP NC, NN
82	ADD A, D	AA	XOR D	D320	OUT (N), A
83	ADD A, E	AB	XOR E	D48405	CALL NC, NN
84	ADD A, H	AC	XOR H	D5	PUSH DE
85	ADD A, L	AD	XOR L	D620	SUB N
86	ADD A, (HL)	AE	XOR (HL)	D7	RST 10H
87	ADD A, A	AF	XOR A	D8	RET C
88	ADC A, B	B0	OR B	D9	EXX
89	ADC A, C	B1	OR C	DA8405	JP C, NN
8A	ADC A, D	B2	OR D	DB20	IN A, (N)
8B	ADC A, E	B3	OR E	DC8405	CALL C, N
8C	ADC A, H	B4	OR H	DE20	SBC A, N
8D	ADC A, L	B5	OR L	DF	RST 18H
8E	ADC A, (HL)	B6	OR (HL)	E0	RET PO
8F	ADC A, A	B7	OR A	E1	POP HL
90	SUB B	B8	CP B	E28405	JP PO, NN
91	SUB C	B9	CP C	E3	EX (SP), HL
92	SUB D	BA	CP D	E48405	CALL PO, NN
93	SUB E	BB	CP E	E5	PUSH HL
94	SUB H	BC	CP H	E620	AND N
95	SUB L	BD	CP L	E7	RST 20 H
96	SUB (HL)	BE	CP (HL)	E8	RET PE
97	SUB A	BF	CP A	E9	JP (HL)
98	SBC A, B	C0	RET NZ	EA8405	JE PE NN
99	SBC A, C	C1	POP BC	EB	EX DE, HL
9A	SBC A, D	C28405	JP NZ, NN	EC8405	CALL PE, NN
9B	SBC A, E	C38405	JP NN	EE20	XOR N
9C	SBC A, H	C48405	CALL NZ, NN	EF	RST 28H
9D	SBC A, L	C5	PUSH BC	F0	RET P
9E	SBC A, (HL)	C620	ADD A, N	F1	POP AF
9F	SBC A, A	C7	RST O	F28405	JP P, NN

FIG. 15-1 (cont'd.)

OBJ CODE	SOURCE STATEMENT	OBJ CODE	SOURCE STATEMENT	OBJ CODE	SOURCE STATEMENT
F3	D1	CB1C	RR H	CB4C	BIT 1, H
F48405	CALL P, NN	CB1D	RRL	CB4D	BIT 1, L
F5	PUSH AF	CB1E	RR (HL)	CB4E	BIT 1, (HL)
F620	OR N	CB1F	RR A	CB4F	BIT 1, A
F7	RST 30H	CB20	SLA B	CB50	BIT 2, B
F8	RET M	CB21	SLA C	CB51	BIT 2, C
F9	LD SP, HL	CB22	SLA D	CB52	BIT 2, D
FA8405	JP M, NN	CB23	SLA E	CB53	BIT 2, E
FB	E1	CB24	SLA H	CB54	BIT 2, H
FC8405	CALL M, NN	CB25	SLA L	CB55	BIT 2, L
FE20	CP N	CB26	SLA (HL)	CB56	BIT 2, (HL)
FF	RST 38H	CB27	SLA A	CB57	BIT 2, A
CB00	RLC B	CB28	SRA B	CB58	BIT 3, B
CB01	RLC C	CB29	SRA C	CB59	BIT 3, C
CB02	RLC D	CB2A	SRA D	CB5A	BIT 3, D
CB03	RLC E	CB2B	SRA E	CB5B	BIT 3, E
CB04	RLC H	CB2C	SRA H	CB5C	BIT 3, H
CB05	RLC L	CB2D	SRA L	CB5D	BIT 3, L
CB06	RLC (HL)	CB2E	SRA (HL)	CB5E	BIT 3, (HL)
CB07	RLC A	CB2F	SRA A	CB5F	BIT 3, A
CB08	RRC B	CB38	SRL B	CB60	BIT 4, B
CB09	RRC C	CB39	SRL C	CB61	BIT 4, C
CB0A	RRC D	CB3A	SRL D	CB62	BIT 4, D
CB0B	RRC E	CB3B	SRL E	CB63	BIT 4, E
CB0C	RRC H	CB3C	SRL H	CB64	BIT 4, H
CB0D	RRC L	CB3D	SRL L	CB65	BIT 4, L
CB0E	RRC (HL)	CB3E	SRL (HL)	CB66	BIT 4, (HL)
CB0F	RRC A	CB3F	SRL A	CB67	BIT 4, A
CB10	RL B	CB40	BIT 0, B	CB68	BIT 5, B
CB11	RL C	CB41	BIT 0, C	CB69	BIT 5, C
CB12	RL D	CB42	BIT 0, D	CB6A	BIT 5, D
CB13	RL E	CB43	BIT 0, E	CB6B	BIT 5, E
CB14	RL H	CB44	BIT 0, H	CB6C	BIT 5, H
CB15	RL L	CB45	BIT 0, L	CB6D	BIT 5, L
CB16	RL (HL)	CB46	BIT 0, (HL)	CB6E	BIT 5, (HL)
CB17	RL A	CB47	BIT 0, A	CB6F	BIT 5, A
CB18	RR B	CB48	BIT 1, B	CB70	BIT 6, B
CB19	RR C	CB49	BIT 1, C	CB71	BIT 6, C
CB1A	RR D	CB4A	BIT 1, D	CB72	BIT 6, D
CB1B	RR E	CB4B	BIT 1, E	CB73	BIT 6, E

FIG. 15-1 (cont'd.)

OBJ CODE	SOURCE STATEMENT	OBJ CODE	SOURCE STATEMENT	OBJ CODE	SOURCE STATEMENT
CB74	BIT 6, H	CB9C	RES 3, H	CBC4	SET 0, H
CB75	BIT 6, L	CB9D	RES 3, L	CBC5	SET 0, L
CB76	BIT 6, (HL)	CB0E	RES 3, (HL)	CBC6	SET 0, (HL)
CB77	BIT 6, A	CB9F	RES 3, A	CBC7	SET 0, A
CB78	BIT 7, B	CBA0	RES 4, B	CBC8	SET 1, B
CB79	BIT 7, C	CBA1	RES 4, C	CBC9	SET 1, C
CB7A	BIT 7, D	CBA2	RES 4, D	CBCA	SET 1, D
CB7B	BIT 7, E	CBA3	RES 4, E	CBCB	SET 1, E
CB7C	BIT 7, H	CBA4	RES 4, H	CBCC	SET 1, H
CB7D	BIT 7, L	CBA5	RES 4, L	CBCD	SET 1, L
CB7E	BIT 7, (HL)	CBA6	RES 4, (HL)	CBCE	SET 1, (HL)
CB7F	BIT 7, A	CBA7	RES 4, A	CBCF	SET 1, A
CB80	RES 0, B	CBA8	RES 5, B	CBD0	SET 2, B
CB81	RES 0, C	CBA9	RES 5, C	CBD1	SET 2, C
CB82	RES 0, D	CBAA	RES 5, D	CBD2	SET 2, D
CB83	RES 0, E	CBAB	RES 5, E	CBD3	SET 2, E
CB84	RES 0, H	CBAC	RES 5, H	CBD4	SET 2, H
CB85	RES 0, L	CBAD	RES 5, L	CBD5	SET 2, L
CB86	RES 0, (HL)	CBAE	RES 5, (HL)	CBD6	SET 2, (HL)
CB87	RES 0, A	CBAF	RES 5, A	CBD7	SET 2, A
CB88	RES 1, B	CBB0	RES 6, B	CBD8	SET 3, B
CB89	RES 1, C	CBB1	RES 6, C	CBD9	SET 3, C
CB8A	RES 1, D	CBB2	RES 6, D	CBDA	SET 3, D
CB8B	RES 1, E	CBB3	RES 6, E	CBDB	SET 3, E
CB8C	RES 1, H	CBB4	RES 6, H	CBDC	SET 3, H
CB8D	RES 1, L	CBB5	RES 6, L	CBDD	SET 3, L
CB8E	RES 1, (HL)	CBB6	RES 6, (HL)	CBDE	SET 3, (HL)
CB8F	RES 1, A	CBB7	RES 6, A	CBDF	SET 3, A
CB90	RES 2, B	CBB8	RES 7, B	CBE0	SET 4, B
CB91	RES 2, C	CBB9	RES 7, C	CBE1	SET 4, C
CB92	RES 2, D	CBBA	RES 7, D	CBE2	SET 4, D
CB93	RES 2, E	CBBB	RES 7, E	CBE3	SET 4, E
CB94	RES 2, H	CBBC	RES 7, H	CBE4	SET 4, H
CB95	RES 2, L	CBBD	RES 7, L	CBE5	SET 4, L
CB96	RES 2, (HL)	CBBE	RES 7, (HL)	CBE6	SET 4, (HL)
CB97	RES 2, A	CBBF	RES 7, A	CBE7	SET 4, A
CB98	RES 3, B	CBC0	SET 0, B	CBE8	SET 5, B
CB99	RES 3, C	CBC1	SET 0, C	CBE9	SET 5, C
CB9A	RES 3, D	CBC2	SET 0, D	CBEA	SET 5, D
CB9B	RES 3, E	CBC3	SET 0, E	CBEB	SET 5, E

FIG. 15-1 (cont'd.)

OBJ CODE	SOURCE STATEMENT	OBJ CODE	SOURCE STATEMENT	OBJ CODE	SOURCE STATEMENT
CBEC	SET 5, H	CBF1	SET 6, C	CBF6	SET 6, (HL)
CBED	SET 5, L	CBF2	SET 6, D	CBF7	SET 6, A
CBEE	SET 5, (HL)	CBF3	SET 6, E	CBF8	SET 7, B
CBEF	SET 5, A	CBF4	SET 6, H	CBF9	SET 7, C
CBF0	SET 6, B	CBF5	SET 6, L	CBFA	SET 7, D

FIG. 15-2 Z-80 CPU Instructions Sorted by Mnemonic

OBJ CODE	SOURCE STATEMENT	OBJ CODE	SOURCE STATEMENT	OBJ CODE	SOURCE STATEMENT
8E	ADC A, (HL)	DD29	ADD IX, IX	CB49	BIT 1, C
DD8E05	ADC A, (IX + d)	DD39	ADD IX, SP	CB4A	BIT 1, D
FD8E05	ADC A, (IY + d)	FD09	ADD IY, BC	CB4B	BIT 1, E
8F	ADC A, A	FD19	ADD IY, DE	CB4C	BIT 1, H
88	ADC A, U	FD29	ADD IY, IY	CB4D	BIT 1, L
89	ADC A, C	FD39	ADD IY, SP	CB56	BIT 2, (HL)
8A	ADC A, D	A6	AND (HL)	DDCB0556	BIT 2, (IX + d)
8B	ADC A, E	DDA605	AND (IX + d)	FDCB0556	BIT 2, (IY + d)
8C	ADC A, H	FDA605	AND (IY + d)	CB57	BIT 2, A
8D	ADC A, L	A7	AND A	CB50	BIT 2, B
CE20	ADC A, N	A0	AND B	CB51	BIT 2, C
ED4A	ADC HL, BC	A1	AND C	CB52	BIT 2, D
ED5A	ADC HL, DE	A2	AND D	CB53	BIT 2, E
ED6A	ADC HL, HL	A3	AND E	CB54	BIT 2, H
ED7A	ADC HL, SP	A4	AND H	CB55	BIT 2, L
86	ADD A, (HL)	A5	AND L	CB5E	BIT 3, (HL)
DD8605	ADD A, (IX + d)	E620	AND N	DDCB055E	BIT 3, (IX + d)
FD8605	ADD A, (IY + d)	CB46	BIT 0, (HL)	FDCB055E	BIT 3, (IY + d)
87	ADD A, A	DDCB0546	BIT 0, (IX + d)	CB5F	BIT 3, A
80	ADD A, B	FDCB0546	BIT 0, (IY + d)	CB58	BIT 3, B
81	ADD A, C	CB47	BIT 0, A	CB59	BIT 3, C
82	ADD A, D	CB40	BIT 0, B	CB5A	BIT 3, D
83	ADD A, E	CB41	BIT 0, C	CB5B	BIT 3, E
84	ADD A, H	CB42	BIT 0, D	CB5C	BIT 3, H
85	ADD A, L	CB43	BIT 0, E	CB5D	BIT 3, L
C620	ADD A, N	CB44	BIT 0, H	CB66	BIT 4, (HL)
09	ADD HL, BC	CB45	BIT 0, L	DDCB0566	BIT 4, (IX + d)
19	ADD HL, DE	CB4E	BIT 1, (HL)	FDCB0566	BIT 4, (IY + d)
29	ADD HL, HL	DDCB054E	BIT 1, (IX + d)	CB67	BIT 4, A
39	ADD HL, SP	FDCB054E	BIT 1, (IY + d)	CB60	BIT 4, B
DD09	ADD IX, BC	CB4F	BIT 1, A	CB61	BIT 4, C
DD19	ADD IX, DE	BC48	BIT 1, B	CB62	BIT 4, D

FIG. 15-2 (cont'd.)

OBJ CODE	SOURCE STATEMENT	OBJ CODE	SOURCE STATEMENT	OBJ CODE	SOURCE STATEMENT
CB63	BIT 4, E	BF	CP A	ED48	IN C, (C)
CB64	BIT 4, H	B8	CP B	ED50	IN D, (C)
CB65	BIT 4, L	B9	CP C	ED58	IN E, (C)
CB6E	BIT 5, (HL)	BA	CP D	ED60	IN H, (C)
DDCB056E	BIT 5, (IX + d)	BB	CP E	ED68	IN L, (C)
FDCB056E	BIT 5, (IY + d)	BC	CP H	34	INC (HL)
CB6F	BIT 5, A	BD	CP L	DD3405	INC (IX + d)
CB68	BIT 5, B	FE20	CP N	FD3405	INC (IY + d)
CB69	BIT 5, C	EDA9	CPD	3C	INC A
CB6A	BIT 5, D	ED89	CPDR	04	INC B
CB6B	BIT 5, E	EDA1	CPI	03	INC BC
CB6C	BIT 5, H	EDB1	CPIR	0C	INC C
CB6D	BIT 5, L	2F	CPL	14	INC D
CB76	BIT 6, (HL)	27	DAA	13	INC DE
DDCB0576	BIT 6, (IX + d)	35	DEC (HL)	1C	INC E
FDCB0578	BIT 5, (IY + d)	DD3505	DEC (IX + d)	24	INC H
CB77	BIT 6, A	FD3505	DEC (IY + d)	23	INC HL
CB70	BIT 6, B	3D	DEC A	DD23	INC IX
CB71	BIT 6, C	05	DEC B	FD23	INC IY
CB72	BIT 6, D	08	DEC BC	2C	INC L
CB73	BIT 6, E	0D	DEC C	33	INC SP
CB74	BIT 6, H	15	DEC D	EDAA	IND
CB75	BIT 6, L	1B	DEC DE	EDBA	INDR
CB7E	BIT 7, (HL)	1D	DEC E	EDA2	INI
DDCB057E	BIT 7, (IX + d)	25	DEC H	EDB2	INIR
FDCB057E	BIT 7, (IY + d)	2B	DEC HL	E9	JP (HL)
CB7F	BIT 7, A	DD28	DEC IX	DDE9	JP (IX)
CB78	BIT 7, B	FD2B	DEC IY	FDE9	JP (IY)
CB79	BIT 7, C	2D	DEC L	DA8405	JP C, NN
CB7A	BIT 7, D	3B	DEC SP	FA8405	JP M, NN
CB7B	BIT 7, E	F3	DI	D28405	JP NC, NN
CB7C	BIT 7, H	102E	DJNZ DIS	C38405	JP NN
CB7D	BIT 7, L	FB	EI	C28405	JP NZ, NN
DC8405	CALL C, NN	E3	EX (SP), HL	F28405	JP P, NN
FC8405	CALL M, NN	DDE3	EX (SP), IX	EA8405	JP PE, NN
D48405	CALL NC, NN	FDE3	EX (SP), IY	E28405	JP PO, NN
CD8405	CALL NN	08	EX AF, AF'	CA8405	JP Z, NN
C48405	CALL NZ, NN	EB	EX DE, HL	382E	JR C, DIS
F48405	CALL P, NN	D9	EXX	182E	JR DIS
EC8405	CALL PE, NN	76	HALT	302E	JR NC, DIS
E48405	CALL PO, NN	ED46	IM 0	202E	JR NZ, DIS
CC8405	CALL Z, NN	ED56	IM 1	282E	JR Z, DIS
3F	CCF	ED5E	IM 2	02	LD (BC), A
BE	CP (HL)	ED78	IN A, (C)	12	LD (DE), A
DDBE05	CP (IX + d)	DB20	IN A, (N)	77	LD (HL), A
FDBE06	CP (IY + d)	ED40	IN B, (C)	70	LD (HL), B

FIG. 15-2 (cont'd.)

OBJ CODE	SOURCE STATEMENT	OBJ CODE	SOURCE STATEMENT	OBJ CODE	SOURCE STATEMENT
71	LD (HL), C	FD4605	LD B, (IY + d)	66	LD H, (HL)
72	LD (HL), D	47	LD B, A	DD6605	LD H, (IX + d)
73	LD (HL), E	40	LD B, B	FD6606	LD H, (IY + d)
74	LD (HL), H	41	LD B, C	67	LD H, A
75	LD (HL), L	42	LD B, D	60	LD H, B
3620	LD (HL), N	43	LD B, E	61	LD H, C
DD7705	LD (IX + d), A	44	LD B, H, NN	62	LD H, D
DD7005	LD (IX + d), B	45	LD B, L	63	LD H, E
DD7105	LD (IX + d), C	0620	LD B, N	64	LD H, H
DD7205	LD (IX + d), D	ED4B8405	LD BC, (NN)	65	LD H, L
DD7305	LD (IX + d), E	018405	LD BC, NN	2620	LDH, N
DD7405	LD (IX + d), H	4E	LD C, (HL)	2A8405	LD HL, (NN)
DD7505	LD (IX + d), L	DD4E05	LD C, (IX + d)	218405	LD HL, NN
DD360520	LD (IX + d), N	FD4E05	LD C, (IY + d)	ED47	LD I, A
FD7705	LD (IY + d), A	4F	LD C, A	DD2AB405	LD IX, (NN)
FD7005	LD (IY + d), B	48	LD C, B	DD218405	LD IX, NN
FD7105	LD (IY + d), C	49	LD C, C	FD2A8405	LD IY, (NN)
FD7205	LD (IY + d), D	4A	LD C, D	FD218405	LD IY, NN
FD7305	LD (IY + d), E	4B	LD C, E	6E	LD L, (HL)
FD7405	LD (IY + d), H	4C	LD C, H	DD6E05	LD L, (IX + d)
FD7505	LD (IY + d), L	4D	LD C, L	FD6E05	LD L, (IY + d)
FD360520	LD (IY + d), N	0E20	LD C, N	6F	LD L, A
328405	LD (NN), A	56	LD D, (HL)	68	LD L, B
ED438405	LD (NN), BC	DD5605	LD D, (IX + d)	69	LD L, C
ED538405	LD (NN), DE	FD5605	LD D, (IY + d)	6A	LD L, D
228405	LD (NN), HL	57	LD D, A	6B	LD L, E
DD228405	LD (NN), IX	50	LD D, B	6C	LD L, H
FD228405	LD (NN), IY	51	LD D, C	6D	LD L, L
ED738405	LD (NN), SP	52	LD D, D	2E20	LD L, N
0A	LD A, (BC)	53	LD D, E	ED788405	LD SP, (NN)
1A	LD A, (DE)	54	LD D, H	F9	LD SP, HL
7E	LD A, (HL)	55	LD D, L	DDF9	LD SP, IX
DD7E05	LD A, (IX + d)	1620	LD D, N	FDF9	LD SP, IY
FD7E05	LD A, (IY + d)	ED5B8405	LD DE, (NN)	318405	LD SP, NN
3A8405	LD A, (NN)	118405	LD DE, NN	EDA8	LDD
7F	LD A, A	5E	LD E, (HL)	ED88	LDDR
78	LD A, B	DD5E05	LD E, (IX + d)	EDA0	LDI
79	LD A, C	FD5E05	LD E, (IY + d)	EDB0	LDIR
7A	LD A, D	5F	LD E, A	ED44	NEG
7B	LD A, E	58	LD E, B	00	NOP
7C	LD A, H	59	LD E, C	B6	OR (HL)
ED57	LD A, I	5A	LD E, D	DDB605	OR (IX + d)
7D	LD A, L	5B	LD E, E	FDB605	OR (IY + d)
3E20	LD A, N	5C	LD E, H	B7	OR A
46	LD B, (HL)	5D	LD E, L	B0	OR B
DD4605	LD B, (IX + d)	1E20	LD E, N	B1	OR C

FIG. 15-2 (cont'd.)

OBJ CODE	SOURCE STATEMENT	OBJ CODE	SOURCE STATEMENT	OBJ CODE	SOURCE STATEMENT
B2	OR D	CB8B	RES 1, E	CBB7	RES 6, A
B3	OR E	CB8C	RES 1, H	CBB0	RES 6, B
B4	OR H	CB8D	RES 1, L	CBB1	RES 6, C
B5	OR L	CB96	RES 2, (HL)	CBB2	RES 6, D
F620	OR N	DDCB0596	RES 2, (IX + d)	CBB3	RES 6, E
EDBB	OTDR	FDCB0596	RES 2, (IY + d)	CBB4	RES 6, H
EDB3	OTIR	CB97	RES 2, A	CBB5	RES 6, L
ED79	OUT (C), A	CB90	RES 2, B	CBBE	RES 7, (HL)
ED41	OUT (C), B	CB91	RES 2, C	DDCB05BE	RES 7, (IX + d)
ED49	OUT (C), C	CB92	RES 2, D	FDCB05BE	RES 7, (IX + d)
ED51	OUT (C), D	CB93	RES 2, E	CBBF	RES 7, A
ED59	OUT (C), E	CB94	RES 2, H	CBB8	RES 7, B
ED61	OUT (C), H	CB95	RES 2, L	CBB9	RES 7, C
ED69	OUT (C), L	CB9E	RES 3, (HL)	CBBA	RES 7, D
D320	OUT (N), A	DDCB059E	RES 3, (IX + d)	CBBB	RES 7, E
EDAB	OUTD	FDCB059E	RES 3, (IY + d)	CBBC	RES 7, H
EDA3	OUTI	CB9F	RES 3, A	CBBD	RES 7, L
F1	POP AF	CB98	RES 3, B	C9	RET
C1	POP BC	CB99	RES 3, C	D8	RET C
D1	POP DE	CB9A	RES 3, D	F8	RET M
E1	POP HL	CB9B	RES 3, E	D0	RET NC
DDE1	POP IX	CB9C	RES 3, H	C0	RET NZ
FDE1	POP IY	CB9D	RES 3, L	F0	RET P
F5	PUSH AF	CBA6	RES 4, (HL)	E8	RET PE
C5	PUSH BC	DDCB05AB	RES 4, (IX + d)	E0	RET PO
D5	PUSH DE	FDCB05AB	RES 4, (IY + d)	C8	RET Z
E5	PUSH HL	CBA7	RES 4, A	ED4D	RETI
DDE5	PUSH IX	CBA0	RES 4, B	ED45	RETN
FDE5	PUSH IY	CBA1	RES 4, C	CB16	RL (HL)
CB86	RES 0, (HL)	CBA2	RES 4, D	DDCB0516	RL (IX + d)
DDCB0586	RES 0, (IX + d)	CBA3	RES 4, E	FDCB0516	RL (IY + d)
FDCB0586	RES 0, (IY + d)	CBA4	RES 4, H	CB17	RL A
CB87	RES 0, A	CBA5	RES 4, L	CB10	RL B
CB80	RES 0, B	CBAE	RES 5, (HL)	CB11	RL C
CB81	RES 0, C	DDCB05AE	RES 5, (IX + d)	CB12	RL D
CB82	RES 0, D	FDCB05AE	RES 5, (IY + d)	CB13	RL E
CB83	RES 0, E	CBAF	RES 5, A	CB14	RL H
CB84	RES 0, H	CBA8	RES 5, B	CB15	RL L
CB85	RES 0, L	CBA9	RES 5, C	17	RLA
CB8E	RES 1, (HL)	CBAA	RES 5, D	CB06	RLC (HL)
DDCB058E	RES 1, (IX + d)	CBAB	RES 5, E	DDCB0506	RLC (IX + d)
FDCB058E	RES 1, (IY + d)	CBAC	RES 5, H	FDCB0506	RLC (IY + d)
CB8F	RES 1, A	CBAD	RES 5, L	CB07	RLC A
CB88	RES 1, B	CBB6	RES 6, (HL)	CB00	RLC B
CB89	RES 1, C	DDCB05B6	RES 6, (IX + d)	CB01	RLC C
CB8A	RES 1, D	FDCB05B6	RES 6, (IY + d)	CB02	RLC D

FIG. 15-2 (cont'd.)

OBJ CODE	SOURCE STATEMENT	OBJ CODE	SOURCE STATEMENT	OBJ CODE	SOURCE STATEMENT
CB03	RLC E	DE20	SBC A, N	CBE6	SET 4, (HL)
CB04	RLC H	ED42	SBC HL, BC	DDCB05E6	SET 4, (IX + d)
CB05	RLC L	ED52	SBC HL, DE	FDCB05E6	SET 4, (IY + d)
07	RLCA	ED62	SBC HL, HL	CBE7	SET 4, A
ED6F	RLD	ED72	SBC HL, SP	CBE0	SET 4, B
CB1E	RR (HL)	37	SCF	CBE1	SET 4, C
DDCB051E	RR (IX + d)	CBC6	SET 0, (HL)	CBE2	SET 4, D
FDCB051E	RR (IY + d)	DDCB05CS	SET 0, (IX + d)	CBE3	SET 4, E
CB1F	RR A	FDCB05C6	SET 0, (IY + d)	CBE4	SET 4, H
CB18	RR B	CBC7	SET 0, A	CBE5	SET 4, L
CB19	RR C	CBC0	SET 0, B	CBEE	SET 5, (HL)
CB1A	RR D	CBC1	SET 0, C	DDCB05EE	SET 5, (IX + d)
CB1B	RR E	CBC2	SET 0, D	FDCB05EE	SET 5, (IY + d)
CB1C	RR H	CBC3	SET 0, E	CBEF	SET 5, A
CB1D	RR L	CBC4	SET 0, H	CBE8	SET 5, B
1F	RRA	CBC5	SET 0, L	CBE9	SET 5, C
CB0E	RRC (HL)	CBCE	SET 1, (HL)	CBEA	SET 5, D
DDCB050E	RRC (IX + d)	DDCB05CE	SET 1, (IX + d)	CBEB	SET 5, E
FDCB050E	RRC (IY + d)	FDCB05CE	SET 1, (IY + d)	CBEC	SET 5, H
CB0F	RRC A	CBCF	SET 1, A	CBED	SET 5, L
CB08	RRC B	CBC8	SET 1, B	CBF6	SET 6, (HL)
CB09	RRC C	CBC9	SET 1, C	DDCB05F6	SET 6, (IX + d)
CB0A	RRC D	CBCA	SET 1, D	FDCB05F6	SET 6, (IY + d)
CB0B	RRC E	CBCB	SET 1, E	CBF7	SET 6, A
CB0C	RRC H	CBCC	SET 1, H	CBF0	SET 6, B
CB0D	RRC L	CBCD	SET 1, L	CBF1	SET 6, C
0F	RRCA	CBD6	SET 2, (HL)	CBF2	SET 6, D
ED67	RRD	DDCB05D6	SET 2, (IX + d)	CBF3	SET 6, E
C7	RST 0	FDCB05D6	SET 2, (IY + d)	CBF4	SET 6, H
D7	RST 10H	CBD7	SET 2, A	CBF5	SET 6, L
DF	RST 18H	CBD0	SET 2, B	CBFE	SET 7, (HL)
E7	RST 20H	CBD1	SET 2, C	DDCB05FE	SET 7, (IX + d)
EF	RST 28H	CBD2	SET 2, D	FDCB05FE	SET 7, (IY + d)
F7	RST 30H	CBD3	SET 2, E	CBFF	SET 7, A
FF	RST 38H	CBD4	SET 2, H	CBF8	SET 7, B
CF	RST 8	CBD5	SET 2, L	CBF9	SET 7, C
9E	SBC A, (HL)	CBD8	SET 3, B	CBFA	SET 7, D
DD9E05	SBC A, (IX + d)	CBDE	SET 3, (HL)	CBFB	SET 7, E
FD9E05	SBC A, (IY + d)	DDCB05DE	SET 3, (IX + d)	CBFC	SET 7, H
9F	SBC A, A	FDCB05DE	SET 3, (IY + d)	CBFD	SET 7, L
98	SBC A, B	CBDF	SET 3, A	CB26	SLA (HL)
99	SBC A, C	CBD9	SET 3, C	DDCB0526	SLA (IX + d)
9A	SBC A, D	CBDA	SET 3, D	FDCB0526	SLA (IY + d)
9B	SBC A, E	CBDB	SET 3, E	CB27	SLA A
9C	SBC A, H	CBDC	SET 3, H	CB20	SLA B
9D	SBC A, L	CBDD	SET 3, L	CB21	SLA C

FIG. 15-2 (cont'd.)

OBJ CODE	SOURCE STATEMENT	OBJ CODE	SOURCE STATEMENT	OBJ CODE	SOURCE STATEMENT
CB22	SLA D	FDCB053E	SRL (IY + d)	93	SUB E
CB23	SLA E	CB3F	SRL A	94	SUB H
CB24	SLA H	CB38	SRL B	95	SUB L
CB25	SLA L	CB39	SRL C	D620	SUB N
CB2E	SRA (HL)	CB3A	SRL D	AE	XOR (HL)
DDCB052E	SRA (IX + d)	CB3B	SRL E	DDAE05	XOR (IX + d)
FDCB052E	SRA (IY + d)	CB3C	SRL H	FDAE05	XOR (IY + d)
CB2F	SRA A	CB3D	SRL L	AF	XOR A
CB28	SRA B	96	SUB (HL)	A8	XOR B
CB29	SRA C	DD9605	SUB (IX + d)	A9	XOR C
CB2A	SRA D	FD9605	SUB (IY + d)	AA	XOR D
CB2B	SRA E	97	SUB A	AB	XOR E
CB2C	SRA H	90	SUB B	AC	XOR H
CB2D	SRA L	91	SUB C	AD	XOR L
CB3E	SRL (HL)	92	SUB D	EE20	XOR N
DDCB053E	SRL (IX + d)				

FIG. 15-3 ASCII code.

HEX CODE	MEANING	COMMENTS
00	NUL	null
01	SOH	start of heading
02	STX	start text
03	ETX	end text
04	EOT	end of transmission
05	ENQ	enquiry
06	ACK	acknowledgment
07	BEL	bell
08	BS	back space
09	HT	horizontal tab
0A	LF	line feed
0B	VT	vertical tab
0C	FF	form feed
0D	CR	carriage return
0E	SO	shift out
0F	SI	shift in
10	DLE	data link escape
11	DC1	direct control 1
12	DC2	direct control 2
13	DC3	direct control 3
14	DC4	direct control 4

FIG. 15-3 (cont'd.)

HEX CODE	MEANING	COMMENTS
15	NAK	negative acknowledgment
16	SYN	synchronous idle
17	ETB	end of transmission block
18	CAN	cancel
19	EM	end of medium
1A	SUB	substitute
1B	ESC	escape
1C	FS	form separator
1D	GS	group separator
1E	RS	record separator
1F	US	unit separator
20	(special)	—
21	!	—
22	"	—
23	#	—
24	$	—
25	%	—
26	&	—
27	'	—
28	(	—
29	)	—
2A	*	—
2B	+	—
2C	,	—
2D	-	—
2E	.	—
2F	/	—
30	0	—
31	1	—
32	2	—
33	3	—
34	4	—
35	5	—
36	6	—
37	7	—
38	8	—
39	9	—
3A	:	—
3B	;	—
3C	>	—

FIG. 15-3 (cont'd.)

HEX CODE	MEANING	COMMENTS
3D	=	—
3E	<	—
3F	?	—
40	@	—
41	A	—
42	B	—
43	C	—
44	D	—
45	E	—
46	F	—
47	G	—
48	H	—
49	I	—
4A	J	—
4B	K	—
4C	L	—
4D	M	—
4E	N	—
4F	O	—
50	P	—
51	Q	—
52	R	—
53	S	—
54	T	—
55	U	—
56	V	—
57	W	—
58	X	—
59	Y	—
5A	Z	—
5B	[	—
5C	/	—
5D	]	—
5E	.	—
5F	|	—
60	$\wedge$	—
61	a	—
62	b	—
63	c	—
64	d	—

FIG. 15-3 (cont'd.)

HEX CODE	MEANING	COMMENTS
65	e	—
66	f	—
67	g	—
68	h	—
69	i	—
6A	j	—
6B	k	—
6C	l	—
6D	m	—
6E	n	—
6F	o	—
70	p	—
71	q	—
72	r	—
73	s	—
74	t	—
75	u	—
76	v	—
77	w	—
78	x	—
79	y	—
7A	z	—
7B	{	—
7C	|	—
7D	}	—
7E	~	—
7F	DEL	—

BAUDOT TELETYPEWRITER CODE

This five-bit code is obsolete and is not in general use in newly designed equipment. But there is a considerable amount of older equipment on the market and still in use. Many surplus commercial and military teletypewriters are used by amateur computer enthusiasts, and they also remain in service in older systems. The Teletype Corporation still offers Baudot coding on their new machines as an option for owners of older systems.

FIG. 15-4 Baudot code.

B5	B4	B3	B2	B1	REGULAR BLANK	SHIFTED BLANK
0	0	0	0	0		
0	0	0	0	1	E	3
0	0	0	1	0	linefeed	linefeed
0	0	0	1	1	A	-
0	0	1	0	0	space	space
0	0	1	0	1	S	Bell
0	0	1	1	0	I	8
0	0	1	1	1	U	7
0	1	0	0	0	Car. Ret.	Car. Ret.
0	1	0	0	1	D	$
0	1	0	1	0	R	4
0	1	0	1	1	J	'
0	1	1	0	0	N	,
0	1	1	0	1	F	!
0	1	1	1	0	C	:
0	1	1	1	1	K	(
1	0	0	0	0	T	5
1	0	0	0	1	Z	"
1	0	0	1	0	L	)
1	0	0	1	1	W	2
1	0	1	0	0	H	#
1	0	1	0	1	Y	6
1	0	1	1	0	P	0
1	0	1	1	1	Q	1
1	1	0	0	0	O	9
1	1	0	0	1	B	?
1	1	0	1	0	G	&
1	1	0	1	1	(figures)	(figures)
1	1	1	0	0	M	.
1	1	1	0	1	X	/
1	1	1	1	0	V	;
1	1	1	1	1	(letters)	(letters)

EBCDIC CODE

This code is used by IBM on some of their equipment. It must be considered when one is interfacing IBM systems, IBM-compatible equipment, or trying to use surplus IBM *Selectric* typewriters (not all of which used EBCDIC; some also used BCD, while others used correspondence code).

FIG. 15-5 EBCDIC code.

CHARACTER	HEX CODE	CHARACTER	HEX CODE
A	C1	K	D2
B	C2	L	D3
C	C3	M	D4
D	C4	N	D5
E	C5	O	D6
F	C6	P	D7
G	C7	Q	D8
H	C8	R	D9
I	C9	S	E2
J	D1	T	E3
U	E4	4	4
V	E5	5	5
W	E6	6	6
X	E7	7	7
Y	E8	8	8
Z	E9	9	9
0	0		
1	1		
2	2		
3	3		

8080/Z80 INSTRUCTION EQUIVALENCY (SAME OP-CODES)

Eight-bit load group

8080	Z80
MOV	LD (all combinations)
MVI	LD
LDA	LD A, (nn)
STA	LD (nn),A
LDAX	LD LD A, (zz)
LDAI	LD A,I
LDAR	LD A,r
STAI	LD I,A
STAR	LD r,A

Sixteen-bit load group

8080	Z80
LXI	LD rr,nn
LBCD	LD BC, (nn)
LDED	LD DE, (nn)
LHLD	LD HL, (nn)
LIXD	LD IX, (nn)
LIYD	LD IY, (nn)
LSPD	LD SP, (nn)
SBCD	LD (nn), BC
SDED	LD (nn),DE
SHLD	LD (nn),HL
SIXD	LD (nn),IX
SIYD	LD (nn),IY
SSPD	LD (nn),SP
SPHL	LD (nn), HL
SPIX	LD (nn),IX
SPIY	LD (nn),IY
PUSH	PUSH (all mnemonics)
POP	POP (all mnemonics)

Exchange, Transfer, Search Group

8080	Z80
XCHG	EX DE,HL
EXAF	EX AF,AF'
EXX	EXX
XTHL	EX (SP),HL
XTIX	EX (SP),IX
XTIY	EX (SP),IY
LDI	LDI
LDIR	LDIR
LDD	LDD
LDDR	LDDR
CCI	CPI
CCIR	CPIR

CCD   CPD

CCDR   CPDR

Eight-bit Arithmetic/Logical Group

8Ø8Ø	Z8Ø
ADD	ADD (all combinations)
ADI	ADD A, n
ADC	ADC
ACI	ADC A, n
SUB	SUB
SUI	SUB A, n
SBC	SBC
SBI	SBC A, n
ANA	AND
ANI	AND A, n
ORA	OR
ORI	OR A, n
XRA	XOR
XRI	XOR A, n
CMP	CP
CPI	CP A, n
INR	INC r
INR M	INC (HL)
INR d(ii)	INC (Iii+d)
DCR r	DEC r
DCR M	DEC (HL)
DCR d(ii)	DEC (Iii+d)

General-purpose Arithmetic/Control Group

8080	Z80
DAA	DAA
CMA	CPL
NEG	NEG
CMC	CCF
STC	SCF
NOP	NOP
DI	DI

HALT	HALT
EI	EI
IMØ	IMØ
IM1	IM1
IM2	IM2

Rotate and Shift Group

8080	Z80
DAD	ADD
DADC	ADC
DSBC	SBC HL,rr
DADX	ADD IX,tt
DADY	ADD IY,tt
INX rr	INC rr
INX ii	INC ii
DCX rr	DEC rr
DCX ii	DEC ii
RLC	RLCA
RAL	RLA
RRC	RRCA
RAR	RRA
RLCR r	RLC r
RLCR M	RLC (HL)
RLCR d(ii)	RLC (Iii+d)
RALR	RL
RRCR	RRC s
RARR	RR s
SLAR	SLA
SRAR	SRA
SRLR	SRL
RLD	RLD
RRD	RRD

Bit Test, Bit Set, Bit Reset Group

8080	Z80
BIT b,r	BIT b,r
BIT b,M	BIT b, (HL)

BIT b,d(ii)	BIT b,d(ii)
SET b,r	SET b,r
SET b,M	SET b, (HL)
SET b,d(ii)	SET b,d(ii)
RES b,s	RES b,s

Jump Group

8080	Z80
JMP	JP
JZ	JP Z
JNZ	JP NZ,nn
JC	JP C,nn
JNC	JP NC,nn
JPO	JP PO,nn
JPE	JP PE,nn
JP	JP P,nn
JM	JP M,nn
JO	JP PE,nn
JNO	JP PO,nn
JMPR	JR,e
JRZ	JR Z,e
JRNZ	JR NZ,e
JRC	JR C,e
JRNC	JR NC,e
DJNZ	DJNZ e
PCHL	JP (HL)
PCIX	JP (IX)
PCIY	JP (IY)

Call/Return Group

8080	Z80
Call nn	Call nn
CZ nn	CALL Z,nn
CNZ	CALL NZ,nn
CC nn	CALL C,nn
CNC	CALL NC
CPO	CALL PO

CPE	CALL PR
CP	CALL P
CM	CALL M,nn
CO	CALL PE,nn
CNO	CALL PO,nn
RET	RET
RZ	RET Z
RNZ	RET NZ
RC	RET C
RNC	RET NC
RPO	RET PO
RPE	RET PE
RP	RET P
RM	RET M
RO	RET PE
RNO	RET PO
RETI	RETI
RETN	RETN
RST n	RST n

Input/Output Group

8080	Z80
IN n	IN A, (n)
INP r	IN r, (C)
INI	INI
INIR	INIR
INDR	INDR
OUT n	OUT (n), A
OUTP	OUT (C), r
OUTI	OUTI
OUTIR	OTIR
OUTD	OUTD
OUTDR	OTDR

Not all of the Z80 instructions have equivalents in the 8080 system. Those listed above use the same op-codes, so they can be plugged into either type of microcomputer. The principal difference between the software of the two different types of uP chip lies in the *timing*. 8080 software will execute on Z80 machines unless timing is important.

16
Z8 and Z8000 Machines

As microprocessor chips go, the Z80 is "old." Its actual age is not very great, but in the fast-moving digital IC market, a few years puts whiskers on any design. The Z80 is, however, still one of the best eight-bit microprocessor chips, and it is used in quite a few microcomputers. Its instruction set makes it one of the best selections for users of eight-bit machines.

Zilog, Inc. has introduced two new (actual three) microprocessor devices: the Z8 and the Z8000. We say "actually three" because the Z8000 is available in two different versions, Z8001 and Z8002. This chapter will introduce these devices, although it will not be an exhaustive treatment. As this is written, only the preliminary information is published by Zilog, and only recently have Z8000 devices been offered for sale.

THE Z8 DEVICE

The Z8 device is, unlike the Z80, a single-chip microprocessor. One feature of the Z8 is that it can be reconfigured under program control to be three different devices. It can, for example be used as a regular microprocesser that is capable of addressing up to 124K of external memory (as opposed to 64K in the Z80). It can also be configured as a stand-alone, ready-to-run microcomputer with 2K of internal ROM. Finally, it can be a parallel processing element in a system that contains other microprocessors, computers, or peripheral controller IC devices.

The internal clock rate of the Z8 microprocessor operates at 4 mHz, but requires an external clock rate of 8 mHz. Since most Z8 instructions can be executed in six to ten machine cycles, the average execution time will be 1.5 to 2.5 microseconds.

The Z8 offers six vectored interrupts that can be prioritized and masked, if needed.

Figure 16-1 shows a block diagram of the internal architecture of the Z8 device. Notice that the Z8 contains its own internal *universal asynchronous receiver/transmitter* (UART), needed for serial input/output. The port-3 lines P30/P37 are programmable as a full-duplex serial I/O. One of the timers used in the Z8 (T∅) is the baud-rate generator for the UART and operates at a frequency that is 16 times the desired baud rate. The maximum baud rate is 62,500 bits per second. One of the many Z8 registers (R240) is used in conjunction with the UART. The data to be transmitted are first assembled in register R240, and are then shifted to the outside world via P37. Serial input data are received through the pin P30.

The Z8 automatically adds a start bit and two stop bits (a relatively common format) to the data stream.

The two timers are designated T∅ and T1. Each of these timers is operated from its own 6-bit prescalers that can divide the input frequency by any programmable ratio from 1 to 64. Registers R243 and R245 are assigned to

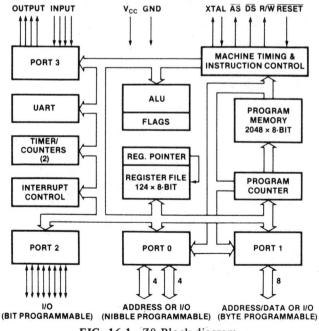

FIG. 16-1 Z8 Block diagram.

program the prescalers. The counters are designed to decrement from the preset value, and when the counter (R244 and R242) reaches zero, an interrupt request is generated. These are designated IRQ4 and IRQ5 for T$\emptyset$ and T1, respectively.

The UART and two timers are used primarily to free the Z8 from the housekeeping chores these circuits handle, allowing more for the real-time operations.

One of the strongest aspects of the Z8 microprocessor chip is the register-file organization. The register-file consists of a 144-byte array. The system contains 124 general-purpose registers (designated R4–R127) and 16 control or status registers (R240–R255). Note that any of the general-purpose registers are able to function as index registers (as opposed to two in the older Z80), accumulators, and address pointers. The normal Z8 instructions can access the registers with an eight-bit address field.

Note that the flexibility of the Z8 allows us to write to a register when the register is defined as a destination in the instruction, and read from a register when it is defined as a source.

The memory addressed by the internal address pointers includes 65,536 bytes of external memory. The first 2047 bytes, however, are on-chip *read only memory* (ROM).

Z8 PINOUTS

Figure 16-2 shows the pin-outs of the standard 40-pin production version of the Z8 microprocessor chip. The following gives the definitions of these pins.

P$\emptyset\emptyset$–P$\emptyset$7 P1$\emptyset$–P17 P2$\emptyset$–P27 P3$\emptyset$–P37	I/O Port Lines. Thirty-two TTL-compatible input/output lines are supplied. These are arrayed in the form of four eight-bit ports, and can be program-controlled. Ports 1/2 can be used as external memory interface, and port 2 can be used as an open-drain output.
$\overline{\text{AS}}$	This line is an active-low output that is used as the address strobe. This output line is pulsed (i.e., *strobed*) once for any internal (ROM) or external (RAM or ROM) program fetches or external data transfers. $\overline{\text{AS}}$ can be placed in a high-impedance, tri-state condition under program control.
$\overline{\text{DS}}$	This pin is similar to the previous instruction. It is an active-low output that goes LOW once for each external memory transfer. The data on port-1 are valid during write cycles when $\overline{\text{DS}}$ is LOW. Like $\overline{\text{AS}}$, $\overline{\text{DS}}$ can be made tri-state under program control. Under some conditions, this output is used as an instruction synchronization signal, and goes LOW during the last clock pulse before an op-code fetch.

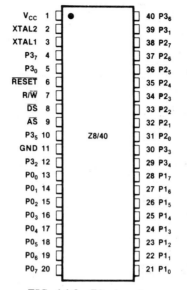

FIG. 16-2   Z8 pinouts.

R/W̄   This active-low output is similar to the R/W̄ pin on the Z80 device. It is LOW for write operations and HIGH at all other times. This output can be made tri-state under program control.

XTAL-1   Pins for an external clock crystal (8 mHz maximum), external
XTAL-2   clock (8 mHz maximum), RC network, LC network.

RESET   This active-low input provides its main function in much the same way as the Z80 reset. It is a hardware jump to location ∅∅ ∅∅ hex. This pin on the Z8 has certain other functions as well. If RESET is brought to a potential greater than Vcc+ the Z8 is forced into a test mode. The reset also acts to protect the register file during power up and power down sequences.

Z8000-SERIES DEVICES (Z8001 AND Z8002)

There are actually two versions of the 16-bit Z8000 microprocessor. The Z8001 is a 48-pin DIP device that allows up to 8 mega-bytes of external memory (provided that an external memory manager is used). The Z8002 is a 40-pin DIP device that can address only 64K of memory. Both of these NMOS devices have 17,500 transistors in 0.06 in.^{2} of silicone chip.

The Z8000 devices contain 24 two-byte (16-bit) on-chip registers. Of these, 16 of the registers are general-purpose registers.

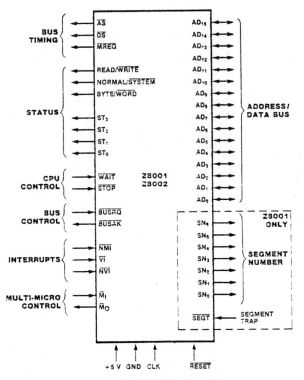

FIG. 16-3 Z8000 pinouts.

The instruction set supports seven different data types that range from single-bit operations to the handling of four-byte (32-bit) word lengths. There are eight addressing modes.

The Z8001 and Z8002 are essentially the same machine, except that the Z8001 is used for larger systems (up to 8,000,000 bytes). The Z8002 is used for smaller applications in which 64K bytes of memory are sufficient. Figure 16-3 shows a pin-out diagram for the Z8000 series devices. More about this device will be available in the near future from Zilog, Inc. as production quantities are just now available.

17
The Z80 Instruction Set

The Z80 instruction set is presented in this chapter, so that you can study the instructions on a one-by-one basis. We will give you the mnemonic for each instruction, a description of what it does, and the code for each. The codes will be listed in octal, hexadecimal, binary, and decimal form to facilitate your work when you are referring to them from another person's program. It invariably seems that when I study a program to see how it works, the code is given in one number system (say octal), while my list of the instructions is written in another (i.e., hexadecimal).

1. **ADC A, n**

    $A \leftarrow A + n + CF$

This is a two-byte instruction in which the contents of the accumulator are added to the operand n, defined by the second byte, and the result is stored in the accumulator.

Code:

Hexadecimal:	CE n
Octal:	316
Decimal:	206
Binary:	11001110

Form:

    CE

    n

Example:

If the accumulator contains 03H, and the instruction is CE 56H, then the result will be stored in the accumulator as 03 + 56 = 59.

Condition bits:

    S   SET if result stored in accumulator is negative
    Z   SET if result is zero
    H   SET if carry from bit-3, RESET otherwise
    P/V   RESET if no overflow, SET if overflow
    N   RESET
    C   SET if carry from bit-7

2.   **ADC A, A**

     A ← A + A + CF

This instruction adds the contents of the accumulator to the contents of the accumulator, and stores the result in the accumulator.

Code:

    Hex.: 8F
    Oct.: 217
    Dec.: 143
    Bin.: 10001111

See **ADC A,n** for condition bits.

3.   **ADC A, B**

     A ← A + B + CF

This instruction adds the contents of the accumulator to the contents of the B register, and stores the result in the accumulator.

Code:

    Hex.: 88

Oct.:   210

Dec.:   136

Bin.:   10001000

See **ADC A,n** for condition bits.

4.   **ADC A,C**

     A ← A + C + CF

This instruction adds the contents of the accumulator to the contents of the C register, and stores the result in the accumulator.

Code:

Hex.:   89

Oct.:   211

Dec.:   137

Bin.:   10001001

See **ADC A,n** for condition bits.

5.   **ADC A,D**

     A ← A + D + CF

This instruction adds the contents of the accumulator to the contents of the D register, and stores the result in the accumulator.

Code:

Hex.:   8A

Oct.:   212

Dec.:   138

Bin.:   10001010

See **ADC A,n** for condition bits.

6.   **ADC A,E**

     A ← A + E + CF

This instruction adds the contents of the E register to the contents of the accumulator, and stores the result in the accumulator.

Code:

    Hex.: 8B
    Oct.: 213
    Dec.: 139
    Bin.: 10001011

See **ADC A,n** for the condition bits.

7.   ADC A,H

$$A \leftarrow A + H + CF$$

This instruction adds the contents of the H register to the contents of the accumulator, and stores the result in the accumulator.

Code:

    Hex.: 8C
    Oct.: 214
    Dec.: 140
    Bin.: 10001100

See **ADC A,n** for condition bits.

8.   ADC A,L

$$A \leftarrow A + L + CF$$

This instruction adds the contents of the L register to the contents of the accumulator, and stores the result in the accumulator.

Code:

    Hex.: 8D
    Oct.: 215
    Dec.: 141
    Bin.: 10001101

See **ADC A,n** for condition bits.

9.   ADC A, (HL)

$$A \leftarrow A + (HL) + CF$$

This instruction adds the contents of the memory location addressed by the contents of the HL register pair to the contents of the accumulator, and stores the result in the accumulator.

Code:

> Hex.:   8E
> Oct.:   216
> Dec.:   142
> Bin.:   10001110

See **ADC A,n** for the condition bits.

Example:

The contents of the accumulator are A2h, the contents of the H register are 6Fh, and the contents of the L register are 03h. The contents of memory location 6F 03 are 03h. After the execution of this instruction, the contents of location 6F 03, as addressed by the HL register pair, are added to the contents of the accumulator (i.e., A2h + 03h = A5h), and the result, A5h, is stored in the accumulator. See Fig. 17-1.

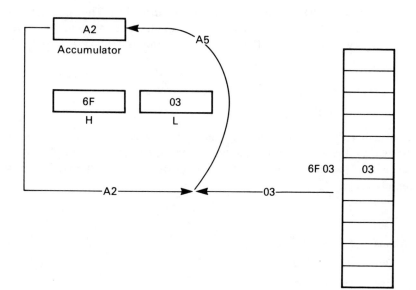

FIG. 17-1

10. ADC A, (IX + d)

$A \leftarrow A + (IX + d) + CF$

This is a three-byte instruction that causes the contents of a memory location addressed by the sum of the contents of the IX register plus a displacement d, to be added to the contents of the accumulator, and the result to be stored in the accumulator.

Code:

Hex.: DD 8E d

Oct.: 335 216 d

Dec.: 221 142 d

Bin.: 11011101 10001110 d

See **ADC A,n** for condition bits.

Form:

DD

8E

d

Example:

The instruction is DD 8E 5F (i.e., the value of d is 5Fh). The contents of the IX register are 43 56, the contents of the accumulator are A2, and the contents of the memory location (IX + d) are 03. This location is 4365h.

11. ADC A, (IY + d)

$A \leftarrow A + (IY + d) + CF$

This is a three-byte instruction that causes the contents of a memory location addressed by the sum of the contents of the IY register and a displacement d to be added to the contents of the accumulator; the result is stored in the accumulator.

Code:

Hex.: FD 8E d

Oct.: 375 216 d

Dec.: 253 142 d

Bin.: 11111101 10001110 d

See **ADC A,n** for the condition bits.

Form:

> FD
> 8E
> d

12.   ADC HL,BC

HL ← HL + BC + CF

This is a two-byte instruction that causes the contents of the BC register to be added to the contents of the HL register and the carry flag (i.e., the C flag in the F register); the result is stored in register HL.

Code:

> Hex.: ED 4A
> Oct.: 355 112
> Dec.: 237 074
> Bin.: 11101101 01001010

Condition bits:

> S   SET if result is negative, RESET if result is positive or zero.
> Z   SET if result is zero, RESET if result is positive or negative.
> H   SET for carry bit from bit 11, RESET otherwise.
> P/V   SET for overflow condition, RESET for nonoverflow.
> N   RESET.
> C   SET if carry from bit 15, RESET if no carry.

13.   ADC HL,DE

HL ← HL + DE + CF

This is a two-byte instruction that causes the contents of the BC register to be added to the carry flag CF and the contents of the HL register. The result is stored in the HL register.

Code:

> Hex.: ED 5A
> Oct.: 355 132
> Dec.: 237 090
> Bin.: 11101101 01011010

See **ADC HL,BC** for condition bits.

14.   **ADC HL, HL**

HL ← HL + HL + CF

This is a two-byte instruction that adds together the contents of the HL register, HL register, and the carry flag, and stores the result in the HL register.

Code:

Hex.: ED 6A
Oct.: 355 152
Dec.: 237 206
Bin.: 11101101 01101010

Form:

ED
6A

Example:

The contents of register pair HL are 2037h, and the carry flag CF is SET (i.e., 1). After this instruction is executed, the HL register will contain

Contents of HL		2037h
Contents of HL		2037h
Carry flag	+	1
New contents of register HL		406Fh

See **ADC HL, BC** for condition bits.

15.   **ADC HL, SP**

HL ← HL + SP + CF

This is a two-byte instruction that adds together the contents of the HL register, the SP register, and the carry flag CF, and stores the result in the HL register.

Code:

Hex.: ED 7A
Oct.: 355 172
Dec.: 237 122
Bin.: 11101101 01111010

Form:

ED

7A

See **ADC HL,BC** for condition bits.

16.   ADD A, (HL)

A ← A + (HL)

This instruction adds the contents of memory location addressed by the contents of the HL register pair to the contents of the accumulator, and stores the result in the accumulator.

Code:

Hex.:   86

Oct.:   206

Dec.:   134

Bin.:   10000110

Example:

The contents of the accumulator are A2, and the contents of the HL register are 6F23. Memory location 6F23 contains 03. After the execution of the instruction, the accumulator will contain

Contents of accumulator:	A2
Contents of 6F23h:	+ 03
Contents of accumulator	A5

Condition bits:

S   SET if result is negative.

Z   SET if result is zero, RESET if result is nonzero.

H   SET on carry from bit 3, RESET otherwise.

P/V   SET for overflow, RESET for nonoverflow.

N   RESET

C   SET for carry from bit 7, RESET for no carry.

17.   ADD A, (IX + d)

A ← A + (IX + d)

This is a three-byte instruction in which the contents of a memory location addressed by the contents of the IX register and a displacement d are added to the contents of the accumulator, and the result is stored in the accumulator.

Code:

> Hex.: DD 86 d
> Oct.: 335 206 d
> Dec.: 221 134 d
> Bin.: 11011101 10000110 d

Form:

> DD
> 86
> d

Condition bits:

> S   SET if result is negative.
> Z   SET if result is zero.
> H   SET for carry from bit 3.
> P/V   SET for overflow, RESET for nonoverflow.
> N   RESET.
> C   SET for carry from bit 7, RESET for no carry.

18.   ADD A, (IY + d)

   A ← A + (IY + d)

This is a three-byte instruction in which the contents of a memory location addressed by the contents of the IY register plus a displacement d are added to the contents of the accumulator, and the result is stored in the accumulator.

Code:

> Hex.: FD 86 d
> Oct.: 375 206 d
> Dec.: 253 134 d
> Bin.: 11111101 10000110 d

Form:

> FD
>
> 86
>
> d

Condition bits:

See **ADD A, (IX+d).**

19.   ADD A, n

> A ← A + n

This is a two-byte instruction in which integer *n* is added to the contents of the accumulator, and the result is stored in the accumulator.

Code:

> Hex.:   C6 n
>
> Oct.:   306 n
>
> Dec.:   198 n
>
> Bin.:   11000110 n

Form:

> C6
>
> n

Example:

The contents of the accumulator are 3Fh, and the instruction is C6 32. After the execution of this instruction the accumulator will contain

Previous contents of accumulator:	3Fh
n:	+32h
New contents of accumulator:	71h

20.   ADD A, A

> A ← A + A

This instruction adds the contents of the accumulator to the contents of the accumulator, and stores the result in the accumulator.

Code:

Hex.: 87
Oct.: 207
Dec.: 135
Bin.: 10000111

Condition bits:

S   SET if result is negative.
Z   SET if result is zero, RESET if result is nonzero.
H   SET for carry from bit 3, RESET for no carry.
P/V SET for overflow, RESET for nonoverflow.
N   RESET.
C   SET for carry from bit 7, RESET for no carry.

21.   ADD A, B

$A \leftarrow A + B$

This instruction adds the contents of register B to the contents of the accumulator, and stores the result in the accumulator.

Code:

Hex.: 80
Oct.: 200
Dec.: 128
Bin.: 10000000

Condition bits:

See ADD A,A.

Example:

The accumulator contains 06h and register B contains AFh. After the execution of this instruction the accumulator will contain:

Previous contents of accumulator:	06h
Contents of register B:	+AFh
New contents of accumulator:	B5h

22.   ADD A, C

A ← A + C

This instruction adds the contents of register C to the contents of the accumulator, and stores the result in the accumulator.

Code:

Hex.:   81
Oct.:   201
Dec.:   129
Bin.:   10000001

Condition bits:

See **ADD A, A.**

23.   ADD A, D

A ← A + D

This instruction adds the contents of register D to the contents of the accumulator, and stores the result in the accumulator.

Code:

Hex.:   82
Oct.:   202
Dec.:   130
Bin.:   10000010

Condition bits:

See **ADD A,A.**

24.   ADD A, E

A ← A + E

This instruction adds the contents of register E to the contents of the accumulator, and stores the result in the accumulator.

Code:

Hex.:   83

Oct.:   203
Dec.:   131
Bin.:   10000011

Condition bits:

See **ADD A,A.**

25.   **ADD A,H**

A ← A + H

This instruction adds the contents of register H to the contents of the accumulator and stores the result in the accumulator.

Code:

Hex.:   84
Oct.:   204
Dec.:   132
Bin.:   10000100

Condition bits:

See **ADD A,A.**

26.   **ADD A, L**

A ← A + L

This instruction adds the contents of register L to the contents of the accumulator, and stores the result in the accumulator.

Code:

Hex.:   85
Oct.:   205
Dec.:   133
Bin.:   10000101

Condition bits:

See **ADD A,A.**

27.   **ADD HL, BC**

   HL ← HL + BC

This instruction adds the contents of register BC to the contents of register HL, and stores the result in register HL.

Code:

   Hex.: 09
   Oct.: 11
   Dec.: 9
   Bin.: 00001001

Condition bits:

   S   not affected.
   Z   not affected.
   H   SET for carry from bit 11, RESET for no carry.
   P/V   not affected.
   N   RESET.
   C   SET for carry from bit 15, RESET for no carry.

28.   **ADD HL, DE**

   HL ← HL + DE

This instruction adds the contents of register pair DE to the contents of register pair HL, and stores the result in register pair HL.

Code:

   Hex.: 19
   Oct.: 31
   Dec.: 25
   Bin.: 00011001

Condition bits:

See **ADD HL,BC.**

29.   **ADD HL, HL**

   HL ← HL + HL

This instruction adds the contents of register pair HL to the contents of register pair HL, and stores the result in register pair HL.

Code:

Hex.: 29
Oct.: 51
Dec.: 41
Bin.: 00101001

Condition bits:

See **ADD HL, BC.**

30.   ADD HL, SP
HL ← HL + SP

This instruction adds the contents of register pair SP to the contents of register pair HL, and stores the result in register pair HL.

Code:

Hex.: 39
Oct.: 71
Dec.: 57
Bin.: 00111001

Condition bits:

See **ADD HL, BC.**

31.   ADD IX, BC
IX ← IX + BC

This instruction adds the contents of register pair BC to the contents of index register IX, and stores the result in index register IX.

Code:

Hex.: DD 09
Oct.: 335 011
Dec.: 221 009
Bin.: 11011101 00001001

Condition bits:

S	not affected.
Z	not affected.
H	SET for carry from bit 11, RESET for no carry.
P/V	not affected.
N	RESET.
C	SET for carry from bit 15, RESET for no carry.

32.   ADD IX, DE

$$IX \leftarrow IX + DE$$

This two-byte instruction adds the contents of register pair DE to the contents of the index register IX, and stores the result in index register IX.

Code:

Hex.: DD 19
Oct.: 335 031
Dec.: 221 025
Bin.: 11011101 00011001

Condition bits:

See **ADD IX,BC.**

33.   ADD IX, IX

$$IX \leftarrow IX + IX$$

This two-byte instruction adds the contents of index register IX to the contents of index register IX, and stores the result in index register IX.

Code:

Hex.: DD 29
Oct.: 335 051
Dec.: 221 041
Bin.: 11011101 00101001

Condition bits:

See **ADD IX,BC.**

34.   ADD IX, SP

   IX ← IX + SP

This two-byte instruction adds the contents of register pair SP to the contents of the index register IX, and stores the result in index register IX.

Code:

   Hex.: DD 39
   Oct.: 335 071
   Dec.: 221 057
   Bin.: 11011101 00111001

Condition bits:

See **ADD IX, BC.**

35.   ADD IY, BC
   IY ← IY + BC

This two-byte instruction adds the contents of register pair BC to the contents of index register IY, and stores the results in index register IY.

Code:

   Hex.: FD 09
   Oct.: 375 011
   Dec.: 253 009
   Bin.: 11111101 00001001

Condition bits:

See **ADD IX, BC.**

36.   ADD IY, DE
   IY ← IY + DE

This two-byte instruction adds the contents of register pair DE to the contents of index register IY, and stores the result in index register IY.

Code:

   Hex.: FD 19

Oct.: 375 031
Dec.: 253 025
Bin.: 11111101 00011001

Condition bits:

See **ADD IX,BC.**

37.   ADD IY, IY

IY ← IY + IY

This two-byte instruction adds the contents of index register IY to the contents of the index register IY, and stores the result in index register IY.

Code:

Hex.: FD 29
Oct.: 375 051
Dec.: 253 041
Bin.: 11111101 00101001

Condition bits:

See **ADD IX, BC.**

38.   ADD IY, SP

IY ← IY + SP

This two-byte instruction adds the contents of register pair SP to the contents of index register IY, and stores the result in index register IY.

Code:

Hex.: FD 39
Oct.: 375 071
Dec.: 253 057
Bin.: 11111101 00111001

Condition bits:

See **ADD IX, BC.**

39.   AND A

$$A \leftarrow A \wedge A$$

The accumulator A is logical ANDed with accumulator A.

Code:

>   Hex.: A7
>   Oct.: 247
>   Dec.: 167
>   Bin.: 10100111

Condition bits:

>   S   SET if the result is negative.
>   Z   SET if result is zero.
>   H   SET.
>   P/V   SET if parity even, RESET for parity odd.
>   H   RESET.
>   C   RESET.

40.   AND B

$$A \leftarrow A \wedge B$$

This instruction performs a bit-by-bit logical AND operation on the contents of the accumulator, using the contents of the B register. The result is stored in the accumulator.

Code:

>   Hex.: AØ
>   Oct.: 240
>   Dec.: 160
>   Bin.: 10100000

Condition bits:

See **AND A**.

41.   AND C

$$A \leftarrow A \wedge C$$

This instruction performs a bit-by-bit logical AND operation on the contents of the accumulator, using the contenst of register C. The result is stored in the accumulator.

Code:

    Hex.:   A1
    Oct.:   241
    Dec.:   161
    Bin.:   10100001

Condition bits:

See **AND A.**

42.   AND D
A ← A ∧ D

This instruction performs a bit-by-bit logical AND operation on the contents of the accumulator, using the contents of register D. The result is stored in the accumulator.

Code:

    Hex.:   A2
    Oct.:   242
    Dec.:   162
    Bin.:   10100010

Condition bits:

See **AND A.**

43.   AND E
A ← A ∧ E

This instruction performs a bit-by-bit logical AND operation on the contents of the accumulator, using the contents of register E. The result is stored in the accumulator.

Code:

    Hex.:   A3

Oct.:   243
Dec.:   163
Bin.:   10100011

Condition bits:

See **AND A.**

44.   **AND H**

A ← A ∧ H

This instruction performs a bit-by-bit logical AND operation on the contents of the accumulator, using the contents of register H. The result is stored in the accumulator.

Code:

Hex.:   A4
Oct.:   244
Dec.:   164
Bin.:   10100100

Condition bits:

See **AND A.**

45.   **AND L**

A ← A ∧ L

This instruction performs a bit-by-bit logical AND operation on the contents of the accumulator, using the contents of register L. The result is stored in the accumulator.

Code:

Hex.:   A5
Oct.:   245
Dec.:   165
Bin.:   10100101

Condition bits:

See **AND A.**

46.   AND n

A ← A ∧ n

This is a two-byte instruction, in which n is the second byte. This instruction will perform a bit-by-bit logical AND operation on the contents of the accumulator, using byte n.

Code:

    Hex.: E6 n

    Oct.: 346 n

    Dec.: 230 n

    Bin.: 11100110 n

Format:

    op-code

    n

Example:

Assume code as follows (both hex and binary are given):

    E6   11100110

    32   00110010

E6 is the op-code for AND n, while 32H is n. If the contents of the accumulator were A7H before this instruction were encountered, then the CPU would perform a bit-by-bit logical AND operation between A7H (the contents of the accumulator) and 32H, the value of n. The result would be 22H:

$$A7 \quad 32 \quad\quad = 22$$

$$10100111 \quad 00110010 = 00100010$$

Condition bits:

See **AND A.**

47.   AND (HL)

A ← A ∧ (HL)

This instruction performs a bit-by-bit logical AND operation on the contents of the accumulator, using the contents of a memory location whose address is held in register pair HL. The result is stored in the accumulator.

Code:

> Hex.: A6
> Oct.: 246
> Dec.: 166
> Bin.: 10100110

Condition bits:

See **AND A.**

48. **AND (IX + d)**

$A \leftarrow A \wedge (IX + d)$

This is a three-byte instruction that performs a bit-by-bit logical AND operation on the contents of the accumulator, using the contents of a memory location whose address is given by the sum of an integer d and the contents of the IX register.

Code:

> Hex.: DD A6 d
> Oct.: 335 246 d
> Dec.: 221 166 d
> Bin.: 11011101 10100110 d

Condition bits:

See **AND A.**

49. **AND (IY + d)**

$A \leftarrow A \wedge (IY + d)$

This is a three-byte instruction that performs a bit-by-bit logical AND operation on the contents of the accumulator, using the contents of a memory location whose address is given by the sum of the contents of register IY and the displacement integer d.

Code:

> Hex.: FD A6 d
> Oct.: 375 246 d

Dec.:   253 166 d

Bin.:   11111101 10100110 d

Condition bits:

See **AND A.**

50.   BIT b, r

This set of instructions is used to test specific bits in specified registers. The bit number, 0-7, is specified by b, while the register is specified by r. The first byte of the op-code is CB, while the second byte is formed from the codes for the bits to be tested and the codes for the register.

Table b			Table r	
BIT	**CODE**		**REGISTER**	**CODE**
0	000		B	000
1	001		C	001
2	010		D	010
3	011		E	011
4	100		H	100
5	101		L	101
6	110		A	111
7	111			

Format:

Byte 1   1 1 0 0 1 0 1 1   CB

0 1   (b)   (r)

Example:

The instruction used to test bit 6 of the E register would be (for bit 6, b = 110, for register E, r = 011):

1 1 0 0 1 0 1 1   CB

0 1 1 1 0 0 1 1   73

When this instruction has been executed, the Z flag in the F register is set to the complement of the indicated bit.

Condition bits:

S   (Unknown).

Z   SET if bit b of register r is Ø, RESET otherwise.

H   SET.

P/V   (Unknown).

N   RESET.

C   Unaffected.

51.   BIT 0, (HL)

This two-byte instruction tests bit 0 of the byte at a memory location whose address is pointed to by the contents of the HL register pair. The Z flag in the F register will contain the complement of this bit.

Code:

Hex.:   CB 46

Oct.:   313 106

Dec.:   203 070

Bin.:   11001011 01000110

Condition bits:

S   (Unknown)

Z   SET if bit is 0, RESET if bit is 1.

H   SET.

P/V   (Unknown).

N   RESET.

C   Unaffected.

52.   BIT 1, (HL)

This two-byte instruction tests bit 1 of the byte at a memory location whose address is pointed to by the contents of the HL register pair. The Z flag in the F register will contain the complement of this bit.

Code:

Hex.:   CB 4E

Oct.:   313 116

Dec.:   203 078

Bin.:   11001011 01001110

Condition bits:

See **BIT 0, (HL)**.

53.   BIT 2, (HL)

This two-byte instruction tests bit 2 of the byte at a memory location whose address is pointed to by the contents of the HL register pair. The Z flag in the F register will contain the complement of this bit.

Code:

> Hex.: CB 56
> Oct.: 313 126
> Dec.: 203 086
> Bin.: 11001011 01010110

Condition bits:

See **Bit Ø, (HL).**

54.   BIT 3, (HL)

This two-byte instruction tests bit 3 of the byte at a memory location whose address is pointed to by the contents of the HL register pair. The Z flag in the F register will contain the complement of this bit.

Code:

> Hex.: CB 5E
> Oct.: 313 136
> Dec.: 203 094
> Bin.: 11001011 01011110

Condition bits.:

See **BIT Ø, (HL).**

55.   BIT 4, (HL)

This two-byte instruction tests bit 4 of the byte at a memory location whose address is pointed to by the contents of register pair HL. The Z flag in the F register will contain the complement of this bit.

Code:

> Hex.: CB 66
> Oct.: 313 146

Dec.:   203 102

Bin.:   11001011 01100110

Condition bits:

See **BIT 0, (HL).**

56.   BIT 5, (HL)

This two-byte instruction tests bit 5 of the byte at a memory location whose address is pointed to by the contents of register pair HL. The Z flag in the F register will contain the complement of this bit.

Code:

Hex.:   CB 6E

Oct.:   313 156

Dec.:   203 110

Bin.:   11001011 01101110

Condition bits:

See **BIT 0, (HL).**

57.   BIT 6, (HL)

This two-byte instruction tests bit 6 of the byte at a memory location whose address is pointed to by the contents of register pair HL. The Z flag in the F register will contain the complement of this bit.

Code:

Hex.:   CB 76

Oct.:   313 166

Dec.:   203 118

Bin.:   11001011 01110110

Condition bits:

See **BIT 0, (HL).**

58. BIT 7, (HL)

This two-byte instruction tests bit 7 of the byte at a memory location whose address is pointed to by the contents of register pair HL. The Z flag in the F register will contain the complement of this bit.

Code:

      Hex.: CB 7E
      Oct.: 313 176
      Dec.: 203 126
      Bin.: 11001011 01111110

Condition bits:

See **BIT Ø, (HL)**.

59. BIT Ø, (IX + d)

This four-byte instruction tests bit Ø of the byte at a memory location pointed to by the contents of the IX register and the two's complement of integer *d*. The Z flag in the F register will contain the complement of this bit.

Code:

      Hex.: DD CB d 46
      Oct.: 335 313 d 106
      Dec.: 221 203 d 070

Condition bits:

      S   (Unknown).
      Z   SET if bit is Ø, RESET if bit is 1.
      H   SET.
      P/V   (Unknown).
      N   RESET.
      C   (Unaffected).

60. BIT 1, (IX + d)

This four-byte instruction tests bit 1 of the byte at a memory location pointed to by the contents of the IX register and the two's complement of integer *d*. The Z flag in the F register will contain the complement of this bit.

Code:

> Hex.: DD CB d 4E
> Oct.: 335 313 d 116
> Dec.: 221 203 d 078
> Bin.: 11011101 11001011 d 01001110

Condition bits:

See **BIT 0, (IX + d)**.

61.   BIT 2, (IX + d)

This four-byte instruction tests bit 1 of the byte at a memory location pointed to by the contents of the IX register and the two's complement of integer d. The Z flag in the F register will contain the complement of this bit.

Code:

> Hex.: DD CB d 56
> Oct.: 335 313 d 126
> Dec.: 221 203 d 086
> Bin.: 11011101 11001011 d 01010110

Condition bits:

See **Bit 0, (IX + d)**.

62.   BIT 3, (IX + d)

This four-byte instruction tests bit 3 of the byte at a memory location pointed to by the contents of the IX register and the two's complement of integer d. The Z flag in the F register will contain the complement of this bit.

Code:

> Hex.: DD CB d 5E
> Oct.: 335 313 d 136
> Dec.: 221 203 d 094
> Bin.: 11011101 11001011 d 01011110

Condition bits:

See **BIT 0, (IX + d)**.

63.   BIT 4, (IX + d)

This four-byte instruction tests bit 4 of the byte at a memory location pointed to by the contents of the IX register and the two's complement of integer d. The Z flag in the F register will contain the complement of this bit.

Code:

> Hex.: DD CB d 66
> Oct.: 335 313 d 146
> Dec.: 221 203 d 102
> Bin.: 11011101 11001011 d 01100110

Condition bits:

See **BIT Ø, (IX + d)**.

64.   BIT 5, (IX + d)

This four-byte instruction tests bit 5 of the byte at a memory location pointed to by the contents of the IX register and the two's complement of the integer d. The Z flag in the F register will contain the complement of this bit.

Code:

> Hex.: DD CB d 6E
> Oct.: 335 313 d 156
> Dec.: 221 203 d 110
> Bin.: 11011101 11001011 d 01101110

Condition bits:

See **BIT Ø, (IX + d)**

65.   BIT 6, (IX + d)

This four-byte instruction tests bit 6 of the byte at a memory location pointed to by the contents of the IX register and the two's complement of integer d. The Z flag in the F register will contain the complement of this bit.

Code:

> Hex.: DD CB d 76
> Oct.: 335 313 d 166

Dec.: 221 203 d 118

Bin.: 11011101 11001011 d 01110110

Condition bits:

See **BIT Ø, (IX + d)**.

66.   BIT 7, (IX + d)

This four-byte instruction tests bit 7 of the byte at a memory location pointed to by the contents of the IX register and the two's complement of integer *d*. The Z flag in the F register will contain the complement of this bit.

Code:

Hex.: DD CB d 7E

Oct.: 335 313 d 176

Dec.: 221 203 d 126

Bin.: 11011101 11001011 d 01111110

Condition bits:

See **BIT Ø, (IX + d)**.

67.   BIT Ø, (IY + d)

This four-byte instruction tests bit Ø of the byte at a memory location pointed to by the contents of the IY register and the two's complement of integer *d*. The Z flag in the F register will contain the complement of this bit.

Code:

Hex.: FD CB d 46

Oct.: 375 313 d 106

Dec.: 253 203 d 070

Bin.: 11111101 11001011 d 01000110

Condition bits:

S   (Unknown).

Z   SET if bit is Ø, RESET if bit is 1.

H   SET.

P/V   (Unknown).

N   RESET.

C   (Unaffected).

68.   BIT 1, (IY + d)

This four-byte instruction tests bit 1 of the byte at a memory location pointed to by the contents of the IY register and the two's complement of the integer d. The Z flag in the F register will contain the complement of this bit.

Code:

    Hex.: FD CB d 4E
    Oct.: 375 313 d 116
    Dec.: 253 203 d 078
    Bin.: 11111101 11001011 d 01001110

Condition bits:

See **BIT 0, (IY + d)**.

69.   BIT 2, (IY + d)

This four-byte instruction tests bit 2 of the byte at a memory location pointed to by the contents of register IY and the two's complement of integer d. The Z flag in the F register will contain the complement of this bit.

Code:

    Hex.: FD CB d 56
    Oct.: 375 313 d 126
    Dec.: 253 203 d 086
    Bin.: 11111101 11001011 d 01010110

Condition bits:

See **BIT 0, (IY + d)**.

70.   BIT 3, (IY + d)

This four-byte instruction tests bit 3 of the byte at a memory location pointed to by the contents of the IY register and the two's complement of integer d. The Z flag in the F register will contain the complement of this bit.

Code:

> Hex.:   FD CB d 5E
> Oct.:   375 313 d 136
> Dec.:   253 203 d 094
> Bin.:   11111101 11001011 d 01011110

Condition bits:

See **BIT 0̸, (IY + d)**.

71.   BIT 4, (IY + d)

This four-byte instruction tests bit 4 of the byte at a memory location pointed to by the contents of the IY register and the two's complement of the integer d. The Z flag in the F register will contain the complement of this bit.

Code:

> Hex.:   FD CB d 66
> Oct.:   375 313 d 146
> Dec.:   253 203 d 102
> Bin.:   11111101 11001011 d 01100110

Condition bits:

See **BIT 0̸, (IY + d)**.

72.   BIT 5, (IY + d)

This four-byte instruction tests bit 5 of the byte at a memory location pointed to by the contents of the IY register and the two's complement of integer d. The Z flag in the F register will contain the complement of this bit.

Code:

> Hex.:   FD CB d 6E
> Oct.:   375 313 d 156
> Dec.:   253 203 d 110
> Bin.:   11111101 11001011 d 01101110

Condition bits:

See **BIT 0̸, (IY + d)**.

73.   BIT 6, (IY + d)

This four-byte instruction tests bit 6 of the byte at a memory location pointed to by the contents of the IY register and the two's complement of integer *d*. The Z flag of the F register will contain the complement of this bit.

Code:

> Hex.:   FD CB d 76
> Oct.:   375 313 d 166
> Dec.:   253 203 d 118
> Bin.:   11111101 11001011 d 01110110

Condition bits:

See **Bit 0̸, (IY + d)**.

74.   BIT 7, (IY + d)

This four-byte instruction tests bit 7 of the byte at a memory location pointed to by the contents of the IY register and the two's complement of integer *d*. The Z flag in the F register will contain the complement of this bit.

Code:

> Hex.:   FD CB d 7E
> Oct.:   375 313 d 176
> Dec.:   253 203 d 126
> Bin.:   11111101 11001011 d 01111110

Condition bits:

See **BIT 0̸, (IY + d)**.

75.   CALL cc, nn

Table of Conditions

CONDITION		cc	FLAG
NZ	nonzero	000	Z
Z	zero	001	Z
NC	noncarry	010	C
C	carry	011	C

CONDITION		cc	FLAG
PO	parity odd	100	P/V
PE	parity even	101	P/V
P	sign positive	110	S
M	sign negative	111	S

If condition cc (part of byte 1) is *true*, then this instruction pushes the contents of the program counter (PC register) out to the external memory stack. The address of an external memory location *nn*, where the first operation code of a subroutine is located, is then loaded into the PC. Byte 2 of the instruction is the low-order byte of this address, while byte 3 of the instruction is the high-order byte of the address.

To return the program at the end of the subroutine, a **RET** instruction must be placed at the end of the subroutine code. This will pop the contents of the stack back to the PC.

If condition cc is *false*, then the program counter (PC) is incremented as usual, and the program continues.

Condition bits:

None affected.

76.   CALL nn

This is a three-byte instruction which, when executed, will push the contents of the program counter (PC) onto the top of an external memory stack. The address of a subroutine (nn) is then loaded into the PC. Byte 2 of the instruction is the lower-order byte of the subroutine address, while byte 3 is the higher-order byte of the subroutine address.

To return from the subroutine, a **RET** instruction must be placed at the end of the subroutine code.

Condition bits:

None affected.

77.   CCF
$$CY \leftarrow \overline{CY}$$

This one-byte instruction caused the carry (C) flag in the F register to be complemented.

Code:

    Hex.: 3F

    Oct.: 77

    Dec.: 63

    Bin.: 00111111

Condition bits:

    S   (Unaffected).

    Z   (Unaffected).

    H   Previous carry copied.

    P/V   (Unaffected).

    N   RESET.

    C   SET if carry was $\emptyset$ before operation, RESET if carry was 1.

78.   CP n

    A − n

This two-byte instruction compares the contents of the accumulator with byte 2 (n). If there is a true, then a flag is SET.

Code:

    (byte 1)   FE

    (byte 2)   n

Condition bits:

    S   SET if result is negative, RESET otherwise.

    Z   SET if result is $\emptyset$, RESET if result is 1.

    H   SET if no borrow from B4, RESET otherwise.

    P/V SET for overflow, RESET otherwise.

    N   SET.

    C   SET for no borrow, RESET otherwise.

79.   CP B

    A − B

This one-byte instruction compares the contents of the accumulator with the contents of register B. If there is a true, then a flag is set.

Code:

    Hex.: B8
    Oct.: 271
    Dec.: 185
    Bin.: 10111000

Condition bits:

See **CP n.**

80. CP C
A – C

This one-byte instruction compares the contents of the accumulator with the contents of register C. If there is a true, then a flag is set.

Code:

    Hex.: B9
    Oct.: 271
    Dec.: 185
    Bin.: 10111001

Condition bits:

See **CP n.**

81. CP D
A – D

This one-byte instruction compares the contents of the accumulator with the contents of register D. If a true exists, then a flag is set.

Code.:

    Hex.: BA
    Oct.: 272
    Dec.: 186
    Bin.: 10111010

Condition bits:

See **CP n.**

82.   CP E

   A – E

This one-byte instruction compares the contents of the accumulator with the contents of register D. If a true exists, then a flag is set.

Code:

   Hex.:   BB
   Oct.:   273
   Dec.:   187
   Bin.:   10111011

Condition bits:

See **CP n.**

83.   CP H

   A – H

This one-byte instruction compares the contents of the accumulator with the contents of register H. If a true exists, then a flag is set.

Code:

   Hex.:   BC
   Oct.:   274
   Dec.:   188
   Bin.   10111100

Condition bits:

See **CP n.**

84.   CP L

   A – L

This one-byte instruction compares the contents of the accumulator and the contents of register L. If a true exists, then a flag is set.

Code:

   Hex.:   BD
   Oct.:   275

Dec.:   189

Bin.:   10111101

Condition bits:

See **CP n.**

85.   **CP A**

A - A

This one-byte instruction compares the contents of the accumulator with the contents of the accumulator. If a true exists, then a flag is set.

Code:

Hex.:   BF

Oct.:   277

Dec.:   191

Bin.:   10111111

Condition bits:

See **CP n.**

86.   **CP (HL)**

A - (HL)

This one-byte instruction compares the contents of the accumulator with the contents of a memory location pointed to by the contents of register pair HL.

Code:

Hex.:   BE

Oct.:   276

Dec.:   190

Bin.:   10111110

Condition bits:

See **CP n.**

87.   CP (IX + d)

A – (IX + d)

This three-byte instruction compares the contents of the accumulator with the contents of a memory location pointed to by the contents of the IX register and integer *d*.

Code:

Hex.: DD BE d

Oct.:   335 276 d

Dec.:   221 190 d

Bin: 11011101 10111110 d

Condition bits:

See **CP n.**

88.   CP (IY + d)

A – (IY + d)

This three-byte instruction compares the contents of the accumulator with the contents of a memory location pointed to by the contents of the IY register and integer *d*.

Code:

Hex.: FD BE d

Oct.:   375 276 d

Dec.:   253 190 d

Bin.:   11111101 10111110 d

Condition bits:

See **CP n.**

89.   CPD

A ← (HL), HL ← HL– 1, BC ← BC– 1

The contents of the accumulator are compared with the contents of a memory location pointed to by the contents of the HL register pair. If a true exists, then a condition flag is set.

The contents of register pair HL is then decremented. The contents of the byte counter (register pair BC) are decremented.

Code:

Hex.: ED A9
Oct.: 355 251
Dec.: 237 169
Bin.: 11101101 10101001

Condition bits:

S   SET if result is negative.
Z   SET if A ← (HL) = Ø.
H   SET if no borrow from bit 4, RESET otherwise.
P/V   SET for BC- 1 ≠ Ø, RESET otherwise.
N   SET.
C   (Unaffected).

90.   CPDR
A ← (HL), HL ← HL- 1, BC ← BC- 1

This two-byte instruction is similar to the CPD instruction given earlier; it is a compare and decrement operation. The contents of a memory location pointed to by the HL register pair are compared with the contents of the accumulator. If the compare is a *true* condition, a condition bit is set. Both register pair HL and register pair BC (byte counter) are decremented by this instruction.

If the new value in register BC is zero, or if the contents of the accumulator and the contents of HL are equal, then the instruction is terminated.

If neither condition is met, i.e., if BC is not zero, and if the contents of the accumulator are not equal to the contents of HL, then the program counter is decremented by 2, and the instruction is repeated. Note that execution of this instruction causes the PC to *increment*, by 2, and the failed test causes it to decrement by 2; this puts the PC back at the original point where the CPDR instruction was encountered.

We can make this instruction test all 64K of memory by initializing the BC register pair to zero prior to this instruction. This will cause it to fail the BC = 0? test, so it will loop until all 64K are tested, or a match is found.

Data interrupts will be recognized after each iteration.

Code:

Hex.: ED B9

Oct.:   355 237
Dec.:   237 185
Bin.:   11101101 10111001

Condition bits:

S   SET if the result is negative, RESET otherwise.
Z   SET for A = (HL).
H   SET if there is no borrow from bit 4, RESET otherwise.
P/V   SET if BC– 1 is nonzero, RESET otherwise.
N   SET.
C   (Unaffected).

91.   CPI

A ← (HL), HL ← HL+1, BC ← BC– 1

This instruction is similar to CPD, except that the HL register is *incremented* instead of decremented. The contents of a memory location addressed by the contents of the HL register pair are compared with the contents of the accumulator. A true compare causes a condition bit to be SET. After the comparison, the HL register is incremented, while the BC register is decremented.

Code:

Hex.:   ED A1
Oct.:   355 241
Dec.:   237 161
Bin: 11101101 10100001

Condition bits:

S   SET if result is negative.
Z   SET for A = (HL).
H   SET for no borrow from bit 4.
P/V   SET if BC– 1 is nonzero.
N   SET.
C   (Unaffected).

92.   CPIR

A ← (HL), HL ← HL+1, BC ← BC– 1

This two-byte instruction is similar to the CPDR instruction (90). The description for CPIR is the same as for CPDR, exect that the HL register is *incremented* instead of decremented. The condition bits are also the same.

Code:

    Hex.: ED B1
    Oct.: 355 261
    Dec.: 237 177
    Bin.: 11101101 10110001

93.   **CPL**

    $A \leftarrow \overline{A}$

This one-byte instruction causes the contents of the accumulator to be complemented.

Code:

    Hex.: 2F
    Oct.: 057
    Dec.: 047
    Bin.: 00101111

Condition bits:

    H   SET.
    N   SET.
    S, Z, P/V, and C unaffected.

94.   **DAA**

This one-byte instruction decimal adjusts the accumulator, so that the correct representation for BCD is obtained.

Code:

    Hex.: 27
    Oct.: 047
    Dec.: 039
    Bin.: 00100111

Condition bits:

S   SET if the MSB of the accumulator is 1 after execution, RESET otherwise.

Z   SET if the accumulator is zero after execution of the instruction.

H   (See table below.)

P/V   SET if the accumulator has even parity after execution.

H   (Unaffected).

C   (See table below.)

Operation Table for DAA Instruction

USED WITH INSTRUC-TION	C BEFORE	C AFTER	H BEFORE DAA	HEX IN LOWER DIGIT (B3-BØ)	HEX IN UPPER DIGIT (B7-B4)	NUMBER ADDED TO BYTE
	0	0	0	0-9	0-9	00
	0	0	0	A-F	0-8	06
	0	0	1	0-3	0-9	06
	0	1	0	0-9	A-F	60
ADD	0	1	0	A-F	9-F	66
ADC	0	1	1	0-3	A-F	66
INC	1	1	0	0-9	0-2	00
	1	1	0	A-F	0-2	FA
	1	1	1	0-3	0-3	A0
NEG	0	0	0	0-9	0-9	00
SUB	0	0	1	6-F	0-8	FA
SBC	1	1	0	0-9	7-F	A0
	1	1	1	6-F	6-F	9A

95.   DEC IX

IX ← IX- 1

This two-byte instruction decrements the IX index register.

Code:

Hex.:   DD 2B

Oct.:   335 221

Dec.:   053 043

Bin.:   11111101 00101011

Condition bits:

All unaffected.

96.   DEC IY

IY ← IY-1

This two-byte instruction causes the contents of the IY index register to be decremented.

Code:

Hex.: FD 2B
Oct.: 375 053
Dec.: 253 043
Bin.: 11111101 00101011

Condition bits:

None affected.

97.   DEC B

B ← B-1

This one-byte instruction decrements the contents of register B.

Code:

Hex.: 05
Oct.: 005
Dec.: 5
Bin. 00000101

Condition bits:

S   Set if result is negative, RESET otherwise.
Z   Set if the result is zero, RESET if nonzero.
H   SET if there is no borrow from bit 4, RESET otherwise.
P/V SET if contents of register was 80 (hex) before operation, RESET otherwise.
N   SET.
C   (Unaffected).

98.   DEC C

C ← C-1

This one-byte instruction decrements the contents of register C.

Code:

> Hex.: ØD
> Oct.: 015
> Dec.: 13
> Bin.: 00001101

Condition bits:

See **DEC B.**

99.   DEC D

> D ← D-1

This one-byte instruction decrements the contents of register D.

Code:

> Hex.: 15
> Oct.: 025
> Dec.: 21
> Bin.: 00010101

Condition bits:

See **DEC B.**

100.   DEC E

> E ← E-1

This one-byte instruction decrements the contents of register E.

Code:

> Hex.: 1D
> Oct.: 035
> Dec.: 29
> Bin.: 00011101

Condition bits:

See **DEC B.**

101.   DEC H

H ← H-1

This one-byte instruction decrements the contents of register H.

Code:

Hex.: 25
Oct.: 045
Dec.: 37
Bin.: 00100101

Condition bits:

See **Dec. B.**

102.   DEC L

L ← L-1

This one-byte instruction decrements the contents of register L.

Code:

Hex.: 2D
Oct.: 055
Dec.: 45
Bin.: 00101101

Condition bits:

See **DEC B.**

103.   DEC A

A ← A - 1

This one-byte instruction decrements the contents of the accumulator.

Code:

Hex.: 3D
Oct.: 075
Dec.: 61
Bin.: 00111101

Condition bits:

See **DEC B.**

104.   DEC (HL)

(HL) ← (HL) - 1

This one-byte instruction decrements the contents of a memory location pointed to by register pair HL.

Code:

Hex.:   35
Oct.:   065
Dec.:   53
Bin.:   00110101

Condition bits:

See **DEC B.**

105.   DEC (IX + d)

This three-byte instruction decrements the contents of a memory location pointed to by the IX register and integer *d*.

Code:

Hex.:   DD 35 d
Oct.:   335 065 d
Dec.:   221 53 d
Bin.:   11011101 00110101 d

Condition bits:

See **DEC B.**

106.   DEC (IY + d)

This three-byte instruction decrements the contents of a memory location pointed to by the IY register and integer *d*.

Code:

>Hex.:   FD 35 d
>Oct.:   375 065 d
>Dec.:   253 53 d
>Bin.:   11111101 00110101 d

Condition bits:

See **DEC B.**

107.   DEC BC

>BC ← BC-1

The contents of register pair BC are decremented.

Code:

>Hex.:   ØB
>Oct.:   013
>Dec.:   11
>Bin.:   00001011

Condition bits:

All unaffected.

108.   DEC DE

>DE ← DE-1

The contents of register pair DE are decremented.

Code:

>Hex.:   1B
>Oct.:   033
>Dec.:   27
>Bin.:   00011011

Condition bits:

All unaffected.

109.   DEC HL

HL ← HL-1

The contents of register pair HL are decremented.

Code:

    Hex.:   2B
    Oct.:   053
    Dec.:   43
    Bin.:   00101011

Condition bits:

All unaffected.

110.   DEC SP

SP ← SP-1

The contents of register pair SP are decremented.

Code:

    Hex.:   3B
    Oct.:   073
    Dec.:   59
    Bin.:   00111011

Condition bits:

All unaffected.

111.   DJNZ, e

This is a two-byte instruction that decrements register B, and performs a jump operation if the result is nonzero. If the contents of the B register are zero following the decrement operation, then the program falls through to the next instruction in sequence. But if the contents of the B register are nonzero following the decrement operation, then the contents of the program counter (PC) are added to displacement e. (The second byte of the instruction is e-2.) The result of this addition becomes the new contents of the PC, and gives the location of the next instruction to be executed.

Code:

Hex.: 10 e-2
Oct.: 20 e-2
Dec.: 16 e-2
Bin.: 00010000 e-2

Condition bits:

All unaffected.

112.   EI

IFF ← 1

This one-byte instruction enables the maskable interrupt function by setting the interrupt flip-flops.

The maskable interrupt function is not enabled *during* the execution of this instruction.

Code:

Hex.: FB
Oct.: 373
Dec.: 251
Bin.: 11111011

Condition bits:

All unaffected.

113.   EX AF,AF′

AF ⟷ AF′

This one-byte instruction causes the register pair **AF** to exchange its contents with register pair **AF′**.

Code:

Hex.: Ø8
Oct.: 010
Dec.: 08
Bin.: 00001000

Condition bits:

All unaffected.

114.   EX DE, HL
DE ⟷ HL

This is a one-byte instruction that exchanges the contents of the DE and HL register pairs.

Code:

> Hex.: EB
> Oct.: 353
> Dec.: 235
> Bin.: 11101011

Condition bits:

All unaffected.

115.   EX (SP), HL
L ⟷ (SP), H ⟷ (SP + 1)

The low-order byte of the sixteen-bit register-pair (i.e., contents of L) is exchanged with the contents of the memory location pointed to by the stack pointer (SP). The high-order byte (i.e., contents of the H register) is exchanged with the contents of the next sequential memory location.

Code:

> Hex.: E3
> Oct.: 343
> Dec.: 227
> Bin.: 11100011

Condition bits:

All unaffected.

116.   EX (SP), IX
LIX ⟷ (SP), HIX ⟷ (SP + 1)

The low-order byte of the sixteen-bit IX index register is exchanged with the contents of the memory location pointed to by the stack pointer (SP). The high-order byte of the IX index register is exchanged with the contents of the next memory location.

Code:

```
Hex.:  DD E3
Oct.:  335 221
Dec.:  343 227
Bin.:  11011101  11100011
```

Condition bits:

All unaffected.

117.   EX (SP), IY

$$LIY \longleftrightarrow (SP), HIY \longleftrightarrow (SP + 1)$$

The low-order byte of the sixteen-bit IY index register is exchanged with the contents of the memory location pointed to by the stack pointer (SP). The high-order byte of the IY index register is exchanged with the contents of the next sequential memory location.

Code:

```
Hex.:  FD E3
Oct.:  375 343
Dec.:  253 227
Bin.:  11111101  11100011
```

Condition bits:

All unaffected.

118.   EXX

$$BC \longleftrightarrow BC', DE \longleftrightarrow DE', HL \longleftrightarrow HL'$$

The sixteen-bit values stored in the BC, DE, and HL register pairs are exchanged with the sixteen-bit values stored in register pairs BC′, DE′, and HL′, respectively.

Code:

Hex.: D9
Oct.: 331
Dec.: 217
Bin.: 11011001

Condition bits:

All unaffected.

119.   IM Ø

This two-byte instruction sets the interrupt mode Ø that allows the interrupting device to insert any instruction code onto the data bus for immediate execution.

Code:

Hex.: ED 46
Oct.: 355 106
Dec.: 237 070
Bin.: 11101101 01000110

Condition bits:

All unaffected.

120.   IM 1

The IM 1 instruction sets interrupt mode 1, in which the CPU will execute a restart to location 00 38 (hex.), 000 070 (oct.) when interrupt occurs.

Code:

Hex.: ED 56
Oct.: 335 126
Dec.: 237 086
Bin.: 11101101 01010110

Condition bits:

All unaffected.

121. IM 2

Interrupt mode 2. In this two-byte instruction, the CPU places the address of a memory location onto the address bus. The lower-order byte of this address is supplied by the interrupting device, while the high-order byte is the contents of register I. The CPU executes a call to this address.

Code:

> Hex.: ED 5E
> Oct.: 355 136
> Dec.: 237 094
> Bin.: 11101101 01011110

Condition bits:

All unaffected.

122.   IN A, (n)
>   A ← (n)

This two-byte instruction loads the accumulator with the data appearing on input port n (0–256). Operand n, the address of the input port, is placed on the lower-order byte (A$\emptyset$–A7) of the sixteen-bit address bus. The contents of the accumulator are also placed on the high-order byte (A8–A15) of the sixteen-bit address bus during the execution of this instruction. The input port byte is then passed over the data bus to be stored in the accumulator.

Code:

> Hex.: DB n
> Oct.: 333 n
> Dec.: 219
> Bin.: 11011011 n

Condition bits:

None affected.

123.   IN B, (C)
>   B ← (C)

Register C contains the address of an input port (0–256). During the execution of this instruction, the contents of the C register are placed on the lower-order byte (A∅–A7) of the address bus to select an input port. The data present at that port are then passed over the data bus to register B. During the period when the address is on the lower byte of the address bus, the previous contents of register B are passed over the high-order byte of the address bus.

Code:

> Hex. : 4∅
> Oct.:   100
> Dec.:   64
> Bin.:   11101101 01000000

Condition bits:

> S   SET if input data is negative.
> Z   SET if input data is zero.
> H   RESET.
> P/V   SET for even parity.
> N   RESET.
> C   (Unaffected).

124.   IN C, (C)

> C ← (C)

The C register contains the address of an input port (0–256). During the execution of this instruction, the contents of the C register are placed on the lower-order byte (A∅–A7) of the address bus to select an input port. The data present at that port are passed over the data bus to register C. During the period when the address is on the lower byte of the address bus, the previous contents of the C register are passed over the high-order byte of the address bus.

Code:

> Hex.:   48
> Oct.:   110
> Dec.:   72
> Bin.:   11101101 01001000

Condition bits:

See **IN B, (C).**

125. **IN D, (C)**

    D ← (C)

This instruction is identical to **IN B, (C)**, except that the input data are stored in the D register.

Code:

    Hex.: 5Ø

    Oct.: 120

    Dec.: 80

    Bin.: 11101101 01010000

Condition bits:

See **IN B, (C)**.

126. **IN E, (C)**

    E ← (C)

This instruction is identical to **IN B, (C)**, except that the input data are stored in the E register.

Code:

    Hex.: 58

    Oct.: 130

    Dec.: 88

    Bin.: 11101101 01011000

Condition bits:

See **IN B, (C)**.

127. **IN H, (C)**

    H ← (C)

This instruction is identical to **IN B, (C)**, except that the input data are stored in the H register.

Code:

    Hex.: 60

Oct.:   140

Dec.:   96

Bin.:   11101101 01100000

Condition bits:

See **IN B, (C)**.

128.   IN L, (C)

L ← (C)

This instruction is identical to **IN B, (C)**, except that the input data are stored in the L register.

Code:

Hex.:   68

Oct.:   150

Dec.:   104

Bin.:   11101101 01101000

Condition bits:

See **IN B, (C)**.

129.   IN A, (C)

A ← (C)

This instruction is identical to **IN B, (C)**, except that the input data are stored in the accumulator.

Code:

Hex.:   70

Oct.:   160

Dec.:   112

Bin.:   11101101 01111000

Condition bits:

See **IN B, (C)**.

130.   INC (HL)

(HL) ← (HL) + 1

This one-byte instruction will increment the contents of a memory location pointed to by the contents of the HL register pair.

Code:

Hex.: 34
Oct.: 64
Dec.: 52
Bin.: 00110100

Condition bits:

S   SET if result negative.
Z   SET for zero result, RESET otherwise.
H   SET if carry from bit 3.
P/V   SET if contents of HL was 7F (hex) before execution.
N   RESET.
C   (Unaffected).

131.   INC (IX + d)

(IX + d) ← (IX + d) + 1

This three-byte instruction increments the contents of a memory location pointed to by the contents of the IX index register and integer *d*.

Code:

Hex.: DD 34 d
Oct.: 335 064 d
Dec.: 221 052 d
Bin.: 11011101 00110100 d

Condition bits:

See **INC (HL)**.

132.   INC (IY + d)

(IY + d) ← (IY + d) + 1

This three-byte instruction increments the contents of a memory location pointed to by the contents of the IY index register and integer *d*.

Code:

    Hex.: FD 34 d
    Oct.: 375 064 d
    Dec.: 253 052 d
    Bin.: 11111101 00110100 d

Condition bits:

See **INC (HL)**.

133.   **INC IX**

      IX ← IX + 1

This two-byte instruction increments the contents of the IX index register.

Code:

    Hex.: DD 23
    Oct.: 335 043
    Dec.: 221 035
    Bin.: 11011101 00100011

Condition bits:

None affected.

134.   **INC IY**

      IY ← IY + 1

This two-byte instruction increments the contents of the IY index register.

Code:

    Hex.: FD 23
    Oct.: 375 043
    Dec.: 253 035
    Bin.: 11111101 00100011

Condition bits:

None affected.

135.   **INC A**

  $A \leftarrow A + 1$

This one-byte instruction increments the contents of the accumulator.

Code:

  Hex.: 3C
  Oct.: 074
  Dec.: 60
  Bin.: 00111100

Condition bits:

  S SET if result is negative.
  Z SET for zero result.
  H SET for carry from bit 3.
  P/V SET if register contents were 7F (hex) before execution.
  N RESET.
  C (unaffected).

136.   **INC B**

  $B \leftarrow B + 1$

This one-byte instruction increments the contents of the B register.

Code:

  Hex.: 04
  Oct.: 04
  Dec.: 04
  Bin.: 00000100

Condition bits:

See **INC A.**

137.   INC C

C ← C + 1

This one-byte instruction increments the contents of the C register.

Code:

Hex.: 0C
Oct.: 014
Dec.: 12
Bin.: 00001100

Condition bits:

See **INC A**.

138.   INC D

D ← D + 1

This one-byte instruction increments the contents of the D register.

Code:

Hex.: 14
Oct.: 024
Dec.: 20
Bin.: 00010100

Condition bits:

See **INC A**.

139.   INC E

E ← E + 1

This one-byte instruction increments the contents of the E register.

Code:

Hex.: 1C
Oct.: 034

Dec.: 28
Bin.: 00011100

Condition bits:

See **INC A.**

140. **INC H**

H ← H + 1

This one-byte instruction increments the contents of the H register.

Code:

Hex.: 24
Oct.: 044
Dec.: 36
Bin.: 00100100

Condition bits:

See **INC A.**

141. **INC L.**

L ← L + 1

This one-byte instruction increments the contents of the L register.

Code:

Hex.: 2C
Oct.: 054
Dec.: 44
Bin.: 00101100

Condition bits:

See **INC A.**

142. **INC BC**

BC ← BC + 1

This one-byte instruction increments the contents of register pair BC.

Code:

Hex.: 03
Oct.: 03
Dec.: 03
Bin.: 00000011

Condition bits:

None affected.

143. INC DE

DE ← DE + 1

This one-byte instruction increments the contents of register pair DE.

Code:

Hex.: 13
Oct.: 23
Dec.: 19
Bin.: 00010011

Condition bits:

None affected.

144. INC HL

HL ← HL + 1

This one-byte instruction increments the contents of register pair HL.

Code:

Hex.: 23
Oct.: 43
Dec.: 35
Bin.: 00100011

Condition bits:

None affected.

145.   INC SP

SP ← SP + 1

This one-byte instruction increments the contents of register pair SP (stack pointer).

Code:

Hex.:   33
Oct.:   063
Dec.:   51
Bin.:   00110011

Condition bits:

None affected.

146.   IND

(HL) ← (C), B ← B - 1, HL ← HL - 1

The address (0-256) of an input port is stored in the C register. During the execution of this instruction, the contents of the C register are passed over the lower byte (A∅-A7) of the address bus. At the same time, the contents of register B (used as a byte counter) are passed over the high-order byte of the address bus (A8-A15). The data present at the designated input port are written into the CPU. Then the data are written to a memory location pointed to by the contents of the HL register pair. Following this, both the B and HL registers are decremented.

Code:

Hex.:   ED AA
Oct.:   355 252
Dec.:   237 170
Bin.:   11101101 10101010

Condition bits:

S   (condition unknown)
Z   SET if B - 1 is zero.
H   (condition unknown)
P/V   (condition unknown)
N   SET
C   (unaffected)

147.   INDR

$(HL) \leftarrow (C), B \leftarrow B-1, HL \leftarrow HL-1$

This two-byte instruction is identical to IND except as follows:

1. If $B - 1 = 0$, then the instruction is terminated, and the next instruction in sequence is executed.
2. If $B - 1 \neq 0$, then the program counter (PC) is decremented by 2, and the INDR instruction is repeated.
3. If B is set to zero prior to this instruction, then the INDR instruction will input 256 bytes of data.
4. Interrupts will be recognized after each loop of this instruction.

Code:

Hex.: ED BA
Oct.: 355 272
Dec.: 237 186
Bin.: 11101101 10111010

Condition bits:

S   (condition unknown)
Z   SET
H   (condition unknown)
P/V   (condition unknown)
N   SET
C   (unaffected)

148.   INI

$(HL) \leftarrow (C), B \leftarrow B-1, HL \leftarrow HL+1$

This instruction is the same as the IND instruction, except that the contents of the HL register are incremented rather than decremented.

Code:

Hex.: ED A2
Oct.: 355 237
Dec.: 237 162
Bin.: 11101101 10100010

Condition bits:

See **IND.**

149.   INIR

(HL) ← (C), B ← B- 1, HL ← HL + 1

This instruction is the same as the **INDR** instruction, except that the contents of the HL register are incremented instead of decremented.

Code:

Hex.: ED B2
Oct.: 355 262
Dec.: 237 178
Bin.: 11101101 10110010

Condition bits:

See **IND**.

150.   JP cc, nn

If cc = TRUE, then PC ← nn

If condition cc (see table) is true, then operand nn is loaded into the program counter (PC). Operand nn is a sixteen-bit address at which the next instruction is located. This is a three-byte instruction in which the first byte is the op-code given in the table for the relevant instruction, and n and n are used to specify the address given to the PC. The second byte (one n) is the lower-order byte of the sixteen-bit address, and the third byte is the high-order byte of the address.

If the condition being tested is false, then the program will increment to the next instruction in sequence.

CONDITION	FLAG	CODE			
		HEX.	OCT.	DEC.	BINARY
Nonzero	Z	C2	302	194	11000010
Zero	Z	CA	312	202	11001010
No carry	C	D2	322	210	11010010
Carry	C	DA	332	218	11011010
Parity Odd	P/V	E2	342	226	11100010
Parity Even	P/V	EA	352	234	11101010
Sign +	S	F2	362	242	11110010
Sign –	S	FA	372	250	11111010

Format example:

We want to use the JP NZ,nn instruction to jump to memory location 1F 25 (hex) if the Z flag indicates that a result from a previous calculation is nonzero.

The proper format is

BYTE	CODE	COMMENTS
1	C2	op-code for JP NZ, nn
2	25	hex for n1
3	1F	hex for n2

If this code series is encountered, the Z flag in the F register will be tested. If the result is zero, then the program will continue on its way (i.e., fall through to byte 4), but if the result is nonzero, then it will jump to location IF 25 (hex), and continue with the instruction found at that location.

Condition bits:

None affected.

151.   JP (HL)

PC ← HL

This is an unconditional jump to a memory location specified by the contents of the HL register pair. When this instruction is encountered, the program counter is loaded with the contents of the HL register pair. The next instruction is fetched from the location stored in PC after execution.

Code:

Hex.:   E9
Oct.:   351
Dec.:   233
Bin.:   11101001

Condition bits:

None affected.

152.   JP (IX)

PC ← IX

This two-byte instruction loads the program counter (PC) with the contents of the IX index register pair. The next instruction is fetched from the new location loaded into the PC.

Code:

Hex.: DD E9
Oct.: 335 351
Dec.: 221 233
Bin.: 11011101 11101001

Condition bits:

None affected.

153.   JP (IY)
        PC ← IY

This two-byte instruction loads the program counter (PC) with the contents of the IY index register pair. The next instruction is fetched from the new location loaded into the PC.

Code:

Hex.: FD E9
Oct.: 375 351
Dec.: 253 233
Bin.: 11111101 11101001

Condition bits:

None affected.

154.   JP nn
        PC ← nn

This three-byte instruction is an unconditional jump to a memory location nn. The next instruction is fetched from this location.

Code:

Hex.: C3 n n
Oct.: 303 n n
Dec.: 195 n n
Bin.: 11000011 n n

Condition bits:

None affected.

Format example:

To call for an unconditional jump to location 1F 25, the following code would be required:

BYTE	CODE	COMMENTS
1	C3	Op-code for JP nn
2	25	
3	1F	

155.   JR e

PC ← PC + e

This two-byte instruction loads the program counter with a displacement value e. The next instruction is fetched from the location calculated as the contents of the PC + e.

Format:

Byte 1	00011000	(op-code for JR e)
Byte 2	(e-2)	Value of e decremented twice, to account for the fact that the PC loaded from JR e, a *two-byte* instruction.

Code:

Hex.:   18

Oct.:   030

Dec.:   24

Bin.:   00011000

Condition bits:

None affected.

156.   JR C, e

If C = 0, then continue

If C = 1, then PC ← PC + e

This two-byte instruction is identical to JR, e, except that it is conditional on the carry flag (C) being SET (i.e., C = 1). The same code format is used as in JR e.

Code:

Hex.: 38 e-2
Oct.: 070 e-2
Dec.: 56 e-2
Bin.: 00111000 e-2

Condition bits:

None affected.

157.   JR NC, e

This two-byte instruction is the same as JR e, except that it is conditional on the carry flag (C) being reset (C = 0).

Code:

Hex.: 30
Oct.: 60
Dec.: 48
Bin.: 00110000

Condition bits:

None affected.

158.   JR NZ, e

If Z = 1, then continue
If Z = 0, then PC ← PC + e

This two-byte instruction is the same as the JR, e instruction except that it is conditional on the zero flag (Z) being reset.

Code:

Hex.: 20
Oct.: 40
Dec.: 32
Bin.: 00100000

Condition bits:

None affected.

159.   **JR Z, e**

      If Z = 0, then continue

      If Z = 1, then PC ← PC + e

This two-byte instruction is the same as JR, e except that it is conditional on the zero flag (Z), instead of the carry flag, being SET (i.e., Z = 1).

Code:

    Hex.: 28

    Oct.: 50

    Dec.: 40

    Bin.: 00101000

Condition bits:

None affected.

160.   **LD A, (BC)**

      A ← (BC)

The accumulator is loaded with the contents of the memory location pointed to by the contents of the BC register pair.

Code:

    Hex.: 0A

    Oct.: 012

    Dec.: 10

    Bin.: 00001010

Condition bits:

None affected.

161.   **LD A, (DE)**

The accumulator is loaded with the contents of a memory location pointed to by the contents of the DE register pair.

Code:

>   Hex.:   1A
>   Oct.:   032
>   Dec.:   26
>   Bin.:   00011010

Condition bits:

None affected.

162.   LD A, (nn)

This is a three-byte instruction that loads the accumulator with the contents of a memory location specified by the following two bytes (nn).

Code:

>   Hex.:   3A
>   Oct.:   072
>   Dec.:   58
>   Bin.:   00111010

Condition bits:

None affected.

Format example:

Load the accumulator with the contents of memory location 1F 25 (hex).

BYTE	CODE	COMMENTS
1	3A	Op-code for LD A, (nn)
2	25	Low-order byte in address
3	1F	High-order byte in address

163.   LD A, I
   A ← I

The contents of interrupt register I are loaded into the accumulator (register A).

Code:

    Hex.: ED 57

    Oct.: 355 127

    Dec.: 237 087

    Bin.: 11101101 01010111

Condition bits:

    S   SET if I is negative.

    Z   SET if I is zero, RESET otherwise.

    H   RESET

    P/V Contains the contents of the second interrupt flip-flop IFF2 (will be 1 or 0).

    N   RESET

    C   (unaffected)

164.   LD A, R

    A ← R

The accumulator is loaded with the contents of the memory refresh register R.

Code:

    Hex.: ED 5F

    Oct.: 355 137

    Dec.: 237 095

    Bin.: 11101101 01011111

Condition bits:

    S   SET if R is negative.

    Z   SET if R is zero.

    H   RESET

    P/V Contains contents of the second interrupt flip-flop (1 or 0).

    N   RESET

    C   (unaffected)

165.   LD (BC), A

    (BC) ← A

The contents of a memory location pointed to by the contents of register pair BC are loaded with the contents of the accumulator.

Code:

> Hex.: 02
>
> Oct.: 02
>
> Dec.: 02
>
> Bin.: 00000010

Condition bits:

None affected.

166.   LD BC, nn

> BC ← nn

Register pair BC is loaded with the two-byte integer nn. The low-order byte is the first n integer.

Code:

> Hex.: 01
>
> Oct.: 01
>
> Dec.: 01
>
> Bin.: 00000001

Condition bits:

None affected.

167.   LD DE, nn

> DE ← nn

Register pair DE is loaded with the two-byte integer nn. The low-order byte is the first n integer.

Code:

> Hex.: 11
>
> Oct.: 21
>
> Dec.: 17
>
> Bin.: 00010001

Condition bits:

None affected.

168.   LD HL, nn

　　HL ← nn

This instruction loads register pair HL with the two-byte integer nn. The low-order byte is the first n integer.

Code:

　　Hex.: 21
　　Oct.: 41
　　Dec.: 33
　　Bin.: 00100001

Condition bits:

None affected.

169.   LD SP, nn

　　SP ← nn

This instruction loads the stack pointer (register pair SP) with the two-byte integer nn. The low-order byte is the first n integer.

Code:

　　Hex.: 31
　　Oct.: 61
　　Dec.: 49
　　Bin.: 00110001

Condition bits:

None affected.

170.   LD BC, (nn)

　　HBC ← (nn + 1), LDD ← (nn)

This instruction loads the contents of a memory address given by the two-byte integer nn into the low-order byte of register pair BC, and the contents of memory location nn + 1 into the high-order byte of the BC register pair.

Code:

> Hex.: 4B
> Oct.: 113
> Dec.: 75
> Bin.: 01001011

Condition bits:

None affected.

171. **LD DE, (nn)**

HDE ← (nn + 1), LDE ← (nn)

This instruction loads the contents of a memory address given by the two-byte integer nn into the low-order byte of register pair DE, and the contents of the memory location nn + 1 into the high-order byte of register pair DE.

Code:

> Hex.: 5B
> Oct.: 133
> Dec.: 91
> Bin.: 01011011

Condition bits:

None affected.

172. **LD HL, (nn)**

This instruction loads the contents of a memory address given by the two-byte integer nn into the low-order byte of the HL register pair. The contents of memory location nn + 1 are loaded into the high-order byte of register pair HL.

Code:

> Hex.: 6B
> Oct.: 153
> Dec.: 107
> Bin.: 01101011

Condition bits:

None affected.

173.   LD SP, (nn)

HSP ← (nn + 1), LSP ← (nn)

This instruction loads the contents of a memory location given by the two-byte integer nn into the low-order byte of the stack pointer (SP register pair), and the contents of memory location nn + 1 into the high-order byte of the SP.

Code:

    Hex.: 7B
    Oct.: 173
    Dec.: 123
    Bin.: 01111011

Condition bits:

None affected.

174.   LD (DE), A

This instruction loads a memory location pointed to by the contents of register pair DE with the contents of the accumulator.

Code:

    Hex.: 12
    Oct.: 22
    Dec.: 18
    Bin.: 00010010

Condition bits:

None affected.

175.   LD (HL), n

(HL) ← n

The memory location pointed to by the contents of the HL register pair are loaded with integer n.

Code:

    Hex.:   36
    Oct.:   66
    Dec.:   54
    Bin.:   00110110

Condition bits:

None affected.

176.   LD HL, nn

The contents of a memory location specified by two-byte integer nn are loaded into the low-order byte of the register pair HL. The contents of memory location nn + 1 are loaded into the high-order byte of HL.

Code:

    Hex.:   2A n n
    Oct.:   52 n n
    Dec.:   42 n n
    Bin.:   00101010 n n

Condition bits:

None affected.

177.   LD (HL), A
         (HL) ← A

The contents of the accumulator are loaded into a memory location pointed to by the contents of the HL register pair.

Code:

    Hex.:   77
    Oct.:   167
    Dec.:   119
    Bin.:   01110111

Condition bits:

None affected.

178.   LD (HL), B

(HL) ← B

The contents of the B register are loaded into a memory location pointed to by the contents of the HL register pair.

Code:

Hex.:   70
Oct.:   160
Dec.:   112
Bin.:   01110000

Condition bits:

None affected.

179.   LD (HL), C

(HL) ← C

The contents of the C register are loaded into a memory location pointed to by the contents of the HL register pair.

Code:

Hex.:   71
Oct.:   161
Dec.:   113
Bin.:   01110001

Condition bits:

None affected.

180.   LD (HL), D

(HL) ← D

The contents of the D register are loaded into the memory location pointed to by the contents of the HL register pair.

Code:

Hex.:   72
Oct.:   162

Dec.: 114
Bin.: 01110010

Condition bits:

None affected.

181. LD (HL), E
(HL) ← E

The contents of the E register are loaded into the memory location pointed to by the HL register pair.

Code:

Hex.: 73
Oct.: 163
Dec.: 115
Bin.: 01110011

Condition bits:

None affected.

182. LD (HL), H
(HL) ← L

The contents of the H register are loaded into the memory location pointed to by the contents of the HL register pair.

Code:

Hex.: 74
Oct.: 164
Dec.: 116
Bin.: 01110100

Condition bits:

None affected.

183. LD (HL), L
(HL) ← L

The contents of the L register are loaded into the memory location pointed to by the HL register pair.

Code:

> Hex.: 75
> Oct.: 165
> Dec.: 117
> Bin.: 01110101

Condition bits:

None affected.

184.   LD I, A

   $I \leftarrow A$

The contents of the accumulator are loaded into interrupt vector I.

Code:

> Hex.: ED 47
> Oct.: 355 107
> Dec.: 237 071
> Bin.: 11101101 01000111

Condition bits:

None affected.

185.   LD IX, (nn)

   $HIX \leftarrow (nn + 1), LIX \leftarrow (nn)$

The contents of an address given by two-byte integer nn are loaded into the low-order byte of index register IX. The contents of memory location nn + 1 are loaded into the high-order byte of index register IX.

Code:

> Hex.: DD 2A n n
> Oct.: 335 052 n n
> Dec.: 221 042 n n
> Bin.: 11011101 00101010 n n

Condition bits:

None affected.

186.   **LD IX, nn**

   IX ← nn

Two-byte integer nn is loaded into index register IX. The first n integer is loaded into the low-order byte of IX, and the second n integer is loaded into the high-order byte of IX.

Code:

> Hex.: DD 21 n n
> Oct.: 335 041 n n
> Dec.: 221 033 n n
> Bin.:   11011101 00100001 n n

Condition bits:

None affected.

187.   **LD (IX + d), n**

   (IX + d) ← n

The memory location pointed to by the contents of the IX index register, and the displacement integer d is loaded with integer n.

Code:

> Hex.: DD 36 d n
> Oct.: 335 066 d n
> Dec.: 221 054 d n
> Bin.:   11011101 00110110 d n

Condition bits:

None affected.

188.   **LD (IX + d), A**

   (IX + d) ← A

The contents of the accumulator are loaded into memory location pointed to by the contents of the IX index register and displacement integer d.

Code:

> Hex.: DD 77 d
> Oct.: 335 167 d
> Dec.: 221 119 d
> Bin.: 11011101 01110111 d

Condition bits:

None affected.

189. LD (IX + d), B

(IX + d) ⟵ B

The contents of register B are loaded into a memory location pointed to by the contents of the IX index register and displacement integer d.

Code:

> Hex.: DD 70 d
> Oct.: 335 160 d
> Dec.: 221 112 d
> Bin.: 11011101 01110000 d

Condition bits:

None affected.

190. LD (IX + d), C

(IX + d) ⟵ C

The contents of register C are loaded into a memory location pointed to by the contents of the IX register and displacement integer d.

Code:

> Hex.: DD 71 d
> Oct.: 335 161 d

Dec.: 221 113 d

Bin.: 11011101 01110001 d

Condition bits:

None affected.

191.   LD (IX + d), D

(IX + d) ←— D

The contents of the D register are loaded into a memory location pointed to by the contents of the IX index register and a displacement integer e.

Code:

Hex.: DD 72 d

Oct.: 335 162 d

Dec.: 221 114 d

Bin.: 11011101 01110010 d

Condition bits:

None affected.

192.   LD (IX + d), E

(IX + d) ←— E

The contents of the E register are loaded into a memory location pointed to by the contents of the IX index register and displacement integer e.

Code:

Hex. : DD 73 d

Oct.: 335 163 d

Dec.: 221 115 d

Bin.: 11011101 01110011 d

Condition bits:

None affected.

193.   LD (IX + d), H

(IX + d) ← H

The contents of the H register are loaded into a memory location pointed to by the contents of the IX index register and a displacement integer d.

Code:

    Hex.: DD 74 d

    Oct.: 335 164 d

    Dec.: 221 116 d

    Bin.:   11011101 01110100 d

Condition bits:

None affected.

194.   LD (IX + d), L

(IX + d) ← L

The contents of the L register are loaded into a memory location pointed to by the contents of the IX index register and a displacement integer d.

Code:

    Hex.: DD 75 d

    Oct.: 335 165 d

    Dec.: 221 117 d

    Bin.:   11011101 01110101 d

Condition bits:

None affected.

195.   LD IY, nn

IY ← nn

Two-byte integer nn is loaded into index register IY. The first n integer is the low-order byte of IY, while the second n integer is the high-order byte of IY.

Code:

Hex.: FD 21 n n
Oct.: 375 041 n n
Dec.: 253 033 n n
Bin.: 11111101 00100001 n n

Condition bits:

None affected.

196.   LD IY, (nn)

HIY ← (nn + 1), LIY ← (nn)

The low-order byte of the IY index register is loaded with the contents of a memory location specified by two-byte integer nn. The low-order byte of the IY index register is loaded with the contents of memory location nn + 1.

Code:

Hex.: FD 2A n n
Oct.: 375 052 n n
Dec.: 253 042 n n
Bin.: 11111101 00101010 n n

Condition bits:

None affected.

197.   LD (IY + d), n

(IY + d) ← n

One-byte integer n is loaded into the memory location pointed to by the contents of the IY index register and displacement integer d.

Code:

Hex.: FD 36 d n
Oct.: 375 066 d n
Dec.: 253 054 d n
Bin.: 11111101 00110110 d n

Condition bits:

None affected.

198. LD (IY + d), A

(IY + d) ← A

The contents of the accumulator are loaded into a memory location pointed to by the contents of the IY index register and two's complements of displacement integer d.

Code:

Hex.: FD 77 d

Oct.: 375 167 d

Dec.: 253 119 d

Bin.: 11111101 01110111 d

Condition bits:

None affected.

199. LD (IY + d), B

(IY + d) ← B

The contents of the B register are loaded into a memory location pointed to by the contents of the IY index register and the two's complement of the displacement integer d.

Code:

Hex.: FD 70 d

Oct.: 375 160 d

Dec.: 253 112 d

Bin.: 11111101 01110000 d

Condition bits:

None affected.

200. LD (IY + d), C

(IY + d) ← C

The contents of the C register are loaded into the memory location pointed to by the contents of the IY index register and the two's complement of the d displacement integer.

Code:

    Hex.: FD 71 d

    Oct.: 375 161 d

    Dec.: 253 113 d

    Bin.: 11111101 01110001 d

Condition bits:

None affected.

201.   LD (IY + d), D

     (IY + d) ← D

The contents of the D register are loaded into the memory location pointed to by the IY index register and the two's complement of the displacement integer d.

Code:

    Hex.: FD 72 d

    Oct.: 375 162 d

    Dec.: 253 114 d

    Bin.: 11111101 01110010 d

Condition bits:

None affected.

202.   LD (IY + d), E

     (IY + d) ← E

The contents of the E register are loaded into the memory location pointed to by the IY index register and the two's complement of the displacement integer d.

Code:

    Hex.: FD 73 d

    Oct.: 375 163 d

    Dec.: 253 115 d

    Bin.: 11111101 01110011 d

Condition bits:

None affected.

---

203.   LD (IY + d), H

(IY + d) ← H

The contents of the H register are loaded into the memory location pointed to by the IY index register and the two's complement of the displacement integer d.

Code:

> Hex.: FD 74 d
> Oct.: 375 164 d
> Dec.: 253 116 d
> Bin.: 11111101 01110100 d

Condition bits:

None affected.

---

204.   LD (IY + d), L

(IY + d) ← L

The contents of the L register are loaded into the memory location pointed to by the contents of the IY index register and the two's complement of the displacement integer d.

Code:

> Hex.: FD 75 d
> Oct.: 375 165 d
> Dec.: 253 117 d
> Bin.: 11111101 01110101 d

Condition bits:

None affected.

---

205.   LD (nn), A

(nn) ← A

The contents of the accumulator are loaded into a memory location pointed to by the two-byte integer nn.

Code:

>Hex.: 32 n n
>Oct.: 062 n n
>Dec.: 50 n n
>Bin.: 00110010 n n

Condition bits:

None affected.

206.   LD (nn), BC

>(nn) ← BC

The low-order byte of register pair BC is loaded into the memory location specified by two-byte integer nn. The high-order byte of the BC register pair is loaded into the next sequential memory location (nn + 1).

Code:

>Hex.: ED 43 n n
>Oct.: 355 103 n n
>Dec.: 237 067 n n
>Bin.: 11101101 01000011 n n

Condition bits:

None affected.

207.   LD (nn), DE

>(nn) ← DE

The low-order byte of register pair DE is loaded into the memory location specified by the two-byte integer nn. The high-order byte of the DE register pair is loaded into the next sequential memory location (nn + 1).

Code:

>Hex.: ED 53 n n
>Oct.: 355 123 n n

Dec.:   237 083 n n

Bin.:   11101101 01010011 n n

Condition bits:

None affected.

208.   LD (nn), HL

(nn) ← HL

The low-order byte of register pair HL is loaded into the memory location specified by two-byte integer nn. The high-order byte of register pair HL is loaded into the next sequential memory location (nn + 1).

Code:

Hex.:   ED 63 n n

Oct.:   355 143 n n

Dec.:   237 099 n n

Bin.:   11101101 01100011 n n

Condition bits:

None affected.

209.   LD (nn), SP

(nn) ← SP

The low-order byte of the stack pointer (SP register) is loaded into the memory location specified by two-byte integer nn. The high-order byte of the SP is loaded into the next sequential memory location (nn + 1).

Code:

Hex.:   ED 73 n n

Oct.:   355 163 n n

Dec.:   237 115 n n

Bin.:   11101101 01110011 n n

Condition bits:

None affected.

210.   LD (nn), HL

(nn) ← L, (nn + 1) ← H

The low-order byte of the HL register pair is loaded into memory location pointed to by two-byte integer nn. The high-order byte of the HL register pair is loaded into memory location nn + 1.

Code:

Hex.: 22 n n
Oct.: 042 n n
Dec.: 34 n n
Bin.: 00100010 n n

Condition bits:

None affected.

211.   LD (nn), IX

(nn) ← LIX, (nn + 1) ← HIX

The low-order byte of register pair IX is located into the memory location pointed to by the two-byte integer nn. The high-order byte of the IX register pair is loaded into the next sequential memory location nn + 1.

Code:

Hex.: DD 22 n n
Oct.: 335 042 n n
Dec.: 221 034 n n
Bin.: 11011101 00100010 n n

Condition bits:

None affected.

212.   LD (nn), IY

(nn) ← LIY, (nn + 1) ← HIY

The low-order byte of index register pair IY is loaded into the memory location pointed to by the two-byte integer nn. The high-order byte of index register IY is loaded into the next sequential memory location (nn + 1).

Code:

    Hex.: FD 22 n n
    Oct.: 375 042 n n
    Dec.: 253 034 n n
    Bin.: 11111101 00100010 n n

Condition bits:

None affected.

213.   LD R, A
   R ← A

The contents of the accumulator are loaded into the memory refresh register R.

Code:

    Hex.: ED 4F
    Oct.: 355 117
    Dec.: 237 079
    Bin.: 11101101 01001111

Condition bits:

None affected.

214.   LD A, (HL)
   A ← (HL)

The byte located at a memory location pointed to by the contents of the HL register pair is loaded into the accumulator.

Code:

    Hex.: 7E
    Oct.: 176
    Dec.: 126
    Bin.: 01101110

Condition bits:

None affected.

215.   LD B, (HL)

B ← (HL)

The byte located at a memory location pointed to by the contents of the HL register pair is loaded into register B.

Code:

Hex.: 46
Oct.: 106
Dec.: 070
Bin.: 01000110

Condition bits:

None affected.

216.   LD C, (HL)

C ← (HL)

The byte located at a memory location pointed to by the contents of the HL register are loaded into the C register.

Code:

Hex.: 4E
Oct.: 116
Dec.: 078
Bin.: 01001110

Condition bits:

None affected.

217.   LD D, (HL)

D ← (HL)

The byte located at a memory location pointed to by the contents of the HL register pair are loaded into the D register.

Code:

Hex.: 56

Oct.:   126
Dec.:   086
Bin.:   01010110

Condition bits:

None affected.

218.   LD E, (HL)

E ← (HL)

The contents of a memory location pointed to by the contents of the HL register are loaded into register E.

Code:

Hex.:   5E
Oct.:   136
Dec.:   094
Bin.:   01011110

Condition bits:

None affected.

219.   LD H, (HL)

H ← (HL)

The contents of the memory location pointed to by the contents of the HL register pair are loaded into register H.

Code:

Hex.:   66
Oct.:   146
Dec.:   102
Bin.:   01100110

Condition bits:

None affected.

220. **LD L, (HL)**

L ← (HL)

The contents of the memory location pointed to by the contents of the HL register pair are loaded into the L register.

Code:

Hex.: 6E
Oct.: 146
Dec.: 102
Bin.: 01101110

Condition bits:

None affected.

221. **LD A, (IX + d)**

A ← (IX + d)

The contents of a memory location pointed to by the IX index register and a displacement integer d are loaded into the accumulator.

Code:

Hex.: DD 7E d
Oct.: 335 176 d
Dec.: 221 126 d
Bin.: 11011101 01111110 d

Condition bits:

None affected.

222. **LD B, (IX + d)**

B ← (IX + d)

The contents of a memory location pointed to by the IX index register and a displacement integer d are loaded into register B.

Code:

Hex.: DD 46 d

Oct.:   335 106 d

Dec.:   221 070 d

Bin.:   11011101 01000110 d

Condition bits:

None affected.

223.   LD C, (IX + d)

C ← (IX + d)

The contents of the memory location pointed to by the IX index register and a displacement integer d are located into register C.

Code:

Hex.:   DD 4E d

Oct.:   335 116 d

Dec.:   221 078 d

Bin.:   11011101 01001110 d

Condition bits:

None affected.

224.   LD D, (IX + d)

D ← (IX + d)

The contents of the memory location pointed to by the IX index register and displacement integer d are loaded into register D.

Code:

Hex.:   DD 56 d

Oct.:   335 126 d

Dec.:   221 086 d

Bin.:   11011101 01010110 d

Condition bits:

None affected.

225.   LD E, (IX + d)

E ← (IX + d)

The contents of a memory location pointed to by the IX index register and displacement integer d are loaded into register E.

Code:

Hex.: DD 5E d

Oct.: 335 126 d

Dec.: 221 094 d

Bin.: 11011101 01011110 d

Condition bits:

None affected.

226.   LD H, (IX + d)

H ← (IX + d)

The contents of a memory location pointed to by the IX index register and displacement integer d are loaded into register H.

Code:

Hex.: DD 66 d

Oct.: 335 146 d

Dec.: 221 102 d

Bin.: 11011101 01100110 d

Condition bits:

None affected.

227.   LD L, (IX + d)

L ← (IX + d)

The contents of a memory location pointed to by the IX index register and displacement integer d are loaded into register L.

Code:

Hex.: DD 6E d

Oct.: 335 156 d

Dec.: 221 110 d

Bin.: 11011101 01101110 d

Condition bits:

None affected.

228.   LD A, (IY + d)

A ← (IY + d)

The accumulator is loaded with the contents of the memory location pointed to by the contents of the IY index register and the displacement integer d.

Code:

Hex.: FD 7E d

Oct.: 375 176 d

Dec.: 253 126 d

Bin.:   11111101 01111110 d

Condition bits:

None affected.

229.   LD B, (IY + d)

B ← (IY + d)

The B register is loaded with the contents of the memory location pointed to by the contents of the IY index register and displacement integer d.

Code:

Hex.: FD 46 d

Oct.: 375 106 d

Dec.: 253 070 d

Bin.: 11111101 01000110 d

Condition bits:

None affected.

230.   LD C, (IY + d)

   C ← (IY + d)

The C register is loaded with the contents of the memory location pointed to by the contents of the IY index register and displacement integer d.

Code:

   Hex.: FD 4E d
   Oct.: 375 116 d
   Dec.: 253 078
   Bin.: 11111101 01001110 d

Condition bits:

None affected.

231.   LD D, (IY + d)

   D ← (IY + d)

The D register is loaded with the contents of the memory location pointed to by the contents of the IY index register and displacement integer d.

Code:

   Hex.: FD 56 d
   Oct.: 375 126 d
   Dec.: 253 086 d
   Bin.: 11111101 01010110 d

Condition bits:

None affected.

232.   LD E, (IY + d)

   E ← (IY + d)

The E register is loaded with the contents of the memory location pointed to by the contents of the IY index register and the displacement integer d.

Code:

   Hex.: FD 5E d

Oct.: 375 136 d
Dec.: 253 094 d
Bin.: 11111101 01011110 d

Condition bits:

None affected.

233.   LD H, (IY + d)
H ← (IY + d)

The H register is loaded with the contents of the memory location pointed to by the contents of the IY index register and the displacement integer d.

Code:

Hex.: FD 66 d
Oct.: 375 146 d
Dec.: 253 146 d
Bin.: 11111101 01100110 d

Condition bits:

None affected.

234.   LD L, (IY + d)
L ← (IY + d)

The L register is loaded with the contents of a memory location pointed to by the contents of the IY index register and displacement integer d.

Code:

Hex.: FD 6E d
Oct.: 375 156 d
Dec.: 253 110 d
Bin.: 11111101 01101110 d

Condition bits:

None affected.

235.   LD A, n

A ← n

One-byte integer n is loaded into the accumulator.

Code:

> Hex.: 3E n
> Oct.:   076 n
> Dec.:   062 n
> Bin.:   00111110 n

Condition bits:

None affected.

236.   LD B, n

B ← n

One-byte integer n is loaded into the B register.

Code:

> Hex.:   06 n
> Oct.:   006 n
> Dec.:   6 n
> Bin.:   00000110 n

Condition bits:

None affected.

237.   LD C, n

One-byte integer n is loaded into the C register.

Code:

> Hex.:   0E n
> Oct.:   16 n
> Dec.:   14 n
> Bin.:   00001110 n

Condition bits:

None affected.

238.   LD D, n

D ← n

One-byte integer n is loaded into register D.

Code:

> Hex.:   16 n
> Oct.:   26 n
> Dec.:   22 n
> Bin.:   00010110 n

Condition bits:

None affected.

239.   LD E, n

E ← n

One-byte integer n is loaded into register E.

Code:

> Hex.:   1E n
> Oct.:   36 n
> Dec.:   30 n
> Bin.:   00011110 n

Condition bits:

None affected.

240.   LD H, n

H ← n

One-byte integer n is loaded into register H.

Code:

> Hex.: 26 n
> Oct.: 46 n
> Dec.: 38 n
> Bin.: 00100110 n

Condition bits:

None affected.

241. LD L, n

> $L \leftarrow n$

One-byte integer n is loaded into register L.

Code:

> Hex.: 2E n
> Oct.: 56 n
> Dec.: 46 n
> Bin.: 00101110 n

Condition bits:

None affected.

242. LD r, r′

> $r \leftarrow r'$

The contents of a register r′ are loaded into any other register. Both r and r′ are selected from the table below.

A	111
B	000
C	001
D	010
E	011
H	100
L	101

Format:

$$0 \ 1 \ |\leftarrow r \rightarrow|\leftarrow r' \rightarrow|$$

Example:

Transfer the contents of the C register (code 001) into the D register (code 010). The op-code for this operation (LD C, D) is 01001010.

Condition bits:

None affected.

243.   LD SP, HL

  SP ← HL

The stack pointer SP is loaded with the contents of the HL register pair.

Code:

    Hex.: F9
    Oct.: 371
    Dec.: 249
    Bin.: 11111001

Condition bits:

None affected.

244.   LD SP, IX

  SP ← IX

The stack pointer SP is loaded with the contents of the IX index register.

Code:

    Hex.: DD F9
    Oct.: 335 371
    Dec.: 221 249
    Bin.: 11011101 11111001

Condition bits:

None affected.

245.   LD SP, IY

  SP ← IY

The stack pointer SP is loaded with the contents of the IY index register.

Code:

    Hex.: FD F9
    Oct.: 375 371
    Dec.: 253 249
    Bin.: 11111101 11111001

Condition bits:

None affected.

246.   LDD

    (DE) ← (HL), DE ← DE - 1, HL ← HL - 1, BC ← BC - 1

One byte of data is transferred from the memory location pointed to by the HL register pair to the memory location pointed to by the DE register pair. The BC register is used as a byte counter. The HL, DE, and BC register contents are then decremented.

Code:

    Hex.: ED A8
    Oct.: 355 250
    Dec.: 237 168
    Bin.: 11101101 10101000

Condition bits:

    H   RESET
    P/V   SET if BC - 1 $\neq$ 0.
    N   RESET
    S, Z and C are unaffected.

247.   LDDR

    (DE) ← (HL), DE ← DE - 1, HL ← HL - 1, BC ← BC - 1

This instruction is the same as LDD, except as follows:

1. If decrementing causes BC to go to zero, then the instruction is terminated.
2. If BC is not zero after decrementing, the program counter is decremented by 2, and the instruction is repeated.

3. If BC is set to zero before the instruction, the LDDR instruction will loop through all 64K of memory unless a match is found.
4. Interrupts will be honored after each data transfer.

Code:

Hex.: ED B8
Oct.: 355 270
Dec.: 237 184
Bin.: 11101101 10111000

Condition bits:

H, P/V and N are RESET
S, Z and C are not affected

248.   LDI

(DE) ← (HL), DE ← DE + 1, HL ← HL + 1, BC ← BC - 1

This instruction is identical to the LDD instruction except that the DE and HL registers are incremented instead of decremented.

Code:

Hex.: ED A0
Oct.: 355 240
Dec.: 237 160
Bin.: 11101101 10100000

Condition bits:

S, Z, and C are not affected. H and N are RESET, and P/V is SET if BC - 1 is not zero.

249.   LDIR

(DE) ← (HL), DE ← DE + 1, HL ← HL + 1, BC ← BC - 1

This instruction is the same as the LDI instruction except as follows: (1) If decrementing causes register BC to go to zero, then the instruction is terminated, and the next sequential instruction is executed. (2) If BC is not zero after decrementing, then the program counter (PC) is decremented by 2, and the instruction is repeated. (3) If BC is set initially to zero, then the instruction will loop through 64K. (4) Interrupts will be honored after each data transfer.

Code:

> Hex.: ED B0
> Oct.: 355 260
> Dec.: 237 176
> Bin.: 11101101 10110000

Condition bits:

> S   (unaffected)
> Z   (unaffected)
> H   RESET
> P/V   RESET
> N   RESET
> C   (unaffected)

250.   NEG

> A ← 0 - A

This instruction causes negation of the accumulator contents. This is the same subtracting the contents of the accumulator from zero. 80 (hex) remains unchanged after execution of this instruction.

Code:

> Hex.: ED 44
> Oct.: 355 104
> Dec.: 237 068
> Bin.: 11101101 01000100

Condition bits:

> S   SET if result is negative.
> Z   SET if result is zero.
> H   SET if no borrow from bit 4.
> P/V   SET if accumulator was 80 (hex) before operation.
> N   SET
> C   SET if accumulator was not 00 before operation.

251.   NOP

> (no operation)

Code:

    Hex.: 00
    Oct.: 00
    Dec.: 00
    Bin.:   00000000

Condition bits:

None affected.

252.   **OR B**

     $A \leftarrow A \lor B$

A bit-by-bit logical OR operation is performed between the byte in the B register and the accumulator. The result is stored in the accumulator.

Code:

    Hex.: B0
    Oct.: 260
    Dec.: 176
    Bin.:   10110000

Condition bits:

S	SET if result is negative.
Z	SET if result is zero.
H	SET
P/V	SET for parity even.
N	RESET
C	RESET

253.   **OR C**

     $A \leftarrow A \lor C$

This instruction performs a bit-by-bit logical OR operation between the contents of the accumulator and the contents of the C register. The result is stored in the accumulator.

Code:

    Hex.: B1

Oct.:   261
Dec.:   177
Bin.:   10110001

Condition bits:

See **OR B.**

254.   OR D

A ← A ∨ D

This instruction performs a bit-by-bit logical OR operation between the contents of the accumulator and the contents of the D register. The result is stored in the accumulator.

Code:

Hex.:   B2
Oct.:   262
Dec.:   178
Bin.:   10110010

Condition bits:

See **OR B.**

255.   OR E

A ← A ∨ E

This instruction performs a bit-by-bit logical OR operation between the contents of the accumulator and the contents of the E register. The result is stored in the accumulator.

Code:

Hex.:   B3
Oct.:   263
Dec.:   179
Bin.:   10110011

Condition bits:

See **OR E.**

256.   OR H

A ← A ∨ H

This instruction performs a bit-by-bit logical OR operation between the contents of the accumulator and the contents of the H register. The result is stored in the accumulator.

Code:

Hex.:   B4
Oct.:   264
Dec.:   180
Bin.:   10110100

Condition bits:

See **OR B.**

257.   OR L

A ← A ∨ L

This instruction performs a bit-by-bit logical OR operation between the contents of the accumulator and the contents of the L register. The result is stored in the accumulator.

Code:

Hex.:   B5
Oct.:   265
Dec.:   181
Bin.:   10110101

Condition bits:

See **OR B.**

258.   OR A

A ← A ∨ A

This instruction performs a bit-by-bit logical OR operation between the contents of the accumulator and the contents of the accumulator. The result is stored in the accumulator.

Code:

Hex.: B7

Oct.: 267

Dec.: 183

Bin.: 10110111

Condition bits:

See **OR B.**

259.   OTDR

$(C) \leftarrow (HL), B \leftarrow B-1, HL \leftarrow HL-1$

1. The contents of the accumulator are placed on the address bus to select a memory location. The data stored in that memory location are temporarily stored in the CPU.
2. The byte counter register (B) is decremented, and the contents of the C register are placed on the low-order byte of the address bus (A∅-A7). This selects one of 256 (i.e., 0-255) ports. The decremented value of the B register is placed on the high-order byte (A8-A15) of the address bus.
3. The byte to be output, i.e., that temporarily stored in the CPU, is placed on the data bus so that it can be output to the selected device.
4. Register pair HL is now decremented.
5. If the decremented byte in the B register is nonzero, then the program counter (PC) is decremented by 2, and the instruction is repeated.
6. If the decremented value of B is zero, then the instruction is terminated.
7. If B is set to zero prior to the execution of this instruction, then the program will loop through all 256 bytes of data.
8. Interrupts will be honored after each data transfer.

Condition bits:

S   (unknown)

Z   SET

H   (unknown)

P/V   (unknown)

N   SET

C   (unaffected)

Code: ,

    Hex.: ED B3
    Oct.: 355 263
    Dec.: 237 179
    Bin.: 11101101 10110011

260.   OTIR

This instruction is the same as OTDR, except that the HL register is incremented instead of decremented. The other operations are the same.

Code:

    Hex.: ED B3
    Oct.: 355 263
    Dec.: 237 179
    Bin.: 11101101 10110011

Condition bits:

See **OTDR.**

261.   OUT (C), B

    (C) ← B

The contents of the B register are output through one of 256 (i.e., 0–255) output ports whose address is contained in the C register. The contents of the C register are placed on the low-order byte of the address bus during the operation.

Code:

    Hex.: ED 41
    Oct.: 355 101
    Dec.: 237 065
    Bin.: 11101101 01000001

Condition bits:

None affected.

262.   OUT (C), C

(C) ← C

The contents of the C register are output through one of 256 (i.e., 0-255) ports whose address is contained in the C register.

Code:

    Hex.: 49
    Oct.: 111
    Dec.: 73
    Bin.: 11101101 01001001

Condition bits:

None affected.

263.   OUT (C), D

(C) ← D

The contents of the D register are output through one of 256 (i.e., 0-255) ports, whose address is contained in the C register.

Code:

    Hex.: 51
    Oct.: 121
    Dec.: 81
    Bin.: 11101101 01010001

Condition bits:

None affected.

264.   OUT (C), E

(C) ← E

The contents of the E register are output through one of 256 (i.e., 0-255) ports, whose address is contained in the C register.

Code:

    Hex.: 59
    Oct.: 131

Dec.:   89
Bin.:   11101101 01011001

Condition bits:

None affected.

265.   OUT (C), H

(C) ← H

The contents of the H register are output through one of 256 (i.e., 0-255) ports, whose address is contained in the C register.

Code:

Hex.:   61
Oct.:   141
Dec.:   97
Bin.:   11101101 01100001

Condition bits:

None affected.

266.   OUT (C), L

(C) ← L

The contents of the L register are output through one of 256 (i.e., 0-255) ports, whose address is contained in the C register.

Code:

Hex.:   69
Oct.:   151
Dec.:   105
Bin.:   11101101 01101001

Condition bits:

None affected.

267.   OUT (C), A

(C) ← A

The contents of the accumulator are output through one of 256 (i.e., 0-255) ports, whose address is contained in the C register.

Code:

Hex.: 71
Oct.: 161
Dec.: 113
Bin.: 11101101 01111001

Condition bits:

None affected.

268.   OUT (n), A

(n) ← A

The contents of the accumulator are output to one of 256 (i.e., 0-255) ports designated by one-byte interger n. The port address (n) is placed on the low-order byte of the address bus (A∅-A7), while the contents of the accumulator are placed on the high-order byte of the address bus (A8-A15). The contents of the accumulator are then passed over the data bus to the selected port.

Code:

Hex.: D3 n
Oct.: 323 n
Dec.: 211 n
Bin.: 11010011 n

Condition bits:

None affected.

269.   OUTD

(C) ← (HL), B ← B-1, HL ← HL-1

The contents of a memory location pointed to by the contents of the HL register pair are written to a memory location pointed to by the contents of the C register. The B register is used as a byte counter, and is decremented after each data transfer.

Code:

> Hex.: ED AB
> Oct.: 355 253
> Dec.: 237 171
> Bin.: 11101101 10101011

Condition bits:

> S   (unknown)
> Z   SET if B − 1 = 0.
> H   (unknown)
> P/V (unknown)
> N   SET
> C   (unaffected)

270.   OUTI

> $(C) \leftarrow (HL), B \leftarrow B-1, HL \leftarrow HL+1$

This instruction is the same as OUTD except that the HL register pair is incremented instead of decremented.

Code:

> Hex.: ED A3
> Oct.: 355 243
> Dec.: 237 163
> Bin.: 11101101 10100011

Condition bits:

See **OUTD.**

271.   POP IX

> $LIX \leftarrow (SP), HIX \leftarrow (SP+1)$

The stack pointer (SP) contains the address of an external memory "stack." The contents of the memory location pointed to by the SP are loaded into the low-order byte of the IX index register. The high-order byte of the IX index register is loaded with the contents of the next sequential memory location (SP + 1).

Code:

> Hex.: DD E1
> Oct.: 335 341
> Dec.: 221 225
> Bin.: 11011101 11100001

Condition bits:

None affected.

272.   POP IY

> LIY ← (SP), HIY ← (SP + 1)

This instruction is the same as POP IX, except that the IY index register, instead of the IX register, is used to store the data popped from the external stack.

Code:

> Hex.: FD E1
> Oct.: 375 341
> Dec.: 253 225
> Bin.: 11111101 11100001

Condition bits:

None affected.

273.   POP BC

This instruction is functionally the same as POP IX, except that the BC register pair is used instead of IX.

Code:

> Hex.: C1
> Oct.: 301
> Dec.: 193
> Bin.: 11000001

Condition bits:

None affected.

274.   POP DE

This instruction is functionally the same as POP IX, except that the DE register pair is used instead of the IX.

Code:

      Hex.:   D1
      Oct.:   321
      Dec.:   209
      Bin.:   11010001

Condition bits:

None affected.

275.   POP HL

This instruction is functionally the same as POP IX, except that the HL register pair is used instead of the IX.

Code:

      Hex.:   E1
      Oct.:   341
      Dec.:   225
      Bin.:   11100001

Condition bits:

None affected.

276.   POP AF

This instruction is functionally the same as POP IX, except that the AF register pair is used instead of the IX.

Code:

      Hex.:   F1
      Oct.:   361
      Dec.:   241
      Bin.:   11110001

Condition bits:

None affected.

277. PUSH IX

$(SP - 1) \leftarrow HIX, (SP - 2) \leftarrow LIX$

This instruction pushes the two-byte data held in the IX index register onto the external memory stack. The stack pointer (SP) holds the address of the top of the stack. The high-order byte in the IX register is pushed out to memory location SP – 1, and the low-order byte from the IX register is pushed onto location SP – 2.

Code:

Hex.: DD E5

Oct.: 335 345

Dec.: 221 229

Bin.: 11011101 11100101

Condition bits:

None affected.

278. PUSH IY

This instruction is the same as PUSH IX, except that the IY index register is used in place of the IX index register.

Code:

Hex.: FD E5

Oct.: 375 345

Dec.: 253 229

Bin.: 11111101 11100101

Condition bits:

None affected.

279. PUSH BC

This instruction is functionally the same as PUSH IX, except that the BC register pair is used.

Code:

    Hex.:   C5
    Oct.:   305
    Dec.:   197
    Bin.:   11000101

Condition bits:

None affected.

280.   PUSH DE

This instruction is functionally the same as PUSH IX, except that the DE register pair is used in place of the IX register.

Code:

    Hex.:   D5
    Oct.:   325
    Dec.:   213
    Bin.:   11010101

Condition bits:

None affected.

281.   PUSH HL

This instruction is functionally the same as PUSH IX, except that the HL register pair is used in place of the IX register.

Code:

    Hex.:   E5
    Oct.:   345
    Dec.:   229
    Bin.:   11100101

Condition bits:

None affected.

282.   PUSH AF

This instruction is functionally the same as PUSH IX, except that the AF register pair is used instead of the IX register.

283.   RES b, r

$s_b \leftarrow 0$

The indicated bit (b) in the register selected (r) is RESET (i.e., made $\emptyset$). This is a two-byte instruction in which the second byte is constructed from the table below, as shown.

Format:

BYTE	CODE
1	1 1 0 0 1 0 1 1
2	1 0 $\mid\leftarrow$ b $\rightarrow\mid\leftarrow$ r $\rightarrow\mid$

Table:

BIT	b	REGISTER	r
0	000	B	000
1	001	C	001
2	010	D	010
3	011	E	011
4	100	H	100
5	101	L	101
6	110	A	111
7	111		

Example:

If the instruction is RES 7, B, we would be resetting to zero, bit 7 in register B. The code would be

    byte 1   11001011
    byte 2   10111000

Condition bits:

None affected.

284.   RES b, (HL)

$s_b \leftarrow \emptyset$

The indicated bit (0-7) in a memory location pointed to by the contents of the HL register pair is reset to zero. The code is as given below, with b selected from the bit table in RES b, r.

1 1 0 0 1 0 1 1   (CB hex)

1 0 _ b _ 1 1 0

Condition bits:

None affected.

285.   RES b, (IX + d)

$s_b \leftarrow \emptyset$

The indicated bit (0-7) in a memory location pointed to by the contents of the IX index register, and displacement integer d is reset to zero. The code is given below, with b selected from the bit table in RES b, r.

byte 1	1 1 0 1 1 1 0 1	$(DD_{16}, 335_8)$
byte 2	1 1 0 0 1 0 1 1	$(CB_{16}, 313_8)$
byte 3	_ _ _ d _ _ _ _	
byte 4	1 0 _ b _ 1 1 0	

Condition bits:

None affected.

286.   RES b, (IY + d)

This instruction is the same as RES b, (IX + d), except that the IY register is used instead of the IX register. The code is the same except for byte 1:

1 1 1 1 1 1 0 1 $(FD_{16}, 375_8)$

287.   RET

LPC ← (SP), HPC ← (SP + 1)

This "return" instruction returns program control to the main program after a subroutine. The contents of the program counter *prior to* jumping to the subroutine are stored in an external memory stack. The low-order byte of the PC is loaded with the contents of the location pointed to by the SP, while the high-order byte of the PC is loaded with the contents of the next sequential memory location SP + 1.

Code:

Hex.: C9

Oct.: 311

Dec.: 201

Bin.: 11001001

Condition bits:

None affected.

288.   Ret cc

If cc is true, then LPC ← (SP), HPC ← (SP + 1)

This is a conditional return instruction. If the condition specified is true (see table), then the program control is returned to the main program. The code is constructed from the table below.

Code Table for RET cc Instruction (288)

CONDITION	FLAG INVOLVED	HEX	OCTAL	DECIMAL	BINARY
Nonzero	Z	C0	300	192	11000000
Zero	Z	C8	310	200	11001000
Noncarry	C	D0	320	208	11010000
Carry	C	D8	330	216	11011000
Parity odd	P/V	E0	340	224	11100000
Parity even	P/V	E8	350	232	11101000
Sign +	S	F0	360	240	11110000
Sign –	S	F8	370	248	11111000

289.   RETI

Return from interrupt

This return instruction returns program control to the main program following an interrupt. It will cause the PC to be restored to the previous value. This instruction also serves to notify the interrupting device that the interrupt request has been serviced. It will reset the IFF1 and IFF2 flip-flops.

Code:

Hex.: ED 4D

Oct.:   355 115
Dec.:   237 077
Bin.:   11101101 01001101

Condition bits:

None affected.

290.   RETN

Return from nonmaskable interrupt

This instruction is the same as an RET instruction, except that it is used at the end of a subroutine that services a nonmaskable interrupt. The IFF2 flip-flop contents are copied back into IFF1, which is now restored to its previous condition.

Code:

Hex.:   ED 45
Oct.:   355 105
Dec.:   237 069
Bin.:   11101101 01000101

Condition bits:

None affected.

291.   RL B

$$\text{CF} \leftarrow 7 \leftarrow 0 \leftarrow$$

The contents of the B register are rotated left. The content of bit 0 is shifted into the bit 1 position, the content of bit 1 into the bit 2 position, etc. The content of bit 7 is shifted into the carry flag (C flag is the F register), and the previous content of the carry flag is shifted into the bit 0 position.

Code:

Hex.:   CB 10
Oct.:   313 020
Dec.:   203 016
Bin.:   11001011 00010000

Condition bits:

S	SET if result is negative.
Z	SET if result is zero.
H	RESET
P/V	SET for parity even.
N	RESET
C	Contains the previous data from bit 7 of register.

292.   RL C

$$\llcorner CF \leftarrow 7 \leftarrow 0 \leftarrow\!\!\rfloor$$

This instruction is the same as RL B, except that the C register is used instead of the B register.

Code:

Hex.: CB 11
Oct.:   313 021
Dec.: 203 016
Bin.:   11001011 00010001

Condition bits:

See **RL B**.

293.   RL D

$$\llcorner CF \leftarrow 7 \leftarrow 0 \leftarrow\!\!\rfloor$$

This instruction is the same as RL B, except that the D register is used instead of the B register.

Code:

Hex.: CB 12
Oct.:   313 022
Dec.: 203 018
Bin.:   11001011 00010010

Condition bits:

See **RL B**.

294.   RL E

$$\llcorner CF \leftarrow 7 \leftarrow \emptyset \leftarrow\rfloor$$

This instruction is the same as RL B, except that the E register is used instead of the B register.

Code:

> Hex.: CB 13
> Oct.: 313 023
> Dec.: 203 019
> Bin.:   11001011 00010011

Condition bits:

See **RL B.**

295.   RL H

$$\llcorner CF \leftarrow 7 \leftarrow \emptyset \leftarrow\rfloor$$

This instruction is the same as the RL B instruction, except that the H register is used instead of the B register.

Code:

> Hex.: CB 14
> Oct.: 313 024
> Dec.: 203 020
> Bin.:   11001011 00010100

Condition bits:

See **RL B.**

296.   RL L

$$\llcorner CF \leftarrow 7 \leftarrow \emptyset \leftarrow\rfloor$$

This instruction is the same as RL B, except that the L register is used instead of the B register.

Code:

> Hex.: CB 15

Oct.: 313 025
Dec.: 203 021
Bin.: 11001011 00010101

Condition bits:

See **RL B.**

297. **RL A**

$$\llcorner CF \leftarrow 7 \leftarrow \emptyset \leftarrow\!\rfloor$$

This instruction is the same as RL B, except that the accumulator is used instead of the B register.

Code:

Hex.: CB 17
Oct.: 313 027
Dec.: 203 023
Bin.: 11001011 00010111

Condition bits:

See **RL B.**

298. **RL (HL)**

$$\llcorner CF \leftarrow 7 \leftarrow \emptyset \leftarrow\!\rfloor$$

The contents of the memory location pointed to by the contents of the HL register pair are rotated left. This instruction is otherwise the same as RL B.

Code:

Hex.: CB 16
Oct.: 313 026
Dec.: 203 022
Bin.: 11001011 00010110

Condition bits:

See **RL B.**

299.   RL (IX + d)

$$\llcorner_{CF} \leftarrow 7 \leftarrow 0\lrcorner$$

This instruction causes the contents of a memory location pointed to by the contents of the IX index register and displacement integer d to be rotated left. This instruction is otherwise the same as the RL B instruction.

Code:

> Hex.: DD CB d 16
> Oct.: 335 313 d 026
> Dec.: 221 203 d 022
> Bin.: 11011101 11001011 d 00010110

Condition bits:

See **RL B.**

300.   RL (IY + d)

$$\llcorner_{CF} \leftarrow 7 \leftarrow 0\lrcorner$$

This instruction is the same as RL (IX + d), except that the IY index register is used, instead of the IX index register.

Code:

> Hex.: FD CB d 16
> Oct.: 375 313 d 026
> Dec.: 253 203 022
> Bin.: 11111101 11001011 d 00010110

Condition bits:

See **RL B.**

301.   RLCA

$$CF \leftarrow \lceil 7 \leftarrow 0\leftarrow \rceil$$

The contents of the accumulator are rotated left. Bit 0 is shifted to bit 1 position, bit 1 is shifted to the bit 2 position, etc. Bit 7 is shifted to both the carry flag (C flag in the F register), and the bit 0 position.

Code:

    Hex.: 07
    Oct.: 07
    Dec.: 07
    Bin.: 00000111

Condition bits:

H and N are RESET; C contains the data from bit 7, while S, Z, and P/V are not affected.

302. RLC (HL)

CF ← 7 ← 0 ←

This instruction is the same as RLCA, except that a memory location pointed to by the contents of the HL register are used, instead of the accumulator.

Code:

    Hex.: CB 06
    Oct.: 313 006
    Dec.: 203 006
    Bin.: 00000110

Condition bits:

    S   SET if result is negative.
    Z   SET if result is zero.
    H   RESET
    P/V SET for even parity.
    N   RESET
    C   Contains the data from bit 7.

303. RLC (IX + d)

CF ← 7 ← 0 ←

This instruction is the same as RLCA, except that the contents of a memory location pointed to by the contents of the IX index register and displacement integer d are used instead of the accumulator.

Code:

> Hex.: DD CB d 06
> Oct.: 335 313 d 006
> Dec.: 221 203 d 006
> Bin.: 11011101 11001011 d 00000110

Condition bits:

See **RLC (HL)**.

304. RLC (IY + d)

CF ←⌐ 7 ← Ø←⌐

This instruction is the same as RLCA, except that the contents of a memory location pointed to by the contents of the IY index register and displacement integer d are used instead of the accumulator.

Code:

> Hex.: FD CB d 06
> Oct.: 375 313 d 006
> Dec.: 253 203 d 006
> Bin.: 11111101 11001011 d 00000110

Condition bits:

See **RLC (HL)**.

305. RLC B

CF ←⌐ 7 ← Ø←⌐

This instruction is the same as RLCA, except that the B register is used instead of the accumulator.

Code:

> Hex.: CB ØØ
> Oct.: 313 ØØØ
> Dec.: 2Ø3 ØØØ
> Bin.: 11001011 00000000

Condition bits:

See **RLC A.**

306.   RLC C

CF ←⎣ 7 ← ∅←⎦

This instruction is the same as RLC A, except that the C register is used instead of the accumulator.

Code:

    Hex.: CB 01
    Oct.: 313 001
    Dec.: 203 001
    Bin.: 11001011 00000001

Condition bits:

See **RLC A.**

307.   RLC D

CF ←⎣ 7 ← ∅←⎦

This instruction is the same as RLC A, except that the D register is used instead of the D register.

Code:

    Hex.: CB 02
    Oct.: 313 002
    Dec.: 203 002
    Bin.: 11001011 00000010

Condition bits:

See **RLC A.**

308.   RLC E

CF ←⎣ 7 ← ∅←⎦

This instruction is the same as RLC A, except that the E register is used instead of the accumulator.

Code:

    Hex.: CB 03
    Oct.: 313 003
    Dec.: 203 003
    Bin.: 11001011 00000011

Condition bits:

See **RLC A.**

309.   RLC H

$$CF \leftarrow \boxed{7 \leftarrow 0}\leftarrow$$

This instruction is the same as RLC A, except that the H register is used instead of the accumulator.

Code:

    Hex.: CB 04
    Oct.: 313 004
    Dec.: 203 004
    Bin.: 11001011 00000100

Condition bits:

See **RLC A.**

310.   RLC L

$$CF \leftarrow \boxed{7 \leftarrow 0}\leftarrow$$

This instruction is the same as RLC A, except that the L register is used instead of the accumulator.

Code:

    Hex.: CB 05
    Oct.: 313 005

Dec.: 203 005

Bin.: 11001011 00000101

Condition bits:

See **RLC A.**

311.   RLD

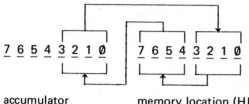

accumulator   memory location (HL)

1. The contents of the lower-order four bits (B$\emptyset$-B7) of memory location (HL) are copied into the high-order four bits of that location.
2. The previous contents of the high-order four bits of memory location (HL) are copied into the lower-order four bits of the accumulator.
3. The previous contents of the low-order four bits of the accumulator are copied into the low-order four bits of memory location (HL).
4. The high-order four bits of the accumulator are unaffected.

Code:

Hex.: ED 6F

Oct.: 355 157

Dec.: 237 111

Bin.: 11101101 01101111

Condition bits:

S   SET if accumulator is negative after execution.

Z   SET if accumulator is zero after execution.

H   RESET

P/V   SET if parity of accumulator after execution is even.

N   RESET

C   (unaffected)

312.   RR B

$$\llcorner 7 \rightarrow \emptyset \rightarrow CF \lrcorner$$

This instruction causes the contents of the B register to rotate right. The contents of bit 7 are shifted to bit 6, the contents of bit 6 are shifted to position bit 5, etc. The contents of bit $\emptyset$ are shifted to carry flag (C flag in the F register). The previous contents of the carry flag are shifted to the bit 7 position.

Code:

> Hex.:   CB 18
> Oct.:   313 030
> Dec.:   203 024
> Bin.:   11001011 00011000

Condition bits:

> S   SET if the result is negative.
> Z   SET if the result is zero.
> H   RESET
> P/V   SET for parity even.
> N   RESET
> C   Contains the previous data from bit $\emptyset$.

313.   RR C

$$\llcorner 7 \rightarrow 0 \rightarrow CF \lrcorner$$

This instruction is the same as RR B, except that the C register is used instead of the B register.

Code:

> Hex.:   CB 19
> Oct.:   313 031
> Dec.:   203 025
> Bin.:   11001011 00011001

Condition bits:

See **RR B.**

314. **RR D**

$$\hookrightarrow 7 \rightarrow 0 \rightarrow CF \rfloor$$

This instruction is the same as RR B, except that the D register is used instead of the B register.

Code:

Hex.: CB 1A
Oct.: 313 032
Dec.: 203 026
Bin.: 11001011 00011010

Condition bits:

See **RR B**.

315. **RR E**

$$\hookrightarrow 7 \rightarrow \emptyset \rightarrow CF \rfloor$$

This instruction is the same as RR B, except that the E register is used instead of the B register.

Code:

Hex.: CB 1B
Oct.: 313 033
Dec.: 203 027
Bin.: 11001011 00011011

Condition bits:

See **RR B**.

316. **RR H**

$$\hookrightarrow 7 \rightarrow \emptyset \rightarrow CF \rfloor$$

This instruction is the same as the RR B instruction, except that the H register is used instead of the B register.

Code:

>   Hex.: CB 1C
>   Oct.: 313 034
>   Dec.: 203 028
>   Bin.: 11001011 00011100

Condition bits:

See **RR B.**

317.   RR L

$$\llcorner\rightarrow 7 \rightarrow \emptyset \rightarrow CF \lrcorner$$

This instruction is the same as the RR B instruction, except that the L register is used instead of the B register.

Code:

>   Hex.: CB 1D
>   Oct.: 313 035
>   Dec.: 203 029
>   Bin.: 11001011 00011111

Condition bits:

See **RR B.**

318.   RR A

$$\llcorner\rightarrow 7 \rightarrow \emptyset \rightarrow CF \lrcorner$$

This instruction is the same as the RR B instruction, except that the accumulator is used instead of register B.

Code:

>   Hex.: CB 1F
>   Oct.: 313 037
>   Dec.: 203 031
>   Bin.: 11001011 00011111

Condition bits:

See **RR B.**

319.   RR (HL)

$$\rightarrow 7 \rightarrow \emptyset \rightarrow CF$$

This instruction is the same as **RR B**, except that the contents of a memory location pointed to by the contents of the HL register pair are used instead of register B.

Code:

    Hex.: CB 1E
    Oct.: 313 036
    Dec.: 203 030
    Bin.: 11001011 00011110

Condition bits:

See **RR B.**

320.   RR (IX + d)

$$\rightarrow 7 \rightarrow \emptyset \rightarrow CF$$

This instruction is the same as **RR B**, except that the contents of a memory location pointed to by the contents of the IX index register and displacement integer d are used instead of the B register.

Code:

    Hex.: DD CB d 1E
    Oct.: 335 313 d 036
    Dec.: 221 203 d 030
    Bin.: 11011101 11001011 d 00011110

Condition bits:

See **RR B.**

321.   RR (IY + d)

$$\hookrightarrow 7 \rightarrow \emptyset \rightarrow CF \rfloor$$

This instruction is the same as **RR B**, except that the contents of the memory location pointed to by the contents of the IY index register and displacement integer d are used instead of the B register.

Code:

    Hex.: 1E CB d 1E
    Oct.: 036 313 d 036
    Dec.: 030 203 d 030
    Bin.: 00011110 11001011 d 00011110

Condition bits:

See **RR B.**

322.   RRCA

$$\hookrightarrow 7 \rightarrow \emptyset \overset{\perp}{\rightarrow} CF$$

This instruction rotates the contents of the register right. The data in bit 7 are shifted to bit 6 position, the data in bit 6 are shifted to the bit 5 position, etc. The data in the bit $\emptyset$ position are shifted to both the carry flag (C flag in the F register) and the bit 7 position.

Code:

    Hex.: 0F
    Oct.: 017
    Dec.: 015
    Bin.: 00001111

Condition bits:

H and N are RESET; S, Z, and P/V are unaffected, and C contains the data from bit $\emptyset$.

323.   RRCB

$$\hookrightarrow 7 \rightarrow \emptyset \overset{\perp}{\rightarrow} CF$$

This instruction is the same as RRCA, except that the B register is used instead of the accumulator.

Code:

Hex.: CB 08
Oct.: 313 010
Dec.: 203 008
Bin.: 11001011 00001000

Condition bits:

S   SET if result is negative.
Z   SET if result is zero.
H   RESET
P/V SET for parity even.
N   RESET
C   Contains data from bit 0 of the register.

324.   RRCC

$$\rightarrow 7 \rightarrow \emptyset \rightarrow CF$$

This instruction is the same as RRCA, except that the C register is used instead of the accumulator.

Code:

Hex.: CB 09
Oct.: 313 011
Dec.: 203 009
Bin.: 11001011 00001001

Condition bits:

See **RRCB**.

325.   RRCD

$$\rightarrow 7 \rightarrow \emptyset \rightarrow CF$$

This instruction is the same as RRCA, except that the D register is used instead of the accumulator.

Code:

>   Hex.: CB 0A
>   Oct.:   313 012
>   Dec.:   203 010
>   Bin.:   11001011 00001010

Condition bits:

See **RRCB.**

326.   RRCE

$$\rightarrow 7 \rightarrow \emptyset \rightarrow CF$$

This instruction is the same as RRCA, except that the E register is used instead of the accumulator.

Code:

>   Hex.: CB 0B
>   Oct.:   313 013
>   Dec.:   203 011
>   Bin.:   11001011 00001011

Condition bits:

See **RRCB.**

327.   RRCH

$$\rightarrow 7 \rightarrow \emptyset \rightarrow CF$$

This instruction is the same as RRCA, except that the H register is used instead of the accumulator.

Code:

>   Hex.: CB 0C
>   Oct.:   313 014
>   Dec.:   203 012
>   Bin.:   11001011 00001100

Condition bits:

See **RRCB.**

328. **RRCL**

$$\rightarrow 7 \rightarrow \emptyset \rightarrow CF$$

This instruction is the same as RRCA, except that the L register is used instead of the accumulator.

Code:

> Hex.: CB 0D
> Oct.: 313 015
> Dec.: 203 013
> Bin.: 11001011 00001101

Condition bits:

See **RRCB.**

329. **RRC (HL)**

$$\rightarrow 7 \rightarrow \emptyset \rightarrow CF$$

This instruction is the same as RRCA, except that the contents of a memory location pointed to by the contents of the HL register pair are used instead of the accumulator.

Code:

> Hex.: CB 0E
> Oct.: 313 016
> Dec.: 203 014
> Bin.: 11001011 00001110

Condition bits:

See **RRCB.**

330. **RRC (IX + d)**

$$\rightarrow 7 \rightarrow \emptyset \rightarrow CF$$

This instruction is the same as RRCA, except that the contents of memory location pointed to by the contents of the IX index register and displacement integer d are used instead of the accumulator.

Code:

> Hex.:   DD CB d 0E
> Oct.:   335 313 d 016
> Dec.:   221 203 d 014
> Bin.:   11011101 11001011 d 00001110

Condition bits:

See **RRCB.**

331.   RRC (IY + d)

$$\hookrightarrow 7 \rightarrow \emptyset \overset{\cdot}{\rightarrow} CF$$

This instruction is the same as **RRCA**, except that the contents of a memory location pointed to by the contents of the IY index register, and a displacement integer d, are used instead of the accumulator.

Code:

> Hex.:   FD CB d 0E
> Oct.:   375 313 d 016
> Dec.:   253 203 d 014
> Bin.:   11111101 11001011 d 00001110

Condition bits:

See **RRCB.**

332.   RRD

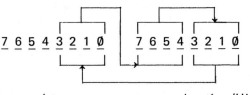

```
7 6 5 4 3 2 1 0     7 6 5 4 3 2 1 0
```

accumulator   memory location (HL)

1. The low-order four bits of the memory location pointed to by the HL register pair are copied into the low-order four bits of the accumulator.
2. The previous contents of the low-order four bits of the accumulator are copied into memory location (HL).

3. The previous contents of the high-order four bits of location (HL) are copied into the low-order four bits of (HL).
4. The high-order four bits of the accumulator are not affected by this instruction.

Code:

Hex.:   ED 67
Oct.:   355 147
Dec.:   237 103
Bin.:   11101101 01100111

Condition bits:

S   SET if result in accumulator after execution is negative.
Z   SET if result in accumulator is zero after execution.
H   RESET
P/V   SET if parity of result in accumulator after execution is even.
N   RESET
C   (unaffected)

333.   RST p

$(SP-1) \leftarrow HPC, (SP-2) \leftarrow (LPC), HPC \leftarrow 0, LPC \leftarrow P$

1. The current contents of the program counter PC are pushed onto the top of an external memory stack.
2. A page $\emptyset$ location given by operand p is loaded into PC.
3. Execution of the program begins with the instruction at the location now pointed to by the PC.
4. Since all addresses used in this instruction are in page $\emptyset$, the high-order byte of the PC is loaded with $\emptyset\emptyset$ (hex), while operand T from the table below is loaded into the low-order byte of the PC.

Code format:

1 1 $|\!\leftarrow T \rightarrow\!|$ 1 1 1

Table:

p (HEX)	T	HEX.	OCT.	DEC.	BIN.
00	000	C7	307	199	11000111
08	001	CF	317	207	11001111

p (HEX)	T	HEX.	OCT.	DEC.	BIN
10	010	D7	327	215	11010111
18	011	DF	337	223	11011111
20	100	E7	347	231	11100111
28	101	EF	357	239	11101111
30	110	F7	367	247	11110111
38	111	FF	377	255	11111111

334.   SBC A, B

$A \leftarrow A - B - CF$

The contents of the B register and the carry flag (C flag in the F register) are subtracted from the contents of the accumulator. The result is stored in the accumulator.

Code:

    Hex.:   98
    Oct.:   230
    Dec.:   152
    Bin.:   10011000

Condition bits:

    S   SET if the result is negative.
    Z   SET if the result is zero.
    H   SET if there is no borrow from bit 4.
    P/V   SET if overflow occurs.
    N   SET
    C   SET if no borrow.

335.   SBC A, C

$A \leftarrow A - C - CF$

This instruction is the same as SBC A, B, except that the C register is used instead of the B register.

Code:

    Hex.:   99
    Oct.:   231

Dec.: 153

Bin.: 10011001

Condition bits:

See **SBC A, B.**

336.   **SBC A, D**

A ← A- D- CF

This instruction is the same as SBC A, D, except that the D register is used instead of the B register.

Code:

Hex.: 9A

Oct.: 232

Dec.: 154

Bin.: 10011010

Condition bits:

See **SBC A, B.**

337.   **SBC A, E**

A ← A- E- CF

This instruction is the same as SBC A, D, except that the D register is used instead of the B register.

Code:

Hex.: 9B

Oct.: 233

Dec.: 155

Bin.: 10011011

Condition bits:

See **SBC A, B.**

338.   SBC A, H

A ← A- H- CF

This instruction is the same as SBC A, B, except that the H register is used instead of the B register.

Code:

Hex.: 9C
Oct.: 234
Dec.: 156
Bin.: 10011100

Condition bits:

See **SBC A, B.**

339.   SBC A, L

A ← A- L- CF

This instruction is the same as SBC A, B, except that the L register is used instead of the B register.

Code:

Hex.: 9D
Oct.: 235
Dec.: 157
Bin.: 10011101

Condition bits:

See **SBC A, B.**

340.   SBC A, A

A ← A- A- CF

This instruction is the same as SBC A, B, except that the accumulator is used instead of the B register.

Code:

Hex.: 9F

Oct.: 237
Dec.: 159
Bin.: 10011111

Condition bits:

See **SBC A, B.**

341. **SBC A, n**

$A \leftarrow A - n - CF$

The one-byte integer n and the carry flag are subtracted from the contents of the accumulator. The result is stored in the accumulator.

Code:

Hex.: DE n
Oct.: 336 n
Dec.: 222 n
Bin.: 11011110 n

Condition bits:

See **SBC A, B.**

342. **SBC A, (HL)**

$A \leftarrow A - (HL) - CF$

The contents of memory location (HL) and the carry flag are subtracted from the accumulator. The result is stored in the accumulator.

Code:

Hex.: 9E
Oct.: 236
Dec.: 158
Bin.: 10011110

Condition bits:

See **SBC A, B.**

343.   SBC A, (IX + d)

A ← A- (IX + d)- d

The contents of a memory location pointed to by the contents of the IX index register and displacement integer d are subtracted from the contents of the accumulator. The result is stored in the accumulator.

Code:

Hex.: DD 9E d
Oct.: 335 236 d
Dec.: 158 221 d
Bin.: 11011101 10011110 d

Condition bits:

See **SBC A, B.**

344.   SBC A, (IY + d)

A ← A- (IY + d)- CF

This is the same as SBC A, (IX + d), except that the IY index register is used instead of the IX index register.

Code:

Hex.: FD 9E d
Oct.: 375 236 d
Dec.: 253 158 d
Bin.: 11111101 10011110

Condition bits:

See **SBC A, B.**

345.   SBC HL, BC

HL ← HL - BC- CF

The contents of the BC register pair and the carry flag are subtracted from the contents of the HL register pair. The result is stored in the HL register pair.

Code:

> Hex.: ED 42
> Oct.: 355 102
> Dec.: 237 066
> Bin.: 11101101 01000010

Condition bits:

> S   SET if result is negative.
> Z   SET if result is zero.
> H   SET if no borrow from bit 12.
> P/V SET if overflow occurs.
> N   SET
> C   SET if no borrow.

346.   SBC HL, DE

> HL ← HL - DE - CF

The contents of the DE register pair and the carry flag are subtracted from the contents of the HL register pair. The result is stored in the HL register pair.

Code:

> Hex.: ED 52
> Oct.: 355 122
> Dec.: 237 082
> Bin.: 11101101 01010010

Condition bits:

See **SBC HL, BC.**

347.   SBC HL, HL

> HL ← HL - HL - CF

The contents of the HL register pair and the carry flag are subtracted from the contents of the HL register pair. The result is stored in the HL register pair.

Code:

> Hex.: ED 62

Oct.:   355 142
Dec.:   237 098
Bin.:   11101101 01100010

Condition bits:

See **SBC HL, BC.**

348.   SBC HL, SP

HL ← HL - SP - CF

The contents of the stack pointer (SP) and the carry flag are subtracted from the contents of the HL register pair. The result is stored in the HL register pair.

Code:

Hex.:   ED 72
Oct.:   355 162
Dec.:   237 114
Bin.:   11101101 01110010

Condition bits:

See **SBC A, B.**

349.   SCF

CF ← 1

The carry flag (C flag in the F register) is SET to 1.

Code:

Hex.: 37
Oct.: 067
Dec.: 055
Bin.: 00110111

Condition bits:

S, Z and P/V are unaffected; H and N are RESET; C is SET.

350.   SET b, (HL)

$(HL)_b \leftarrow 1$

Bit b (0-7) in memory location pointed to by the contents of the HL register pair is set to 1. This is a two-byte instruction in which byte 2 is selected from the table according to which bit is to be set.

Code:

> Hex.:   CB (see table)
> Oct.:   313 (see table)
> Dec.:   203 (see table)
> Bin.:   11001011 (see table)

Table for byte 2 of the instruction:

BIT	HEX.	OCTAL	DECIMAL	BINARY
0	C6	306	198	11000110
1	CE	316	206	11001110
2	D6	326	214	11010110
3	DE	336	222	11011110
4	E6	346	230	11100110
5	EE	356	238	11101110
6	F6	366	246	11110110
7	FE	376	254	11111110

Condition bits:

None affected.

351.   SET b, (IX + d)

$(IX+d)_b \leftarrow 1$

This is the same as the SET b, (HL) instruction, except that the memory location pointed to by the IX index register and displacement integer d is used instead of register pair HL.

Code:

> Hex.:   DD CB d [see table in SET b, (HL)]
> Oct.:   335 313 d [see table in SET b, (HL)]
> Dec.:   221 203 d [see table in SET b, (HL)]
> Bin.:   11011101 11001011 d [see table in SET b, (HL)]

Condition bits:

None affected.

352.   SET b, (IY + d)

$(IY + d)_b \leftarrow 1$

This instruction is the same as SET b, (HL), except that the memory location pointed to by the IY index register, and displacement integer d, are used instead of the HL register pair. This is a four-byte instruction, and byte 4 is selected from the table in SET b, (HL).

Code:

Hex.: FD CB d (table)

Oct.: 375 313 d (table)

Dec.: 253 203 d (table)

Bin.: 11111101 11001011 d (table)

Condition bits:

None affected.

353.   SET b, r

$r_b \leftarrow 1$

The indicated bit b in the selected register r is set to 1. This is a two-byte instruction, in which the second byte is made up by using the values for b and r obtained from the tables below.

Code:

Hex.: CB (table)

Oct.: 313 (table)

Dec.: 203 (table)

Bin.: 11001011 (table)

Table for SET b, r

(format: 1 1 |← b →|← r →)

BIT	/	b	REGISTER	/	r
0		000	B		000
1		001	C		001
2		010	D		010
3		011	E		011
4		100	H		100
5		101	L		101
6		110	A		111
7		111			

Condition bits:

None affected.

354.　SLA B

CF ← 7 ← 0 ← 0

1. The content of bit $\emptyset$ is RESET to zero.
2. The previous contents of bit $\emptyset$ are copied into the bit 1 position. The previous contents of bit 1 are copied into the bit 2 position, etc.
3. The content of the bit 7 position are copied into the carry flag (i.e., C flag in the F register).

Code:

Hex.:　20
Oct.:　040
Dec.:　032
Bin.:　00100000

Condition bits:

S　　　SET if result is negative.
Z　　　SET if result is zero.
H and N　RESET
P/V　　SET for even parity.
C　　　Contains data from bit 7.

355.　SLA C

CF ← 7 ← 0 ← 0

This instruction is the same as SLA B, except that the C register is used instead of the B register.

Code:

    Hex.: 21
    Oct.: 041
    Dec.: 033
    Bin.: 00100001

Condition bits:

See **SLA B.**

356.   **SLA D**

    $CF \leftarrow 7 \leftarrow 0 \leftarrow 0$

This instruction is the same as SLA B, except that the D register is used instead of the B register.

Code:

    Hex.: 22
    Oct.: 042
    Dec.: 034
    Bin.: 00100010

Condition bits:

See **SLA B.**

357.   **SLA E**

    $CF \leftarrow 7 \leftarrow 0 \leftarrow 0$

This instruction is the same as SLA B, except that the E register is used instead of the B register.

Code:

    Hex.: 23
    Oct.: 043
    Dec.: 035
    Bin.: 00100011

Condition bits:

See **SLA B.**

358. SLA H

CF ← 7 ← 0 ← 0

This instruction is the same as SLA B, except that the H register is used instead of the B register.

Code:

Hex.: 24
Oct.: 044
Dec.: 036
Bin.: 00100100

Condition bits:

See **SLA B.**

359. SLA L

CF ← 7 ← 0 ← 0

This instruction is the same as SLA B, except that the L register is used instead of the B register.

Code:

Hex.: 25
Oct.: 045
Dec.: 037
Bin.: 00100101

Condition bits:

See **SLA B.**

360. SLA A

CF ← 7 ← 0 ← 0

This instruction is the same as SLA A, except that the accumulator is used instead of the B register.

Code:

> Hex.:   27
> Oct.:   047
> Dec.:   039
> Bin.:   00100111

Condition bits:

See **SLA B.**

361.   SLA (HL)

> CF ← 7 ← 0 ← 0

This instruction is the same as SLA B, except that the contents of a memory location pointed to by the HL register pair is used instead of the B register.

Code:

> Hex.:   CB 26
> Oct.:   313 046
> Dec.:   203 038
> Bin.:   11001011 00100110

Condition bits:

See **SLA B.**

362.   SLA (IX + d)

> CF ← 7 ← 0 ← 0

This instruction is the same as SLA B, except that the contents of a memory location pointed to by the contents of the IX index register and displacement integer d are used instead of the B register.

Code:

> Hex.:   DD CB d 26
> Oct.:   335 313 d 046
> Dec.:   221 203 d 038
> Bin.:   11011101 11001011 d 00100110

Condition bits:

See **SLA B.**

363.   SLA (IY + d)

CF ← 7 ← 0 ← 0

This instruction is the same as SLA B, except that the contents of the memory location pointed to by the contents of the IY index register, and displacement integer d are used instead of the B register.

Code:

    Hex.: FD CB d 26
    Oct.: 375 313 d 046
    Dec.: 253 203 d 038
    Bin.: 11111101 11001011 d 00100110

Condition bits:

See **SLA B.**

364.   SRA B

7 → 0 → CF

This is an arithmetic shift right instruction. The contents of bit 7 are copied into the bit 6 position, and the bit 6 data are shifted into the bit 5 position, etc. The contents of bit $\emptyset$ are copied into the carry flag. The original content of bit 7 remains unchanged.

Code:

    Hex.: CB 28
    Oct.: 313 050
    Dec.: 203 040
    Bin.: 11011011 00101000

Condition bits:

    S   SET if result is negative.
    Z   SET if result is zero.

H   RESET
P/V   SET for even parity.
N   RESET
C   Data from bit Ø.

365.   SRA C

$$7 \rightarrow Ø \rightarrow CF$$

This instruction is the same as the SRA B instruction, except that the C register is used instead of the B register.

Code:

Hex.: CB 29
Oct.: 313 051
Dec.: 203 041
Bin.: 11011011 00101001

Condition bits:

See **SRA B**.

366.   SRA D

$$7 \rightarrow Ø \rightarrow CF$$

This instruction is the same as SRA B, except that the D register is used instead of the B register.

Code:

Hex.: CB 2A
Oct.: 313 052
Dec.: 203 042
Bin.: 11011011 00101010

Condition bits:

See **SRA B**.

367.   SRA E

$$\boxed{7 \rightarrow 0 \rightarrow CF}$$

This instruction is the same as SRA B, except that the E register is used instead of the B register.

Code:

    Hex.: CB 2B
    Oct.: 313 053
    Dec.: 203 043
    Bin.: 11011011 00101011

Condition bits:

See **SRA B.**

368.   SRA H

$$\boxed{7 \rightarrow \emptyset \rightarrow CF}$$

This instruction is the same as SRA B, except that the H register is used instead of the B register.

Code:

    Hex.: CB 2C
    Oct.: 313 054
    Dec.: 203 044
    Bin.: 11011011 00101100

Condition bits:

See **SRA B.**

369.   SRA L

$$\boxed{7 \rightarrow \emptyset \rightarrow CF}$$

This instruction is the same as SRA B, except that the L register is used instead of the B register.

Code:

     Hex.: CB 2D
     Oct.: 313 055
     Dec.: 203 045
     Bin.: 11011011 00101101

Condition bits:

See **SRA B.**

370.   **SRA A**

   $7 \rightarrow \emptyset \rightarrow CF$

This instruction is the same as SRA B, except that the accumulator is used instead of register B.

Code:

     Hex.: CB 2F
     Oct.: 313 057
     Dec.: 203 047
     Bin.: 11011011 00101111

Condition bits:

See **SRA B.**

371.   **SRA (HL)**

   $7 \rightarrow \emptyset \rightarrow CF$

This instruction is the same as SRA B, except that the content of a memory location pointed to by the contents of the HL register pair are used instead of register B.

Code:

     Hex.: CB 2E
     Oct.: 313 056
     Dec.: 203 046
     Bin.: 11001011 00101110

Condition bits:

See **SRA B.**

372.   SRA (IX + d)

   $\sqsubset 7 \to \emptyset \to \text{CF}$

This instruction is the same as SRA B, except that the contents of memory location (IX + d) are used instead of register B.

Code:

   Hex.: DD CB d 2E
   Oct.: 335 313 d 056
   Dec.: 221 203 d 046

Condition bits:

See **SRA B.**

373.   SRA (IY + d)

   $\sqsubset 7 \to \emptyset \to \text{CF}$

This instruction is the same as SRA B, except that the contents of memory location (IY + d) are used instead of register B.

Code:

   Hex.: FD CB d 2E
   Oct.: 375 313 d 056
   Dec.: 253 203 d 046
   Bin.: 11111101 11001011 d 00101110

Condition bits:

See **SRA B.**

374.   SRL B

   $0 \to 7 \to 0 \to \text{CF}$

The contents of the B register are shifted right. Bit 7 is shifted into the bit 6 position, bit 6 is shifted into the bit 5 position, etc. Bit $\emptyset$ is shifted into the carry flag, and bit 7 is RESET to $\emptyset$.

Code:

> Hex.: CB 38
> Oct.: 313 070
> Dec.: 203 056
> Bin.: 11001011 00111000

Condition bits:

> S   SET if result is negative.
> Z   SET if result is zero.
> H   RESET
> P/V   SET for even parity.
> N   RESET
> C   Data from bit $\emptyset$ of register.

375.   SRL C

> $0 \rightarrow 7 \rightarrow 0 \rightarrow CF$

This instruction is the same as SRL B, except that the C register is used in place of the B register.

Code:

> Hex.: CB 39
> Oct.: 313 071
> Dec.: 203 057
> Bin.: 11001011 00111001

Condition bits:

See **SRL B.**

376.   SRL D

> $0 \rightarrow 7 \rightarrow 0 \rightarrow CF$

This instruction is the same as SRL B, except that the D register is used instead of the B register.

Code:

    Hex.: CB 3A

    Oct.: 313 072

    Dec.: 203 058

    Bin.: 11001011 00111010

Condition bits:

See **SRL B.**

377.   SRL E

$0 \rightarrow 7 \rightarrow 0 \rightarrow CF$

This instruction is the same as SRL B, except that the E register is used instead of the B register.

Code:

    Hex.: CB 3B

    Oct.: 313 073

    Dec.: 203 059

    Bin.: 11001011 00111011

Condition bits:

See **SRL B.**

378.   SRL H

$0 \rightarrow 7 \rightarrow 0 \rightarrow CF$

This instruction is the same as SRL B, except that the H register is used instead of the B register.

Code:

    Hex.: CB 3C

    Oct.: 313 074

    Dec.: 203 060

    Bin.: 11001011 00111100

Condition bits:

See **SRL B**.

379.   **SRL L**

      $0 \to 7 \to 0 \to CF$

This instruction is the same as SRL B, except that the L register is used instead of the B register.

Code:

    Hex.: CB 3D
    Oct.:   313 075
    Dec.:   203 061
    Bin.:   11001011 00111101

Condition bits:

See **SRL B**.

380.   **SRL A**

      $0 \to 7 \to 0 \to CF$

This instruction is the same as SRL B, except that the accumulator is used instead of the B register.

Code:

    Hex.: CB 3F
    Oct.:   313 077
    Dec.:   203 063
    Bin.:   11001011 00111111

Condition bits:

See **SRL B**.

381.   **SRL (HL)**

      $0 \to 7 \to 0 \to CF$

This instruction is the same as SRL B, except that the contents of memory location (HL) are used instead of register B.

Code:

    Hex.: CB 3E
    Oct.: 313 076
    Dec.: 203 062
    Bin.: 11001011 00111110

Condition bits:

See **SRL B.**

382.   SRL (IX + d)

    $0 \rightarrow 7 \rightarrow 0 \rightarrow CF$

This instruction is the same as SRL B, except that a memory location pointed to by the IX index register and displacement integer d are used instead of register B.

Code:

    Hex.: DD CB d 3E
    Oct.: 335 313 d 076
    Dec.: 221 203 d 062
    Bin.: 11011101 11001011 d 00111110

Condition bits:

See **SRL B.**

383.   SRL (IY + d)

    $0 \rightarrow 7 \rightarrow 0 \rightarrow CF$

This instruction is the same as SRL B, except that a memory location pointed to by the IY index register and displacement integer d are used instead of register B.

Code:

    Hex.: FD CB d 3E
    Oct.: 375 313 d 076
    Dec.: 253 203 d 062
    Bin.: 11111101 11001011 d 00111110

Condition bits:

See **SRL B.**

384.   **SUB B**

   A ← A- B

The contents of register B are subtracted from the content of the accumulator.

Code:

   Hex.:   90
   Oct.:   220
   Dec.:   144
   Bin.:   10010000

Condition bits:

   S   SET if result is negative.
   Z   SET if result is zero.
   H   SET if no borrow from bit 4.
   P/V   SET for overflow.
   N   SET
   C   SET if no borrow.

385.   **SUB C**

   A ← A- C

The contents of the C register are subtracted from the contents of the accumulator. The result is stored in the accumulator.

Code:

   Hex.:   91
   Oct.:   221
   Dec.:   145
   Bin.:   10010001

Condition bits:

See **SUB B.**

386.   SUB D

A ← A- D

The contents of the D register are subtracted from the contents of the accumulator. The result is stored in the accumulator.

Code:

Hex.: 92
Oct.: 222
Dec.: 146
Bin.: 10010010

Condition bits:

See **SUB B.**

387.   SUB E

A ← A- E

The contents of the E register are subtracted from the contents of the accumulator. The result is stored in the accumulator.

Code:

Hex.: 93
Oct.: 223
Dec.: 147
Bin.: 10010011

Condition bits:

See **SUB B.**

388.   SUB H

A ← A- H

The contents of the H register are subtracted from the contents of the accumulator. The result is stored in the accumulator.

Code:

Hex.: 94

    Oct.: 224
    Dec.: 148
    Bin.: 10010100

Condition bits:

See **SUB B.**

389.   SUB L

        A ← A- L

The contents of the L register are subtracted from the contents of the accumulator. The result is stored in the accumulator.

Code:

    Hex.: 95
    Oct.: 225
    Dec.: 149
    Bin.: 10010101

Condition bits:

See **SUB B.**

390.   SUB A

        A ← A- A

The contents of the accumulator are subtracted from the contents of the accumulator. The result is stored in the accumulator.

Code:

    Hex.: 97
    Oct.: 227
    Dec.: 151
    Bin.: 10010111

Condition bits:

See **SUB B.**

391. SUB n

A ← A- n

The one-byte integer n is subtracted from the contents of the accumulator. The result is stored in the accumulator.

Code:

>Hex.: D6 n
>Oct.: 326 n
>Dec.: 214 n
>Bin.: 11010110 n

Condition bits:

See **SUB B.**

392. SUB (HL)

A ← A- (HL)

The contents of memory location (HL) are subtracted from the accumulator. The result is stored in the accumulator.

Code:

>Hex.: 96
>Oct.: 226
>Dec.: 150
>Bin.: 10010110

Condition bits:

See **SUB B.**

393. SUB (IX + d)

A ← A- (IX + d)

The contents of a memory location pointed to by the contents of the IX index register and displacement integer d are subtracted from the contents of the accumulator. The result is stored in the accumulator.

Code:

Hex.: DD 96 d
Oct.: 335 226 d
Dec.: 221 150 d
Bin.: 11011101 10010110 d

Condition bits:

See **SUB B.**

394.   SUB (IY + d)

   A ← A- (IY + d)

The contents of a memory location pointed to by the contents of the IY index register and the displacement integer d are subtracted from the contents of the accumulator. The result is stored in the accumulator.

Code:

Hex.: FD 96 d
Oct.: 375 226 d
Dec.: 253 150 d
Bin.: 11111101 10010110 d

Condition bits:

See **SUB B.**

395.   XOR B

   A ← A ⊕ B

This instruction performs a bit-by-bit logical exclusive-OR operation between the contents of the accumulator and the contents of register B. The result is stored in the accumulator.

Code:

Hex.: A8
Oct.: 250
Dec.: 168
Bin.: 10101000

Condition bits:

    S   SET if result is negative.
    Z   SET if result is zero.
    H   SET
    P/V SET for even parity.
    N   RESET
    C   RESET

396.   XOR C

$$A \leftarrow A \oplus C$$

This instruction performs a bit-by-bit logical exclusive OR operation between the contents of the accumulator and the contents of the C register.

Code:

    Hex.: A9
    Oct.: 251
    Dec.: 169
    Bin.: 10101001

Condition bits:

See **XOR B.**

397.   XOR D

$$A \leftarrow A \oplus D$$

This instruction performs a bit-by-bit logical exclusive-OR operation between the contents of the accumulator and the contents of the D register.

Code:

    Hex.: AA
    Oct.: 252
    Dec.: 170
    Bin.: 10101010

Condition bits:

See **XOR B.**

398.   XOR E

$A \leftarrow A \oplus E$

This instruction performs a bit-by-bit logical exclusive-OR operation between the contents of the accumulator and the contents of the E register.

Code:

  Hex.: AB
  Oct.: 253
  Dec.: 171
  Bin.: 10101011

Condition bits:

See **XOR B.**

399.   XOR H

$A \leftarrow A \oplus H$

This instruction performs a bit-by-bit logical exclusive-OR operation between the contents of the accumulator and the contents of the H register.

Code:

  Hex.: AC
  Oct.: 254
  Dec.: 172
  Bin.: 10101100

Condition bits:

See **XOR B.**

400.   XOR L

$A \leftarrow A \oplus L$

This instruction performs a bit-by-bit logical exclusive-OR operation between the contents of the accumulator and the contents of the L register.

Code:

  Hex.: AD

Oct.:   255
Dec.:   173
Bin.:   10101101

Condition bits:

See **XOR B.**

401.   XOR A

$$A \leftarrow A \oplus A$$

This operation performs a bit-by-bit logical exclusive-OR operation between the contents of the accumulator and the contents of the accumulator.

Code:

Hex.:   AF
Oct.:   257
Dec.:   175
Bin.:   10101111

Condition bits:

See **XOR B.**

402.   XOR n

$$A \leftarrow A \oplus n$$

This instruction performs a bit-by-bit logical exclusive-OR operation between the contents of the accumulator and one-byte integer n.

Code:

Hex.:   EE n
Oct.:   356 n
Dec.:   238 n
Bin.:   11101110 n

Condition bits:

See **XOR B.**

403.   XOR (HL)

$A \leftarrow A \oplus (HL)$

This instruction performs a bit-by-bit logical exclusive-OR operation between the contents of the accumulator and the contents of a memory location pointed to by the contents of the HL register pair.

Code:

Hex.: AE
Oct.: 256
Dec.: 174
Bin.: 10101110

Condition bits:

See **XOR B.**

404.   XOR (IX + d)

$A \leftarrow A \oplus (IX + d)$

This instruction performs a bit-by-bit logical exclusive-OR operation between the contents of the accumulator and the contents of a memory location pointed to by the IX index register, and a displacement integer d.

Code:

Hex.: DD AE d
Oct.: 335 256 d
Bin.: 11011101 10101110 d
Dec.: 221 174 d

Condition bits:

See **XOR B.**

405.   XOR (IY + d)

$A \leftarrow A \oplus (IY + d)$

This instruction performs a bit-by-bit logical exclusive-OR operation between the contents of the accumulator and the contents of a memory location pointed to by the contents of the IY index register and a displacement integer d.

Code:

Hex.: FD AE d
Oct.: 375 256 d
Dec.: 253 174 d
Bin.: 11111101 10101110 d

Condition bits:

See **XOR B.**

Index